# Farewell in Splendor

ALSO BY JERROLD M. PACKARD

*Neither Friend Nor Foe*
*Sons of Heaven*
*Peter's Kingdom*
*American Monarchy*
*The Queen & Her Court*

JERROLD M. PACKARD

# *Farewell*  *in* *Splendor*

## The Passing of Queen Victoria and Her Age

A William Abrahams Book

DUTTON

DUTTON
Published by the Penguin Group
Penguin Books USA Inc., 375 Hudson Street,
New York, New York 10014, U.S.A.
Penguin Books Ltd, 27 Wrights Lane,
London W8 5TZ, England
Penguin Books Australia Ltd, Ringwood,
Victoria, Australia
Penguin Books Canada Ltd, 10 Alcorn Avenue,
Toronto, Ontario, Canada M4V 3B2
Penguin Books (N.Z.) Ltd, 182–190 Wairau Road,
Auckland 10, New Zealand

Penguin Books Ltd, Registered Offices:
Harmondsworth, Middlesex, England

First published by Dutton, an imprint of Dutton Signet, a division
of Penguin Books USA Inc.
Distributed in Canada by McClelland & Stewart Inc.

First Printing, January, 1995
10 9 8 7 6 5 4 3 2 1

Insert photographs courtesy of Hulton Deutsch, Hulton Deutsch Collection

 REGISTERED TRADEMARK—MARCA REGISTRADA

LIBRARY OF CONGRESS CATALOGING-IN-PUBLICATION DATA
Packard, Jerrold M.
Farewell in splendor : the passing of Queen Victoria and her age /
Jerrold M. Packard.
p. cm.
"A William Abrahams book."
Includes bibliographical references (p.    ) and index.
ISBN 0-525-93730-7
1. Victoria, Queen of Great Britain, 1819–1901—Death and burial.
2. Funeral rites and ceremonies—Great Britain—History—20th
century. 3. Great Britain—History—1837–1901. 4. Queens—Great
Britain—Biography. I. Title.
DA555.P27 1995
941.081'092—dc20

[B]                                                        94-30225
                                                              CIP

Printed in the United States of America
Set in Galliard
Designed by Julian Hamer

# CONTENTS

# ACKNOWLEDGMENTS

For their generous help, I owe a great debt to the staffs of the British Library and its Newspaper Library, the Lambeth Palace Library, the London Library, the Guildhall Library of the City of London, the Portland State University Library, the University of Washington Library, and the Multnomah County Library. My special thanks go to the staff of the Services Convalescent Home at Osborne House. At Windsor Castle, Oliver Everett, Librarian, and Lady de Bellaigue, Registrar of the Royal Archives, were generous with their assistance, and I wish to extend my sincere thanks to them both. I am grateful to Her Majesty the Queen for permission to make use of the relevant materials at Windsor Castle.

Much of the information in this book concerning Dr. James Reid's medical care of Queen Victoria comes from his diary entries as reproduced in Michaela Reid's *Ask Sir James*. My thanks to Lady Reid for this wonderful book on her husband's grandfather, and for allowing me to see original passages from Sir James's papers.

Special thanks, too, to my friend Rolla Spotts, M.D., for helping me with medical queries.

Finally, the greatest thanks of all to my editor, William Abrahams, and my literary agent, Frederick Hill, who agreed with me it could be done, and stood behind me until it *was* done.

**VICTORIA** & **ALBERT,** *Prince Consort*
1819-1901        1819-1861

**Albert Edward,** & **Alexandra**
EDWARD VII        *of Denmark*
1841-1910        1844-1925

Alice & Louis IV,
1843-1878        *Grand Duke of*
(25)        *Hesse-Darmstadt*
1837-1892
(83)

**Victoria Mary** & **George,**
**(May)** *of Teck*        *Duke of York*
1867-1953        GEORGE V
1865-1936

*Victoria*
1868-1935

Frederick
William
1870-1873

Mary
Victoria
1874-1878

Prince Edward,        Albert Frederick,
EDWARD VIII        GEORGE VI
1894-1972        1895-1952
(265)

*Maud*
1869-1938
(102, 213)
&
*Haakon VII,*
✠ *King*
*of Norway*
1872-1957
(213)

*Alexandra*
*(Alix)*
1872-1918
(158)
&
*Nicholas II,*
✠ *Czar of*
*Russia*
1868-1918
(158)

*Albert Victor,*
*Duke of*
*Clarence*
1864-1892
(26, 100)

*Alexander* & *Louise,*
*Duff,*        *Princess*
*Duke of Fife*        *Royal*
1849-1912        1867-1931
(102, 222)        (102)

1.) Ernest, &
Grand Duke
of Hesse
1868-1937
*(div. 1901)*

*Elisabeth*
1864-1918
(137)
&
Serge,
Grand Duke
of Russia
1857-1905

### *The German Branch*

Frederick        &        Louise of
William III        Mecklenburg-
✠ King        Strelitz
of Prussia        1776-1810
1770-1840

*Augusta* &        *William I,*        *Frederick*
1811-1890        ✠ *King of Prussia,*        *William IV,*
(46)        *Emperor of*        ✠ *King of*
*Germany*        *Prussia,*
1797-1888        1795-1861
(45)        (45)

*Victoria*
1863-1950
(88–89,
155, 158)

*Victoria*        &        **Prince Frederick William,**
*(Vicky),*        **(Fritz)** *Frederick III,*
*Princess Royal*        ✠ *Emperor*
1840-1901        *of Germany,*
1831-1888

**William II,**        *Charlotte*        *Victoria*
✠ *Emperor of*        1860-1919        1866-1929
*Germany,*        (89)        (223)
1859-1941        &        &
&        Bernard        1.) *Adolph*
**Augusta**        of Saxe-        *of Schaumburg-*
**Victoria**        Meiningen,        *Lippe,*
**(Dona),**        1851-1928        1859-1916
*of Schleswig-*        (223)
*Holstein-*
*Sonderburg-*        *Sigismund*        2.) Alexander
*Augustenburg*        1864-1866        Zubkov
1858-1921        (90)        1900-1929
(92, 136)

Henry        &        Irene
of Prussia        of Hesse
1862-1929        1866-1953

*Sophie* & Constantine,
1870-1932        ✠ *King of*
(188)        *Greece*
1868-1923

Margaret & Frederick Charles
1872-1954        of Hesse
1868-1940

Waldemar
1868-1879

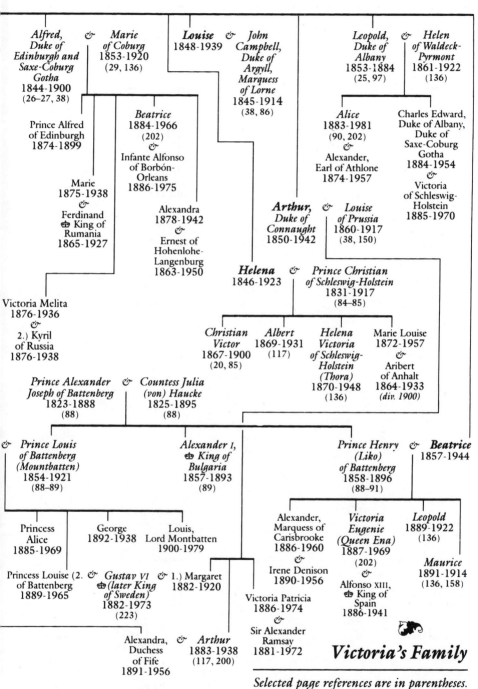

*Victoria's Family*

*Selected page references are in parentheses.*
**Boldface names** *are refered to passim.*
Names in roman *are not mentioned in the text.*
♛ *indicates monarchs of countries other than Great Britain.*

# Monday,
# January 14, 1901

❖  1  ❖

She couldn't have known it, of course, but the Queen—in residence at Osborne House, her estate on the Isle of Wight—was about to perform the last duty of her sixty-three-year, eight month, twelve-day reign, the longest in the thousand-year history of the monarchy. Her task today was to honor Lord Roberts, the kingdom's preeminent soldier. Ill, she would nevertheless, as always, rise to both the occasion and the demands expected of her. Only her doctors knew that Victoria's life could now be measured in days—perhaps even in hours.

Few things in the world could have been less like the splendors of Osborne than the South African veld. But in that desolate wilderness, the future of British imperialism was at stake, the Queen's soldiers entangled in a war whose main aim had become to save their nation from an unprecedented humiliation.

General Roberts, who had until a few weeks before led those armies in South Africa, matched his sovereign in one respect: at only a fraction more than five feet tall, the two could look each other right in the eye.

"Our Bobs" was what most of his countrymen affectionately called him, and his career, to all appearances charmed, was marked by a steady progression from distinction to distinction. He had been born the son of power, his father—Sir Abraham Roberts—having also worn the golden pips of a general. Bobs was, in full, Field Marshal Lord (Frederick Sleigh) Roberts of Kandahar, V.C., K.P., G.C.B., G.C.S.I., G.C.I.E. The first of those initials stood for the Victoria Cross, Britain's highest military mark of valor, that he had achieved at twenty-six for his exploits in the Indian Mutiny. This episode got Roberts's forty-one-year-long career in the Indian Army off to a start to which Kipling, had he been on the spot, might have written an ode. Nationwide fame in England was ensured when the Viceroy chose Roberts to command a punitive column marching on Kabul and Kandahar, flash points in the Afghan War of 1879–80; his leadership further ensured that he would dominate the Subcontinent as no other British officer during his eventful years there.

For his successes the Queen created him Sir Frederick Roberts, Baronet, and a grateful Parliament granted him £100,000, then a sum on whose interest a man could live in conditions approaching opulence. Kipling gave him something still greater, fame in the form of a jaunty jingle whose silly words swept England, "Little Bobs, Bobs, Bobs . . . Pocket Welling-ton." His illustrious career in India, followed in the mid-nineties by a command in Ireland, earned him in 1892 a peerage—as Baron Roberts of Kandahar—and, three years later, the baton of a field marshal.

Every armed conflict produces its stars, and thus far in the Boer War the brightest was the sixty-seven-year-old Bobs. Central to his success was an understanding that the outcome of military campaigns was decided as much in Whitehall as it was on the actual battlefields. Complementing this political sensitivity was a shrewd sartorial acumen. Like many physically small people, he dressed carefully and with panache, the scarlet and gold of a general officer's uniform felicitously accenting his solidly muscular frame. The one human failing he admitted to was a weak stomach, a condition for which he always kept a bottle of sherry near at hand, though he was reputed to strongly disapprove of drinking "in general."

Today's audience with his sovereign was the field marshal's second in less than two weeks. On New Year's Day, Victoria had visited a military hospital on the island to meet a group of injured soldiers recently returned from the fighting, and, the next day, the monarch had followed up this tribute by receiving her most illustrious soldier at her home. For that visit, Roberts had been treated by the cheering islanders like a conquering hero, the luster of his exploits having turned him into another, albeit smaller, Wellington. A more sedate private welcome attended him today at Trinity Pier in East Cowes, where Princess Henry of Battenberg, the Queen's youngest daughter, stood in nervously as her mother's official greeter. After their carriage passed under a triumphal arch outside Osborne specially commissioned for the occasion by the Royal Household, the soldier and the princess entered the estate itself, where Bobs met with a warmhearted welcome from an awaiting sovereign whose strength had clearly waned in the two weeks since his previous audience.

❖ 2 ❖

The woman who greeted Roberts was extraordinary not only in repute, but extraordinary as well to look upon. The features so familiar to millions were most remarkable for being unreinforced by anything approaching physical beauty. There was, however, a formidably authoritarian set to her face, one made even more formidable by shiny silver hair pulled back from a center parting and tucked under the well-known widow's cap. Her skin was white, soft and, in the appropriate places, pertly dimpled. The habitual expression hundreds of photographs immortalized and millions assumed to be unvarying was one of sourness; Bismarck referred to her as a "jolly little body," but perhaps he was one of the few fortunate enough to be granted the favor of her smiles. Roberts would have noticed how modest was the ornamentation worn by a Queen whose hoard of jewelry was the finest in the world; only the gold rings of matrimony and a hair bracelet—her husband's hair, of course—were habitual.

Her dress was today, as always, severe to the point that it astonished visitors. At home, Victoria wore a gown of black "stuff"— usually dull bombazine—of easy fit and unpretentious tailoring, and with only moderate gewgawing in an age when feminine attire was decorated on the principle that more is more. She had not worn a crown or tiara in front of her subjects in forty years, since the last court Drawing Room in Albert's lifetime; her tiara on that occasion incorporated 2,673 white diamonds and 523 rose brilliants, and in the interests of comfort was made with an especially light frame. But such ornaments did not accord with the four decades of mourning she had so exhaustively observed.

After a lifetime of being indulged in every conceivable physical and material whim that she believed her station warranted, the Victoria who was receiving her general had, unsurprisingly, become a woman of settled partialities. She hated a small but strictly applied list of annoyances, a roster that included bishops, loud noises, meeting people she knew when out for an afternoon drive, meeting *any* new people, Gladstone (though it should be noted that this dislike did not prevent the Great Liberal from becoming prime minister four times), smoking (throughout all her homes she had "no smoking" signs conspicuously posted), hot rooms, coal fires, and death duties. She had never "accepted" the telephone, though her son had talked her into allowing two to be installed at Buckingham Palace, a dispensation granted probably only because she was so rarely there. There were plenty of other annoyances to keep her in a near-permanent state of pique. Because she herself never breast-fed her own children, she didn't approve of the practice in others; once when she heard that her daughter Alice breast-fed one of the latter's brood of seven, the Queen ordered that a cow in the royal dairy be named "Princess Alice." One more particular Victoria especially disliked was competition, especially that from her eldest son.

One of the things she *did* like was gold, which she liked very much indeed. She habitually dined off solid-gold plates, even in private, even on her breakfast table, where one of her most beloved bits of bric-a-brac was a little golden egg cup that went everywhere she went. Fortunately, such expensive tastes were easily indulged; Victoria's every fantasy could, if she wished, be made reality.

In the late years of her life, her role as state hostess had generally been desultorily played. In his memoirs, Lord Ribblesdale wrote a telling paragraph on his own, always pointed, impressions, in this case of sharing the royal table. "One way or another, I must have dined a great many times at the Queen's dinner party, and I personally never heard her say anything at dinner which I remembered next morning. Her manners were not affable; she spoke very little at meals; and she ate fast and very seldom laughed. To the dishes she rejected she made a peevish *moue* with crumpled brow more eloquent than words."

❖ 3 ❖

Victoria reigned over a kingdom that was beginning to show dangerous signs of wear. The laissez-faire attitudes of Victorian complacence had produced a conundrum. Britain was a kingdom whose corridors of power seemed paved with gold, yet a nation in which stupefying poverty and social inequity compared with the worst in Europe. Its chief bounty had been peace. No world conflagration had disturbed the general harmony since the threat of Napoleonic France had been crushed eighty-six years earlier. Other than the Crimean campaign of 1859—Britain's sole armed conflict of international gravity since Waterloo had ended the French menace—what few "contained" wars had marred the tranquillity had only helped affirm Victoria's domain as the world's preeminent superpower and the guarantor of its peace.

For the current administration in her reign, the head of the Queen's government had once again come from that clique of aristocrats who firmly grasped most of the nation's engines of power. The Marquess of Salisbury, heir to the great and conservative house of Cecil, had been prime minister, off and on, since 1885; he had been "on" now for six years, governing in the laconic manner of a man who believed he was fulfilling the obligation of his class. Representing the luxurious pelt covering the workaday flesh and bone of the British body politic, a central aim of this Tory government was to make sure the working class remained excluded from any role in the administration of the nation, an aim to which Salisbury's Liberal rivals were almost equally dedicated.

The nation's grandees were men whose position and power rested on the foundation of their great landed estates, a foundation only just being superseded by mercantile leaders of the nation's economy. Yet even as injections of commercial wealth melded with the old land-based power and the first sustained stirrings of organized class conflict were heard, in 1901 the prospects of the highest reaches of society still seemed limitless. A large part of the reason for this phenomenon was that supporting the aristocracy stood a middle class eager to raise itself and thus little interested in weakening the structure into which it aspired. It was this reality that lent to Britain's aristocracy a dynamic missing from its Continental counterparts.

It had been the Reform Act of 1832 that made a secure and ambitious middle class possible. The act transformed a kingdom in which, until then, nearly the entire House of Commons had been returned to power again and again by a numerically insignificant aristocracy. Though the act did not enfranchise the working class, halfway through Victoria's reign the artisan—mainly the urban craftsman who represented the top layer of manual workers—was granted the vote, and, after a few years, other workers, including those on the land, gained the ballot, finally giving nearly every British male the theoretical right to decide who should represent him in Parliament. But to erect a barrier against the working masses' turning this still-fragile franchise into political power, the middle classes raised a collective moistened thumb to the political winds and threw in their lot with their economic and social betters.

By the turn of the century, even as a class struggle was beginning to gum up what had been smoothly running gears of Britain's political machinery, foreign events contrived to further disturb the government. For fifteen months now, Britain had been bleeding over a distant southern African cluster of colonial possessions and semi-possessions. The enemy was shockingly inconsequential, an unruly mob of alien farmers whom the British had expected to put down with the expenditure of little effort. The *Times* summed up the struggle's insignificance in an acid observation that the war seemed to have "begun at teatime"—the nation clearly having expected that it would end by dinner.

Thinly peopled by Britons, indeed thinly settled by Europeans of any kind, the southern part of Africa had turned into a battleground. Intent on wiping out the native peoples who had occupied these lands for thousands of years, the European settlers came to war over their own jealousies and greed. The rival Boers and Britons had organized their fiefdoms into four political entities—two Boer republics, called the Orange Free State and the Transvaal, and two British colonies, called Natal and the Cape Colony. The Boers, an amalgam of Huguenot emigrants from France and Holland (and whose name came from the Dutch word for "farmer"), had centuries ago dug into southern Africa and now considered themselves Africans—at least a special kind of African called "Afrikaners." Their European political ties had long since atrophied, and they were, in fact, now as much an African tribe as any of the black variety that preceded and still surrounded them.

Britain maintained that the two Boer entities were still answerable to the Crown, even though in the 1870s both were given recognition from Whitehall as independent republics, restricted only in their foreign policies. The problems in maintaining such a potentially volatile arrangement were obvious. Boer interests focused on possessing a homeland—predictably, Pretoria and Blomfontein, the Boer capitals, began to agitate to remove every vestige of British control from their affairs. Britain's interests centered on the area's riches—mainly the gold and the diamonds of the Transvaal, the discovery of which had become the principal factor disrupting the Boers' cozy status quo. What was worse, Britain's imperialistic priorities further recognized the geo-strategic importance of controlling the southern tip of the continent.

Though many—perhaps most—Boers hoped that an amicable relationship could be worked out with Britain, an almost comically inept raid led by a hot-headed British physician named Leander Starr Jameson set fire to the waiting tinder of suspicion and rivalry. Enraged by the Boer administration's interference with the movements and rights of "foreigners" in the republics (British subjects in both republics were, unhappily, classified as foreigners), Jameson launched a peremptory "invasion" of the Transvaal. The Boer militia quickly put down the raid. Unfortunately, the Cape Colony's charismatic Prime Minister—Cecil Rhodes—by publicly seeming to support Jameson's goals, squandered the goodwill he had gained with the Boers. The Transvaal's President, Oom ("Uncle") Paul Kruger, shaped in his youth by the arduous Boer trek from the Cape to the interior by which they had distanced themselves from the British, was as hard-headed as Dr. Jameson was hot-headed. Kruger decided his aggrieved farmers were left with no choice but to strike out at their enemies.

Acting in unison with its Orange Free State partner, the government of the Transvaal declared war on Britain. It was an act of seemingly stupefying audacity. Britain possessed not only its own well-trained forces, but also a vast empire on which to call. Yet the odds soon proved less one-sided than they at first seemed. Though the Boer force amounted to something under forty thousand men—this was counting virtually every male capable of shouldering a rifle—the farmers commanded an unrivaled familiarity with the land, and were prepared to sacrifice much, and die if necessary, for what they had come to regard as their inalienable home. Kruger's men knew where they could find every waterhole for their horses and every store of food for their troops, they knew how to ride on the veld, and they knew they were able to count on civilian comfort and support as could no foreign force. Furthermore, they didn't hesitate to cross into British Natal and the Cape to take on their enemy. Perhaps most helpful to their cause, these offspring of the Voortrekkers possessed a powerful weapon in their ability and willingness to engage in guerrilla war, a new kind of fighting the British held up to ridicule as unsportsmanlike but which their enemy employed with stunning effect.

Convention-bound inefficiencies, lack of preparedness, poor generalship and early unwillingness to take their Boer adversaries seriously got the Queen's forces off to a miserable start when the conflict began in 1899. But by the beginning of 1901 the weight of numbers had turned the struggle in Britain's favor. Troops who had only recently traded in their scarlet tunics for the more utilitarian khaki drill came to understand what had to be done to best a dedicated enemy. Caging the Boers' women and children into festering "concentration" camps in which twenty thousand had by this time already died proved effective against Kruger's onslaughts, but it horrified the watching world. A Europe already in sympathy with the Boer cause, a rapport undergirded by antipathy to British arrogance and strength, bitterly reproached Britain while at the same time ignoring the Boer crusade to condemn the black African to slavery or exile—or worse.

At home, painfully aware of the international opprobrium hurled at them (the Boers routinely personified their enemy as the British sovereign, whom they represented as a blowsy, bug-eyed harridan, a view shared in almost every state in Europe), the Queen's subjects had come to regard the war as a fundamental test of national resolve. A single week in December 1899 brought British arms three disastrous defeats in quick succession, prompting ridicule from European neighbors at the spectacle of an empire held hostage to gangs of Bible-spouting, bandolier-draped farmer-warriors. When five months later the besieged town of Mafeking was finally relieved by General Sir Redvers Buller, thus giving Britain a modest victory, the entire nation let itself go in an unseemly but heartfelt celebration.

Still the Boers hung on. Though British victories began to pile up in ever more impressive numbers—Modder River, Kimberley, Paardeberg—the Queen's soldiers failed to finish off Kruger's forces. At the beginning of 1901, Victoria had already had to suffer the knowledge that three thousand of her soldiers were dead. She tried to put on a brave front by remarking in the face of such carnage that "we are not interested in the possibilities of defeat," but the monarch was appalled with the war—with the loss of so many courageous young soldiers, with its cost, with the fact that Britain had become involved in the struggle in the first place—already the longest the nation had known in half a century. After seeing the Queen, Arthur Balfour told his uncle, Prime Minister Lord Salisbury, that Victoria remained in "wonderful good humor." Yet the sovereign noted grimly in her journal after Balfour's visit that the only thing she had to write of was the "lists of casualties."

At the end of December 1900, the field commander in South Africa, Lord Roberts, having endured the loss of his only son Frederick on the Tugela River during the relief at Ladysmith (the young man was posthumously awarded a Victoria Cross), was replaced by General Lord Kitchener. Though Roberts had wrought wonders in his few months in the veld—relieving the Boer siege of Kimberley, capturing Cronjé, occupying Johannesburg and Pretoria—and though he patriotically announced on his steamer voyage home that victory was at hand—final success remained elusive. It would be left to Kitchener to hunt down the remaining twenty-five thousand Boer guerrillas. All Roberts had to do was confront his sovereign and accomplish the unenviable task of explaining to an incredulous Victoria why a half million of her troops were unable to defeat a tenth as many of the enemy.

❖ 4 ❖

B roken away in some prehistoric seismic rending, the Isle of Wight has for aeons floated in the English Channel, looking on the maps like a diamond-shaped pendant. Tethered to its parent only by an armada of ferries, its northern face looks across the river-like strait called the Solent to the green shores of Hampshire. Because its southerly side faces what had been for centuries the traditional Gallic enemy, this 147-square-mile chip of Britain served a string of monarchs as an invaluable linchpin in their kingdom's defense. But it would wait until the middle of the nineteenth century before achieving its greatest luster, when as the most enchanted and private domain of this maritime kingdom's first family, the mighty of the world would come in an unending stream to the island.

The fragment of her realm that decades earlier had achieved an unmatchable rank in the sovereign's regard has been held by generations of its residents as a place where the gods who fashioned Britain dealt most bountifully. The sheltered south is so fertile that myrtles and other delicate plants grow to tropical dimensions, and the outlook from almost any elevated place on the island takes in a comely vista of sea and shore and rolling hills.

The first islanders to arrive were almost certainly Celts, and it was their Celtic word *gwyth*—"channel," or "division"—whence the name *Wight* came. This place of such un-English-like weather, Mediterranean countenance, and relatively pacific inhabitants presented an irresistible temptation to those who would disturb the Celts' peace. The first wave of invaders came from the Continent when troops of the Roman Emperor Claudius claimed the entire Kent coast in the spring of A.D. 43. In less time than it took to requisition it in the name of Caesar, troops under the command of Claudius's successor Vespasian spread out over the island they would call Vectis, erecting villas that became the nuclei of the towns that soon displaced great hunks of the ancient myrtle forests.

With the collapse of Roman authority, a volatile age came to the island, as it did to most of Europe. Here it culminated in the Saxon establishment of a stronghold called Carisbrooke Castle in the heart of the island. With his conquest of the native Saxons in 1066, the Norman conqueror William rewarded an intimate friend, William Fitz-Osbern, Earl of Hereford, with jurisdiction over the Isle of Wight. This Hereford chieftaincy would by a complex series of bequeathals devolve by the end of the thirteenth century onto one Countess Isabella, and out of the direct stewardship of the Crown. The then-King, Edward I, recognized anew the island's strategic importance and bought out the countess, the isle thus coming under direct royal control, the new Lord of the Island— no longer a hereditary tenure but a Crown appointment—charged with the defense of the entire southern regions of the realm.

The French, their wont to be an unending threat to their cross-Channel neighbors, launched periodic raids not only on the island but along much of the nearby English coastline. Carisbrooke Castle, the strongest fortress on the island, turned out to be of little use in thwarting the French outrages, and as the years passed, the King's advisers counseled in favor of far more substantial defenses to ward off the marauding Gauls.

Lack of money remained the Crown's most serious obstacle to a reliable shield against the enemy. Finally, in the 1530s, Henry VIII worked out a solution for both the island's peril and, more importantly, to his kingdom's financial shortcomings. The king simply appropriated the wealth of England's monasteries, and thus was now able to pay for the expensive sort of defenses he needed to keep his enemies at a safe distance. The Isle of Wight assumed a key place in these defenses. With its encircling lines of bows and spears and pikes, harquebuses and cannon, the island's fortifications presented a formidable bulwark against the new menace that had replaced France as its principal threat, the galleons of imperial Spain. The rout of the Spanish Armada at the end of the sixteenth century finally allowed the islanders to transform their economy from that of building defenses to the pursuits of peacetime.

And transform they did. The island had long been overlaid with royal manor houses, but Queen Elizabeth had blocked their sale or transfer while the Armada remained a threat. With the danger gone, these stately residences drew rich buyers anxious to savor both the island's relative warmth and its isolation from London's foul humors. And to service the new manorial lords, what had been hamlets now flowered into prosperous towns rivaling in size those on the mainland.

One such settlement, a pair of villages called West Cowes and East Cowes—the two a chain-ferry apart from each other at the mouth of the river Medina on the island's north coast—grew especially prosperous over the succeeding centuries. It was in the rolling heights overlooking East Cowes that one of the most fetching homes in the kingdom was built in the shelter of a grove of ilex trees. This manor, named for the island's long-ago first liege, was called Osborne House.

By the mid-nineteenth century, the trail of ownership of the land that became Victoria's island estate would stretch over nearly a thousand years, centuries of bequeathals extending from William Fitz-Osbern down through a succession of the island's first families, leading in 1672 to the daughter of a family of gentlefolk named Mann. This daughter married one Captain Robert Blachford, and their estate, on which land a succession of manor houses had been raised and torn down, passed through the Blachford heirs until it came down to the captain's namesake, another Robert Blachford. In the reign of King George III, Robert married Miss Winifred Barrington, and in 1779 the couple built for themselves a graceful Georgian-style manor house on the Osborne land.

This new Osborne House passed in 1790 from Robert and Winifred to their third son, Barrington Pope Blachford. A member of Parliament and a successful businessman—he once handled the arrangements on a cargo of sherry exported by the Duke of Wellington during the Peninsular War—the well-to-do exemplar of fashionable society took as his wife a vigorous young woman named Lady Isabella Fitzroy, youngest daughter of the third and enormously rich Duke of Grafton. The marriage between Barrington and Isabella ended a bit under four years later, when the sudden death of the husband left the wife a rich and still-comely widow, with two young children to comfort her, as well as Osborne House to shelter her in the degree of state befitting the daughter of an English duke.

Within a few years of Lady Isabella's bereavement, the kingdom's young First Couple entered the picture. Although the monarch and her husband had in the early 1840s—shortly after their marriage—been looking for "something cozy" to which they could periodically escape the difficulties of their London palace, the house that Victoria would come to covet fitted that description only when translated into royal terms. The stately Georgian structure of the Blachfords consisted of a series of splendid reception chambers of the kind common to the best manor houses in England. Some sixteen bedrooms, several dressing rooms, a billiard room and an "adequate" wine cellar further ensured its occupants' gracious living. Attached were the kinds of outbuildings that made the home a true estate—laundry, offices, stables, carriage and harness rooms, work offices for the property's overseers.

Victoria's requirement for "cozy" is understandable in light of the circumstances in which the new monarch found herself after coming to the throne. Buckingham Palace, greatly expanded at astronomical expense to the British taxpayer by George IV, was—amazingly—considered by the Queen too small for the "growing" (her fourth child had been born in 1844) Royal Family's needs. How this could be when the mammoth palace contained scores of rooms was a matter of some annoyance to many of those in Parliament, which body was expected to finance the Royal Family's comforts. But perhaps nearer to the heart of the Queen's concerns was the fact that Buckingham Palace overlooked an ulcerating slum to its south, a sight that must have been painfully unedifying to the sensitive young sovereign and her fastidious husband. The Royal Family's neighbors were the subjects of a monarch who had vowed at her coronation to dedicate her life to them—*all* of them—presumably even the poorest. But London's slum-dwellers might have been a different species as far as Victoria and Albert were concerned; the remark of Victoria's ill-fated predecessor Charles I, that a subject and a sovereign were "clean different things," was an observation especially perceptive when the sovereign is compared to the least privileged of her subjects.

In justice to Victoria and Albert, it must be said that great tracts of London *were* a sink of indescribable vileness. The Thames as it oozed past the city was near solid with muck, the sluggish stream giving off such loathsome smells that the lawmakers in Parliament were constrained to drape the legislative building's windows with enormous lime-moistened sheets to render their air reasonably breathable. With hundreds of thousands of fireplaces and stoves spewing noxious soft-coal fumes into the metropolis's skies, respiration became an often lethal undertaking for high and low alike. As for Buckingham Palace, the stultifying vapors turned its masses of royal silverplate a mottled purplish black and ground into the subtle weave of its costly damask-covered furniture. Probably most degrading to the young Queen was the fact that undesirable members of the public sometimes sneaked into her palace for a night's relatively pleasant sleep away from their own wretched hovels.

To escape such unpleasantness, Victoria possessed a number of alternatives to Buckingham Palace. The principal royal retreat was, then as now, Windsor Castle. This venerable seat of Britain's monarchy was certifiably large, had plenty of bedrooms for present and future royal offspring, and was located at some considerable remove from London's prying eyes and routine wretchedness. Unfortunately, it had drawbacks of its own. That the adjacent town impinged on the Queen's passionately sought-after privacy was bothersome, but that the castle's drains and sewers let off a constant and nose-blistering stench was even worse. Sir Jeffry Wyatville, the architect who rebuilt it for Victoria's uncle, the Prince Regent, placed its royal occupants on notice that "there will be great stinks there." These problems were, incidentally, shared quite equitably between Windsor and Buckingham Palace, giving the Queen an unquenchable interest in plumbing arrangements that she maintained until the end of her life.

For escape from the public scrutiny to which a queen was as much victim in the middle of the nineteenth century as is her counterpart at the end of the twentieth, Victoria's search took on an increasingly frenzied tone. After Buckingham Palace and Windsor, there was the Royal Marine Villa at Brighton. But to the royal couple the villa was unthinkable. More familiarly known as the Royal Pavilion, George IV's retreat—built when he was still regent for his mad father—represented a dazzling confection created from a bottomless purse matched by a bottomless willingness to empty that purse. The insurmountable difficulty Victoria faced with the Pavilion was that it stood smack on a public street, in the heart of a crowded and rather downmarket seaside resort. One foot outside her front door, or while passing an undraped window, and Victoria would have been as much on display as any inhabitant of the new royal zoo at Regent's Park. What was worse were the memories that Brighton stirred. Her uncle George, the only royal occupant in the Pavilion's short history, was not a man Victoria wished to be reminded of, much less to emulate. He had used the pavilion for *pleasure*, with his *mistress* as chatelaine. Victoria wished her reputation to remain as far removed as possible from Uncle George's libertinism. A last spadeful of dirt on the Pavilion's undoing was that Victoria intensely disliked it for its architectural excesses—she called it "a strange, odd, Chinese-looking thing."

There *were* other state residences scattered about, palaces in which Victoria could, theoretically, have made a holiday home. She had been born and raised at Kensington Palace, but it was now shabby and hardly a real palace, and besides, like Buckingham Palace it too was in London, and that was where she wanted least to be. The enormous Hampton Court, technically at her disposal, hadn't been used as a royal residence since the time of George II. The Palace of Holyroodhouse in Edinburgh, besides being a very long ways away in a minor part of her realm, stood in a state of decrepitude.

Victoria quite liked the idea of the coast, what with its fresh sea air and all. When she had been a girl, and her mother wished to show her off around the kingdom, there had been a number of trips to the Isle of Wight. After marriage, Victoria more and more recalled these youthful days of soaking in the island's sea breezes and relative privacy. Thus it was that her housing search lighted on the widowed Lady Isabella Blachford's splendid home, which happened in this seventh year of Victoria's reign to be on the market.

Having recently asked Sir Robert Peel, her Prime Minister, for his advice on a holiday home, he told her of a "quite lovely" property in the Isle of Wight, and that she and her Prince might wish to consider it. Sir Robert's suggestion was, of course, Osborne.

Peel added the useful intelligence that the owner couldn't keep the place up after the recent death of her husband. Victoria jumped at Sir Robert's counsel, thinking it would be splendid fun to live in such a place. The asking price of £28,000, furniture included, was, however, a problem. Because the money would come out of their own pockets rather than those of the taxpayers, Albert thought it best if they might *rent* the estate for a trial run, and if they liked it, only then would they make an offer to buy.

In March 1844, with the property still unexplored by either husband or wife, Albert went alone to the island, probably on the assumption that too much fuss would be made if his wife accompanied him. He got up at dawn to be sure to get back to London and Victoria by nightfall, the Queen being anxious to hear all about it as soon as possible. Evidently the Prince liked what he saw, and immediately offered £1,000 for a year's rent, his Germanic confidence of Victoria's eventual approval quite touching. The owner accepted, and from May 1, 1844, the royal couple became the tenants of Lady Isabella Blachford. The *Illustrated London News* reported in its March 23 issue—correctly, as it turned out—that the Queen and Prince Albert had already agreed to purchase the estate for the full asking price, the only proviso that Her Majesty be satisfied with it for the twelve months during which she and her husband would be renters.

It was October before both husband and wife managed to get to Osborne, but when they did, Victoria fell instantly in love with the place, a love likely abetted by her belief that Albert had already done so. She clearly wanted it, but stipulated that the mansion would have to be "added to." Lady Isabella, now living in her town house in London's Berkeley Square, was restless to unload the property as soon as possible and for as much as possible, and the fact that she was dealing with the Queen and Prince Albert didn't seem to faze the aristocratic widow in the least. What she hadn't reckoned on, however, was Albert's needle-sharp pencil. Shortly after the New Year in 1845, the Prince's private secretary, George Anson, wrote Lady Isabella informing her that the Queen *wouldn't* be buying the place—at least not at the £28,000 asking price. The monarch wished to *negotiate*, and Mr. Anson wanted to know what lower price Lady Isabella might consider.

Through her own solicitor the owner communicated that she hadn't any intention of budging on her price, upon which news the Prince came back with a £26,000 offer, excepting only that Lady Isabella could keep her furniture—he and his wife could, after all, bring in all the furniture they might need from the royal residences Victoria already possessed. Her Ladyship finally acceded, although one additional problem had to be worked out. The Queen wanted the outright ownership of the part of the estate called Barton Farm, land to which Lady Isabella held only a long-term lease. Winchester College was the ultimate owner of Barton Farm, and the college's solicitors informed the estate agents that they didn't have the authority to sell the property outright, at least not without an act of Parliament authorizing such a transfer (it was officially church property). The negotiations came to a satisfactory conclusion when at Victoria's request the Prime Minister himself quickly and smoothly saw to the necessary legislation. In the end, Victoria and Albert became the proud owners of Osborne House and its estate of 342 acres for £26,000; an additional £18,560 was paid for the adjoining Barton Farm and *its* estate of 500 acres, the latter deed to come fully into the Royal Family's possession in 1862. The couple would eventually buy a clutch of neighboring farms, and in the end possessed 2,000 prime acres of the northern apex of the Isle of Wight, altogether one of the finest estates in the Queen's entire kingdom.

❖ 5 ❖

With children filling up the family roll call at almost annual intervals, Victoria and Albert at last had a *private* home of their own, one to which escapes would provide the happiest days of their twenty-one-year marriage. Osborne's extravagant acres conferred an enclosed world on them, its gates at a far remove from the mansion, its lawns sweeping straight down from the mansion to the sea, where the family not only had a beach of their own but also a landing stage for the royal yacht, the latter allowing them to enter their holiday kingdom away from the attentions of the Cowes pier. Even if another Brighton-like magnet for visitors were to develop at the very portals of the estate, the royal couple was assured of their own privacy.

The tearing down and rebuilding of the Queen's new house began almost immediately after the new owners took possession. Like only one other royal British residence—Uncle George's Brighton Pavilion—Osborne came to express the reign of but a single sovereign. From the first overturned spade of earth at the beginning of the Blachford mansion's dismantling, to the final alterations at the end of the nineteenth century, Osborne mirrored the wishes and tastes and passing lives of, first, an adoring couple, and later, a reminiscing widow. Though it started out—was indeed planned—as simply a private retreat for the Royal Family, a place to escape the nearly unavoidable opulence and panoply that is part of being a British sovereign, it soon became, inevitably and unmistakably, a royal palace.

Both the virtues and the shortcomings of the reborn Osborne were due to its guiding spirit. From its beginning, the complex that totally replaced Lady Isabella's comparatively simple Georgian home was the creation of the Prince Consort. He saw in its site a reflection of the Neapolitan countryside he had once visited in his youth—the Solent standing in for the Bay of Naples, the rolling hills of the island substituting for those of the Campania.

The couple's priority became to refashion their new property into a setting suitable for a sovereign. No matter how much Victoria thought they might get along in a "snug" nest, her position meant that any home she lived in would by necessity assume a quasi-public character. Albert asked Thomas Cubitt, the London builder who had done much to create Belgravia and Pimlico (and an individual of whom the Queen said "no kinder, better man exists"), to take charge of the technical details of a new house. But the Prince himself would supervise its design, intending to fill it with as much German *Gemütlichkeit* and Italian *scintillare* as he could.

What the Prince sketched for Cubitt to flesh out was a relatively compact, three-story brickwork building. It was to be covered in Roman cement to imitate more expensive Bath stone, an economy greatly appealing to Albert's finely honed parsimony. Skirtings inside the rooms were also made of concrete, genuine wooden ones held to be too great a strain on the royal budget. Tons of cockleshells were employed to insulate the Albertine building venture, though the shells were Cubitt's idea to make the building as fire resistant as possible. When the rooms were finally painted—it took three years to first decide on and then execute the brilliantly colored Renaissance interiors—Victoria and Albert were at last able to start filling them with objects left over from other royal residences, bits from Maple's (London's great middle-class furniture emporium and an establishment much admired by Victoria), and the largesse of an almost-endless buying spree carried out all over Europe.

This initial creation for the royal couple, from the outset known as the "Pavilion," was ready for Victoria and Albert to occupy in September 1846. Two years later, the old Osborne House was razed, and after three more years, the much larger block that made up the combined Main and Household wings was finished, the latter vastly overshadowing the Pavilion in its more classic mass, and the element that completed the metamorphosis of the Blachford estate into Britain's newest royal palace.

❖ 6 ❖

Now, on Monday, January 14, performing what would be her last official duty, Victoria listened sadly and with all the attention she could muster as Lord Roberts described the bitter war Britain found itself fighting. The Queen's two youngest daughters, Louise and Beatrice—the Household censoriously called them the "Petticoats," partly for their simpleminded chirpiness, partly for their attempts to shield their mother from importunate courtiers —had tried to stop the field marshal's visit. This duo of middle-aged princesses had devised a stratagem to interrupt Lord Roberts's audience after twenty minutes. When they told the Queen what they planned to do, expecting quick approval, the sovereign vetoed the idea in as strong terms as her dwindling energy allowed. "Do nothing of the kind," Victoria ordered. "I have a great deal to say to him which I *must* say and a great deal to hear from him. I shall want plenty of time and I won't be interrupted!"

After an hour, Victoria had indeed heard Roberts out. Though his truthful summation of the war was in no way meant to simply gratify royal ears, Victoria came away from the audience gladdened in the knowledge that her 500,000 troops were, at least, doing all that could be expected of them.

Roberts couldn't help but be impressed by the fact that his sovereign looked very old—and very unwell. Further, she seemed easily agitated. As the field marshal recounted events in South Africa to the Queen, the purpose of his visit, Victoria's mind was so distracted that she sat idly pulling the feathers out of her ostrich fan—though Roberts's sitting without being so bidden may well have added to her upset. But what was most unsettling to the Queen was the reality of the enemy's continued resistance to the efforts of her armies, and she knew this was one vexation she could do little about.

After hearing Roberts admit that no final victory to the war was in sight, the Queen shrugged off the gloomy tidings and, surprising the field marshal, bestowed two honors that would elevate him into the most exalted ranks of her subjects. First, she upgraded his barony two notches to an earldom, and, because he had lost his only son, added a rare dispensation that this peerage might one day be passed to the new earl's daughter. Her knowledge that Roberts's only son had died in the fighting was especially painful to a woman who had herself lost a grandson to this dreadful war —Christian Victor, Princess Helena's boy, had died just three months ago of enteric fever at Pretoria.

The second gift Victoria extended added yet two more characters—K.G.—to the impressive list of post-nominal letters that signified the highest his sovereign and his nation had to offer. A Garter knighthood, the most prized of British orders and one reserved almost exclusively for royalty and the greatest noblemen, conferred almost unprecedented honor on Roberts, and was, in fact, the only Garter she ever bestowed on a soldier outside her own family—the first on *any* non-royal soldier since Wellington. Ironically, when he first set out for South Africa only a few months earlier as the new commander, deeply aggrieved at the recent death of his son Freddy, Roberts had remarked to the press that "honors, rewards and congratulations have no value to me. . . ." Now they helped comfort a man who could commiserate with his Queen over the toll the war was taking.

When her newly elevated guest was ushered out of the royal presence, the monarch was so weak from the strain of her meeting that it was all she could do to sit up in the wheelchair that took her back to her bedroom. The little rolling chair had been her main means of locomotion for some weeks now. After tonight, it would be the only way Victoria would ever again be moved.

## CHAPTER II

# Tuesday,
# January 15

❖ 1 ❖

It might have been better had Victoria allowed the Petticoats their intended kindness. Getting through—barely—yesterday's audience with Lord Roberts had been about all the Queen could manage. Having existed for the last month on little more than broth, warm milk and Benger's Food—a patented wheat powder that was mixed with milk and tasted like a combination of farina and library paste—it was small wonder the Queen was today only minimally transportable. Victoria would be eighty-two in May, a remarkable feat for a woman who was born into a world still suffused with medical notions as much whimsical as scientific. Equally, it was extraordinary that a woman who had been old—acted old, been treated old, been thought old—since the day her husband died four decades earlier, a woman whose notion of exercise was being carted around one or another of her estates in a pony-chair, one whose every need or want was instantly carried out by minions, it was extraordinary that so out-of-shape a woman should have gotten to the great age she *had* achieved. That the end was clearly approaching was, medically, unsurprising. What *was* surprising was that her subjects still held the opinion that the monarch would go on forever. Or, at the very least, that few of them could imagine a world without Victoria, a world that only those of her subjects nearing their eighth decade had ever experienced.

### ❖ 2 ❖

The self-contained universe Victoria inhabited in the Isle of Wight encompassed all the ingredients necessary to ensure that its privileged residents would never *have* to set foot outside its closely guarded gates. Given its unique status as the sometime seat of the kingdom's court, everything that was needed from the outside was brought to Osborne—or, more pointedly, to Victoria. This included people, with prominent reference to the members of her government whose personal attendance on the sovereign was required for the constitutional functioning of the Crown and State.

Since the beginning of her four-decade-long widowhood, the style of rule Victoria had adopted was, in essence, one of a desk-bound bureaucrat writ large. That which was expected of British sovereigns—to show themselves and live life as symbol and social overseer—was precisely what she rejected. What she gave to her kingdom was an extravagantly punctilious involvement in the daily, even hourly, minutiae of government's intimate workings. Abjuring all but a marginal involvement in court ceremonial, she lived her life without a backward glance, or even an indication that *her* way was anything but the right, the only way.

A December 1861 letter to her uncle Leopold, her mother's brother and her fellow sovereign as King of the Belgians, set forth Victoria's inflexible resolve with the clarity of a contract:

> I am . . . anxious to repeat *one* thing, and *that one* is *my firm* resolve, my *irrevocable decision*, vz. that *his* wishes—*his* plans— about everything, *his* views about *every* thing are to be *my law*! And *no human power* will swerve me from *what he* decided and wished. . . . I apply this particularly as regards our children— Bertie, etc. . . . I am *also determined* that *no one* person, may *he* be ever so good, ever so devoted among my servants—is to lead or guide or dictate to me. . . . Though miserably weak and utterly shattered, my spirit rises when I think of *any* wish or plan of his is to be touched or changed, or I am *made to do* anything. . . . I won't think of it!

It would take a powerful effort to find a firmer declaration of the path Victoria intended to follow for the rest of her life. In fact, this was precisely how she conducted the four decades remaining of her tenure of the throne—in an unswerving emulation of all that she thought Albert would have wanted. Even now, two weeks into the new century, the Albertinism Victoria had cultivated with such single-minded assiduity still held sway over the monarch, her family, her homes, her outlook on life. If by the last years of that life most of her subjects regarded Albert himself as little more than a hazy memory or a dry subject from a history book, such was anything but the case with the influence he still exercised over their sovereign.

Thrust into a brain-numbing grief in 1861, the monarch had given herself over to a desolation of stupefying proportions, what would likely be regarded today as a severe nervous breakdown. Forging her sorrow into grim enterprise, she made of Albert's memory a kind of personal cult, one in which she demanded her family and household's unqualified membership. Among its bizarre rules was the laying out every night before dinner of her late husband's evening clothes, as though the Prince were still alive. She commanded that his shaving gear be set up every morning before breakfast, insisted that his chamber pot be scoured daily. For four decades, Victoria would each day enter Albert's darkened and airless dressing rooms to fondle these relics, always kept meticulously just-so for the Queen's examination. His portraits, each draped in black crepe, decorated every wall and tabletop; hand-colored photographs of Albert's corpse hung over the Queen's bed in all her residences. The result was that Osborne in particular, the house *he* built, soon came to look like an undertakers' stockist.

Few places were safe from Victoria's commemorative urges: the Scottish glen where Albert shot his last stag was duly marked with a stone cairn. In letters the Queen wrote, she sometimes referred to Albert as "Him," as though a deity. The widow weeds topped by a white chiffon pom-pom that she affected for the rest of her life became a memorial uniform, one as unique and invariable as the white robes of the Roman popes.

The Queen's obsession settled into a drearily inflexible posture. There was no one to gainsay a monarch. Indulged in her morbidity by family, court, ministers and—at first—a public unwilling to criticize the bereaved sovereign, the result was that literally no one could tell the Queen to pull herself together, to become the woman she had been before that black December day. Such an obsession in what was a sentiment-soaked age might have been acquitted had it lasted for a year, or even two. But it never ended, the ranting and weeping only slowly mutating over forty years into a sullen moodiness. It took her secretary until 1863 to cajole Victoria into setting foot in a public place. When she finally did, it was only for the briefest of appearances: swaddled in black, her dumpy figure hooded against prying eyes, the occasion was, unsurprisingly, an unveiling of a statue of Albert. Even at the Prince of Wales's wedding that same year, the Queen hid behind a grille high above the chapel and departed as soon as the ceremony was over. Instead of joining the wedding breakfast, she ate alone before scuttling off to the Royal Mausoleum to stare at "him" for two hours.

With the nation's head of state utterly hidden away at Windsor or Osborne or Balmoral, the increasingly exasperated British began to question the utility of the monarchy altogether. Expressing the general feeling, in 1867 someone stuck a sign on the gate at Buckingham Palace, noting that "these commanding premises are to be let or sold, as a consequence of the late occupant's declining business."

Illness and death slowly settled in alongside grief as the preeminent chords in Victoria's life. In 1871, she watched the Prince of Wales very nearly succumb to typhoid; his recovery from a cliffhanging illness amazingly but effectively stemmed the nation's popular drift toward republicanism. Later that same year, the Queen herself became dangerously ill from strep throat and an underarm abscess. Her second daughter, Princess Alice, died in 1878, and her fourth son, Prince Leopold (the Duke of Albany), followed his sister six years later. Her favorite son-in-law, Fritz, died in 1888 after a ninety-nine-day reign as German Emperor, his passing as severe a blow to the Queen as it would be to future Anglo-German relations. Prince Alfred, her second and most dissolute son, died in 1900. It got so that virtually every day was the anniversary of the death of some member of her enormously extended family, with the Queen insisting on mortuarial obsequies to the fullest. The fact that both husband Albert and daughter

Alice died on December 14 made that particular day the most mordant in the Queen's calendar. Only the 1892 death of Prince Albert Victor, the Prince of Wales's oldest son (and thus the direct heir, once removed, to the throne), a backward and uneducable fop, was likely to have been seen by the Queen as a blessing; Victoria was acutely aware that her grandson's shortcomings might be lethal to the monarchy. She nonetheless raised a monumental wailing at his demise.

Though her sense—both common and constitutional—had been severely compromised by all this grieving, Victoria's lucidity seems to have remained relatively intact. Manipulating her children, especially in matters matrimonial, and taking refuge in what was universally seen as an unseemly relationship with her Scottish servant, John Brown, engaged the Queen's mind sufficiently for her to retain her reason. But her ministers may have questioned even this assessment, as official dealings with Victoria became a near impossibility. Though she treated and was treated by Disraeli with something approaching mutual fairyhood, a relationship cemented for the Queen by the Premier's gushing obsequities, her ill-famed and malignant relationship with Gladstone often approached, indeed sometimes stepped over, the limits of expression proper to a constitutional monarch.

In the last quarter of her reign, the private Victoria had turned into a demanding, self-pitying woman. Obsessed with her health, she wouldn't move between any two of her three principal residences without a vast retinue of medical specialists and body attendants. She thought nothing of awakening in the middle of the night one of her doctors—most often the ever-compliant Sir James Reid—to attend her at bedside to hear some complaint, perhaps about missing a daily bowel movement, or possibly just to demand stronger sleeping medicine.

The monarch who entered the twentieth century had long since become insensitive to the wishes or needs of almost everyone except herself: nothing was allowed to stand in the way of her wants, no one—least of all her surviving children, each now middle-aged—was permitted to thwart her slightest wish. Narrow-minded and reactionary regarding the aspirations of the working classes, Victoria openly disparaged Liberal politicians—Gladstone especially—because of the Liberal Party's attempts to introduce social legislation; the hatred was abetted by the party's efforts to grant some measure of home rule to the Irish, a race for which she had little understanding and less sympathy. Completely close-minded to the issue of women's rights or to women's attempts to win release from legal marital indentureship, the monarch couldn't understand, indeed made no effort to understand, why any woman might be chafing under such bonds, viewing her own freedom from any strictures as proof of the rightness of her views. Above all, Victoria was congenitally incapable of comprehending any viewpoint other than her own, a failing that inevitably ended in bitter invective directed at anyone hazarding to disagree with her in even the smallest degree. Such unchecked self-indulgence created a court regimen at once tyrannical and tedious, unbearable and unreal.

❖ 3 ❖

The Queen's regimented days at Osborne passed with her physical efforts confined to little more than studying state papers and writing—endless letters to endless relatives, instructions to ministers, notes (often curt and almost invariably in the third person) to courtiers. Visits to Osborne were, like sojourns at all her residences, governed by an inflexible calendar. The court would set off for the island refuge every year at the end of December and remain until the end of January, and then repeat the journey in the middle of July for a six-week summer holiday. (To ensure her privacy here, one company from any of the regiments stationed at Parkhurst Barracks would take up quarters at East Cowes in a commodious barracks near the Coast Guard station.)

As a break from the tedious pen-and-ink routine she adhered to as closely here as at any of her palaces, Victoria looked forward to little else as much as the daily pony-chaise drive that had long been a mark of life at Osborne. A lightweight carriage, more a basket on wheels, the rig was harnessed to a yearling and guided by a trusted attendant chosen from her army of retainers. The carts were big enough for the Queen and one companion—an always near-at-hand daughter, or daughter-in-law, or granddaughter, or lady-in-waiting—her voluminous petticoat-stiffened skirts and Indian paisley shawls warding off any offending breeze that might blow up from the Solent, the companion dressed in some dark color in respect of the Queen's wishes of all those who shared her eccentric mortuarial world.

Today the ride would be particularly welcome. The Queen had earlier this morning undergone one of those fatiguing medical scrutinies by which she had been increasingly tortured in the last few weeks. This time the martyrdom involved an eye examination. Her vision had gotten so bad that she was nearly blind before the morning ministrations of belladonna; at Christmas, Princess Beatrice had written her eldest sister Vicky, the German Dowager Empress, that their mother's sight was "so very bad and she could hardly see her pretty presents."

So arrangements were made for Professor Hermann Pagenstecher to subject the Queen to one of the probings she found so annoying but of which she sourly conceded to her ladies the necessity. The esteem the professor had earned in Germany for his miraculous cures some five years earlier had brought him to the attention of his most renowned patient. At the time of his first visit, the German scored a notable success with the Queen. Murmuring in German (which Victoria spoke well) during his examination such reassuring nostrums as "good," "very good," "quite healthy," and "not half as bad as I should have thought," his reassurances were balm to his patient. (The Queen's own English oculist, a less voluble man, omitted such encouragements; she accordingly judged him "cold, harsh, abrupt and unsympathetic.") Pagenstecher kept his more candid report for Sir James Reid, Victoria's primary physician, telling him that "the cataract was a little worse." The German shared in the English doctor's opinion that Victoria was experiencing "cerebral degeneration," Reid's way of saying the monarch was at imminent risk of suffering a stroke.

Victoria's medical inspection now thankfully completed, she could get on with her ride. Today her companion would be her daughter-in-law, Marie of Coburg. Recently widowed and thus humanely released from a dismal and—in Marie's view—unequal marriage, she had for twenty-eight years been the wife of Victoria's second son, Alfred. "Affie," as his family called him, was the Duke of Edinburgh, and had in 1893 become Duke of Saxe-Coburg and Gotha when he reluctantly assumed the throne of his father's toy German duchy. Affie had just fought a long battle against spinal cancer, losing his struggle only six months before. His widowed Russian duchess—Marie was born a daughter of Tsar Alexander II—had been prickly ever since arriving in England a quarter century earlier with a considerably diminished status from that in which she reveled back home as the daughter of the Emperor. When she first arrived in England, the extraordinarily plain young grand duchess imprudently demanded a status above that of the Princess of Wales. Victoria swiftly and in razor-sharp phrases instructed her intended daughter-in-law of the outlandishness of a second son's wife assuming precedence over the heir's consort.

Marie fetched the wheelchair-bound Queen from her cluttered second-floor sitting room office in the Pavilion. The walls of this pleasantly chintz-bestrewn chamber represented the horizons of the Queen's daytime world, the place where she worked and dictated her interminable correspondence to ladies-in-waiting and daughters, and the ever-briefer absences from it were enthusiastically anticipated by Victoria. After the sovereign and her daughter-in-law passed marble busts of Albert that ornamented the corridor outside the sitting room, the two women arrived at a tiny, upholstered elevator that would lower them to the ground floor. After descending in the little steam-powered apparatus, they glided slowly across the brilliantly marble-tiled passage, finally reaching the mansion's impressive porte cochere. There, held at the ready by a servant, a pony-chaise awaited them. With practiced efforts, the servants hoisted the Queen into the contraption, Marie quickly following on her own motive power. What little exercise Victoria could expect on her outing would consist of turning her head from side to side, absorbing once more the familiar trees and fountains and vistas that always evoked reveries of Albert and gay moments that had now faded into gauzy but precious memories. Even this small reward would be denied today, as Queen, duchess and attendant waited long minutes in vain under the canopy for a break in the biting January drizzle. When Victoria decided they had waited long enough, she signaled for Marie to reverse the whole exercise, the sovereign joylessly retracing her route back to the sitting room.

Slowly, this living monument was running down. Nothing thus far was immediately threatening, not in the imminent mortal sense, but the mechanisms that kept Victoria's body operating were, indisputably and now unalterably, congealing. Physician-in-Ordinary Sir James Reid, the nearest and most intimate among the battery that made up Victoria's private medical community, knew that there was no basis for hope that the eighty-one-year-old woman might deflect her body's sprint toward breakdown. Though the doctor had approved the continuation of formal planning for her annual holiday in the south of France (planning which because of Victoria's penchant to bring her own bed, desk, chairs, couch, family pictures, carriage, donkey, and—most importantly—food involved logistics on a martial scale), Reid knew there was no chance the Queen would ever again leave her kingdom. Perhaps the most poignant of the signs the vigilant physician saw were the alterations in her personality over the last few days. Victoria was allowing minor imperfections to go unrebuked, things that even a week ago would have caused irritation or even anger—the unwonted noise, a servant too visible, a bell not answered as quickly as she thought it should be. The Queen's private secretary, taking it on his own responsibility and supported by Reid, had this morning quietly canceled the trip to France, notifying the Excelsior Regina Hotel in Cimiez—an establishment whose royal custom impelled its owners to add the "Regina" to its title—that Her Majesty would not be visiting. The courtier enclosed a check for £800 to cover the costs the hotel had already incurred.

Still Victoria remained, beyond question, the trunk from which every branch, shoot and leaf of the royal oak of Osborne radiated. Like all her residences, so too was this one astonishingly complex. In fact, the Osborne world was operated along much the same lines as a department of state, which, in an only somewhat reduced way, it was. Not only did it house the anointed head of the world's greatest empire, but that head expected her government to come to her wherever she may be, an expectation meticulously observed throughout her reign. Victoria expected to be informed, she took seriously her constitutional duty to approve, and she believed her advice on virtually any situation involving her empire, her kingdom, or her immense and widely scattered family, among which were counted sovereign heads of state, to be a crucial component in the government of her nation.

Since Albert's death, the royal domain on the Osborne estate had grown considerably. The Queen's private mansion itself and its surrounding array of outbuildings, farms, play buildings, and ecclesiastical confections had expanded until the whole had taken on some of the attributes of a self-contained fiefdom. Though Victoria personally ruled Osborne like a small kingdom, as she did each of her homes, the man who managed the monarch and who worked more closely around her than any other adviser was Sir Arthur Bigge. Over the long history of the British monarchy, the courtier caste that Bigge represented had accreted itself around the throne like ivy to an oak, its services becoming indispensable to both the functioning of the throne and to the life of the monarch.

Before the modern ministerial system was firmly settled in the eighteenth century, the highest-ranking courtiers had been, in effect, the kingdom's top officials. In the aggregate, they served as an executive cabinet between the throne and a Parliament not yet endowed from its own ranks with responsible ministers. As the legislature's power gradually expanded at the expense of that of the monarchy and the nation came to be governed solely by Parliament, the executive courtier class faded, with only the highest positions—the sovereign's private secretaries—continuing to act as the intermediary between palace and Parliament. Still, courtiers remained an entrenched and active estate in royal affairs, their numbers replenished from the nation's landed, titled, and moneyed classes.

At the beginning of the twentieth century, few men were more securely entrenched in that class than Arthur Bigge. The future private secretary got his cap set on court life via a youthful friendship with Louis Napoleon, the Prince Imperial and only son of the exiled Emperor Napoleon III and his Empress, Eugénie. Attached to Bigge's battery in the Zulu War of 1879, the Prince was killed in an ambush while participating in a scouting party. Bigge was ordered to accompany the body back to England, such escort an honor routinely accorded royal corpses. Eugénie was at Balmoral, staying with her old friend Victoria, an intimate since the 1850 visit the Queen and Prince Albert made to her husband's court. In the presence of both Queens, the young officer gracefully recounted the tragic and courageous circumstances of his friend's death. Impressed with Bigge's poise, Victoria appointed him on the spot to the position of groom-in-waiting, a kind of super-pageship bestowed on likely young men who hailed from genteel background.

Bigge's background had, in fact, been spotlessly genteel. Born in 1849, the quiet and comely third son of a Northumberland vicar sprang from a family deeply rooted in country life, its branches living in houses with names redolent of the English gentry—Gun Lodge, Fenham Hall, Lye House, and Islip Manor. Arthur trained for an army career at the Royal Military Academy at Sandhurst, sharing classes with the Queen's third son, Prince Arthur. His army career continued in the Royal Artillery, a pursuit which would see him rising to the rank of lieutenant colonel.

Bigge's duty as a groom-in-waiting proved far less arduous than what he had experienced in Africa as a young officer. Because Victoria virtually ignored her junior male Household, preferring to work only with the most senior of her staff, the fledgling courtier grew accustomed to spending ample chunks of his days doing little other than copying out the odd letter for more senior colleagues. Fishing came to be an avenue to help him get through the boring days at whichever royal residence he was attending at the moment. One day at Balmoral the youthful groom was unnerved when the Queen's domineering Highland servant, John Brown, stuck his head into his room to rudely announce that "ye'll not be going fishing today," the plain-spoken head of the monarch's serving retinue adding that "Her Majesty thinks it's about time ye did some work." Despite Bigge's underutilization at court, he was nonetheless promoted to equerry, an honorific denoting somewhat higher status than that of a mere groom-in-waiting. What duties he was assigned he performed with dispatch and tact, and in due time he was again advanced, this time to the far more substantive office of assistant private secretary; together with his new equerryship, the office signified unusual trust from the monarch in someone both so young and so relatively new to court. The assistant secretaryship thus began a fifteen-year run-up to the most important office of all, that of private secretary, to which Bigge was promoted in 1895 on the death of its redoubtable and venerated incumbent, Sir Henry Ponsonby.

As private secretary, Bigge acted as liaison between the sovereign and ministers of state—most importantly the Prime Minister—the private secretary expected to smooth the often fractious relationship that Victoria would develop with the leaders of her governments. Bigge knew that Victoria demanded the same intensity of labor from her most intimate servants that she herself gave; a desk worker of vast and seemingly unquenchable energy, the Queen spared little sympathy for those who wouldn't give as good as she was willing to do.

Throughout the Victorian era, the private secretaryship represented a vital and influential office. Not only was the incumbent required to be a master of diplomatic discretion in explaining the Queen's views to the government and the government's to the Queen, he was expected to attend to the mountains of desk work that flowed in and out of the well-used studies that were the center of the monarch's life in her residences, making sure Victoria's interactions with her ministers were handled smoothly and flawlessly. Not trusting to oral communications, Victoria insisted that all business with both her top ministerial servants and her top Household servants be in writing, and the newfangled typewriting machines that were beginning to be popular in many offices weren't permitted by a Queen who treasured the maintenance of tradition above almost everything. Because of the monarch's failing eyesight in her last years, Bigge had to transform his own handwriting to a large sweeping script that the Queen could readily read, and even developed his own pitch-like black ink to enable the sovereign to more easily make out the documents that flowed across her desk like a stream of oozing lava.

On this cold and dreary January Tuesday, Bigge knew the crisis of his career was in the offing. He had discussed the Queen's health with Reid, who confided to the private secretary that Victoria wouldn't likely last much longer. Accepting the physician's reluctant but trustworthy prognosis, Bigge grieved, both for the woman he admired and for the country he served, and understood the hurricane of massive and largely unforeseeable challenges that would soon be bearing down on Osborne, a hurricane in whose path he stood foursquare.

❖ 4 ❖

Unsuspecting of the storm about to blow out of the Isle of Wight on an empire whose heart it symbolized, London sped along at the usual feverish pace that made it this winter of 1901 both the largest city in the world and the preeminent commercial center of the empire. The name London strictly applied only to the seven hundred acres that was the ancient City, but the true totality of the metropolis spread deep into the viscera of Middlesex and Kent and Surrey, counties that had for centuries been the cockpit of England. Its sweep in both size and population was humbling. From the overflowing streets and sepulchral dwelling blocks stretching nearly across the whole of the metropolis to the bastions of commerce shoulder by uncomfortable shoulder with near-antediluvian squalor, from the bejeweled squares of the aristocracy to the palace of the Queen, London at the turn of the century proffered every virtue and vice, splendor and malignancy known to mankind.

There were, to be sure, many hubs to this colossal conurbation. But a reasonable choice for the capital's center was London Bridge. Some fifty-eight miles upstream from the mouth of the Thames, London Bridge linked two very different worlds: the dull and largely working-class districts of the south bank with the vibrant heart of the City business quarter on the facing shore. In 1832, a modern structure designed by John Rennie was built to span the river, superseding an ancient, shop-encrusted bridge that had been the oldest in the capital. This later structure, its footpaths graced by lampposts cast from the metal of French cannons captured in the Peninsular War, was a five-arched affair, a little over a thousand feet in length, and which cost more than £2 million. But its roadway was already wholly inadequate for the pulsating twentieth-century traffic, and the 22,000 vehicles and 110,000 pedestrians who crossed it daily managed their passage only with considerable patience.

It was the northern end of the bridge—the venerable City of London—that defined the ancient heart of the capital. Separating the metropolis's poor east from its rich west, the City was where Wren's ecclesiastical masterpieces lay thick on the ground: the church of St. Clement's Dane within a throw of St. Martin's-le-Grand within a toss of St. Dunstan, and all within the sound of St. Mary le Bow's bells, those born within the sound of the latter's bells accounted the "truest" Londoners. Overshadowing all else sired by Wren's genius, indeed overshadowing all else in the City's wondrous square mile, was the cathedral church of the empire, the Latin-cruciform mass of St. Paul's. Here in 1897 the Queen herself had progressed in fetchingly modest state to the porch of Wren's masterpiece, there to receive the gratitude of the Archbishop of Canterbury and a thousand of her grandees for the completion of sixty years on the throne.

The City was, of course, more than the ecclesiastical cynosure of the kingdom. The real master over this tightly packed core of London was Almighty Sterling, the world's chief reserve currency and the instrument from which the music-makers of empire truly drew their pitch. Dominating this orchestra were the dung-gray, penal-looking walls of the Old Lady of Threadneedle Street, the Bank of England, within whose windowless stone bulwark lay untold millions of pounds' worth of gold ingots, the precious bricks—resembling dirty blocks of copper—all neatly heaped up on barrows. The issuer of the kingdom's paper money, the banker to the government, the manager of the national debt, and the agent of government in all its business transactions, the Old Lady often took daily into her vaults instruments to the value £50 million. By law the bank was bound to buy all gold bullion brought to it, which value per ounce in the last week of the Queen's life amounted to three pounds, seventeen shillings, nine pence.

Further out from the center, toward the east and a widening Thames, the commercial concourse of London's working classes lay low to the earth like a threadbare carpet. Jack London wrote that to go from west to east in the metropolis meant encountering "a new and different race of people, short of stature, an odd wretched and beer sodden appearance." The fact that the average working-class family spent six shillings a week on drink, fully a third of its income, gave the American writer's observations a doleful pathos.

Not entirely slum—some of the neighborhoods were dignified by neat, however modest, terraced housing in which lived artisans and shopkeepers—the East End was nonetheless pocked by seemingly intractable precincts of poverty that disgraced the kingdom in their want, their principal attention from the government the collection of whatever tax revenue might be wrung from such squalor. In 1901 thirty-five percent of East Enders lived below the official poverty line, reckoned that year at eighteen to twenty-one shillings per week for a middle-size family, meaning around £50 per year. The metropolis's infant mortality of 279 per 1,000 births was over-represented by East Enders. London's legions of prostitutes clustered here, effectively imprisoned in many of the city's 2,200 brothels. Most of the street girls—the "dolly-mops"— couldn't even practice their trade indoors, using polluted alleys instead and giving irrefutable lie to the Victorian era's pretensions of sexual fastidiousness.

Yet even the East End couldn't hold all the destitution this megalopolis possessed in such intimidating quantity. Back across the City, in the western reaches where the prevailing breezes had long ago led the upper and middle classes to migrate and claim as their own, even there Victoria would have been confronted with thousands of her subjects living as rough as the draft animals used to transport the overflowing millions. The West End theater district was where most of London's fifty playhouses and many of its five hundred music halls were concentrated and which entertained a third of a million people nightly from those among the population who could afford to be entertained. Yet this area too was encrusted on all sides with slums that beggared the worst of the East End; the fabulously vile Seven Dials in Soho, a stew within five minutes' walking time of the town palaces of the nobility, had only just begun to be rehabilitated through the efforts of the various Christian societies.

Though the capital possessed the kingdom's first and best police force—London's famous "bobbies"—even those custodians of the law hesitated to enter the Dials. Part of the larger St. Giles rookery of squalor and criminality, the pickpockets and thieves and beggars working the lodemine of the West End could after their felonies disappear into the slum's labyrinthine lanes and there find near-perfect safety from the law. Its so-called Back Settlements were a network of yards and lanes, runway traps and bolt-holes protected by sentries who would instantly sound the alarm if police were to try to enter. None of the Dials' vermin-infested dwellings was wholly private, each instead an open path for criminals and whores on the run, from the police, from jealous competitors, from life.

Walking west from this morass, one entered the world touching on that lived in by the Queen. Comfort, respectability, beauty—all were the hallmarks of *this* West End, albeit hallmarks upheld on the overburdened shoulders of a serving class. Stretching from Mayfair and Tyburnia and the newly fashionable Belgravia, Kensington and Chelsea and further afield to Holland Park and Hampstead, this London was a comparative paradise, the sum of everything good the empire offered its plutocrats. Studded throughout like plump raisins in a sugar cake were the lavish town palaces of the aristocracy, many of which would have made the Queen's Osborne look like small pickings indeed. Gracefully connected with streets that seemed to be paved with gold—Piccadilly and Brompton Road, Bond Street and Park Lane—those upon whom Britain's blessings flowed in its days of glory gorged themselves with every comfort and luxury imaginable in their privileged milieu.

In this quarter too lay the seats of temporal power, both executive and legislative. Though Victoria loathed her capital, it nonetheless generously provided her with an immense and splendid stage setting for those few royal occasions on which the monarch deigned to visit London. Though the ancient St. James's Palace remained the nominal seat of the court, and was indeed the official venue to which diplomatic representatives to the British Crown brought their accreditations, Buckingham Palace reigned as the London headquarters of the monarchy. Huge, ugly on the outside, drafty on the inside, "Buck House," as the Royal Family called it, had never been a place much savored by the Queen. Since Albert's death, she had spent exactly twelve nights in it—this in forty years. But, characteristically, neither did the monarch permit its use as any kind of boardinghouse for visiting relatives; in her absence, which was to say almost always, Buckingham Palace remained empty of all but a small staff of servants employed only occasionally by the Prince of Wales for those giant royal galas for which his own town palace, Marlborough House, proved too small.

Other nearby bits of this splendid district sheltered various members of the Queen's family: the Duke and Duchess of Connaught occupied Clarence House, the appendage of St. James's Palace which the Queen's second son, the Duke of Edinburgh, vacated when he went to assume his patrimony in Coburg; Schomberg House in Pall Mall housed two of Princess Helena's daughters in considerable state; Kensington Palace, Victoria's birthplace across Hyde Park from Buckingham Palace, boarded a number of royal aunts and uncles and cousins, with its ranking residents the Queen's daughter Louise and her husband the Duke of Argyll. The Prince of Wales's son and heir, Prince George, the Duke of York, lived with his wife Mary in another wing of St. James's Palace known as York House.

The center of all this royal and aristocratic honey-making was, in January 1901, the very choicest beehive of all. Built originally by Wren for Queen Anne's great and good friend, Sarah, Duchess of Marlborough, the house named for her was now the nerve center of all that was smart and elegant and *au courant* in London. Home to the Prince and Princess of Wales since the Queen bestowed it on them after their wedding in 1863, Marlborough House drew the kingdom's most fashionable society—the Marlborough Set—that stood atop Britain's social pyramid in the absence of its putative leader, a Queen tucked up tightly elsewhere. Sitting on almost five acres of some of the most valuable land in the world, Marlborough House unendingly welcomed the richest and most powerful, loveliest and handsomest, highest and most mighty of the 500 million people subject to its occupant's mother.

Just across St. James's Park from all this glory and wealth worked the men of power whose role was to govern the Queen's domain. The politicians guiding the destiny of the kingdom were concentrated in Whitehall, a street named for the palace Henry

VIII had built there and whose name was in 1901 eponymous with power and government. The heart of the district was the one-hundred-yard-long Downing Street, the town house at Number 10 housing the prime minister and that next door at Number 11 the chancellor of the exchequer.

With their own working palace at Westminster, the Commons and Lords of the United Kingdom worked at maintaining nothing so much as the status quo. Their seat, a royal palace itself, albeit one the Queen could enter only at the invitation of Parliament, housed the two chambers of Britain's legislature.

Losing power rapidly but not yet an emasculated rump, the collective voice of the Peers of the United Kingdom still rang in the House of Lords with magisterial authority. The Upper House was composed of the Lords Spiritual, Legal, and Temporal, the first the archbishops and a portion of the bishops of the kingdom, the second the highest justices, and the third the hereditary nobility that had been created and magnified by centuries of England's sovereigns and in concert with the forces of primogeniture. Their collective lordships occupied the most splendid legislative chamber in the world. The golden chair at one end of the great hall under a canopy of heraldic devices was the throne of England, the seat from which the Queen—or, since Albert's death, her ministerial surrogate—announced annually the program the government would adopt in the upcoming session of Parliament.

The Lords consisted of a complex, graduated system of ranks and peerages, the latter representing—in theory—the different geographical parts of the United Kingdom. There were five grades of the temporal peerage, two of the spiritual. In the year of Victoria's death the House consisted of 5 royal dukes (Princes of the Blood), 22 non-royal dukes, 22 marquesses, 121 earls, 30 viscounts, and 322 barons, as well as 16 Scottish and 28 Irish representative peers; 2 archbishops and 24 bishops completed the roll.

Though the Upper House recalled Britain's most ancient authority, real parliamentary power was vested, as it had been for centuries, in the Lower House. With the Georgian abolition of the sovereign presiding personally at meetings of the ministers, the representative commoners of the kingdom and the office of Prime Minister came into their own. Though even by 1901 hardly a perfect democracy—the exclusion of the female half of the Queen's subjects conformed with ⟶      e found in nearly every state on ear        ned by the men of the kingdom t          Parliament reflected an enormous            ince the days of Victoria's immedi             ich Britons were justifiably proud.

Yet,                        government of Queen Victoria's re                  he minister from the Lords. Robert A              ᴏᴛ Gascoyne-Cecil, Lord Salisbury, the ninth earl and third marquess of that title, was in 1901 heading his third cabinet as the Queen's First Lord of the Treasury and Prime Minister. A descendant of William Cecil—the famous Lord Burghley, Queen Elizabeth I's Lord High Treasurer—Salisbury felt very much as one with his great ancestor. A dedicated defender of the principle of aristocracy and late Victorian Britain's champion of empire building, Salisbury *understood* the relative weight of Commons to Lords, but never for a moment considered the Lower House superior to the Upper.

Though by 1901 it was plainly an anomaly for the Prime Minister to sit in the Lords—Salisbury's brilliant nephew (and a future Prime Minister) Arthur Balfour took care of the House of Commons in the uncle's stead as its "Leader"—this outsized politician had long years' experience of his own in the Commons. First elected to that body in 1853 at the age of twenty-three—from a completely safe family constituency and one in which he never faced the impertinence of an opponent—he sat in the Lower House for fifteen years until he succeeded to his father's title in 1868 and was thus obliged to forfeit the rough and tumble of the Lower Body for the magisterial solemnity of Lords. Salisbury held the latter as a place better suited to the task of protecting the values that made Britain great, believing the Commons a potential destroyer as its tide of liberal values gradually rose, washing away centuries of accepted verities.

Though the Prime Minister eccentrically feigned complete indifference to politics, he sought power for the one unmatchable gift it afforded: that of fulfilling a mission to preserve his class as the unquestioned governors of the kingdom. This scion of gen erations of nobility was too secure to indulge in overt class prejudices, and never regarded the lower orders as undeserving. He did, though, account them as *different*, a difference for which they could neither be held accountable nor which they could change. It left them, simply, bereft of the capacity to govern themselves with anything like the success that the aristocracy could bring to bear. Salisbury countenanced no nonsense about *political* equality of the classes, believing there were "natural leaders," of which, of course, the upper reaches of society maintained a near-total monopoly. In this view, he held the complete confidence of his monarch, who considered Salisbury one of the "two best prime ministers I ever had"—the other not Disraeli (surprisingly), but Peel. Many disagreed with Victoria, of course; Disraeli described Salisbury as "a great master of gibes and flouts and jeers" —a fair reflection of the marquess's disdain for ordinary mortals and politicians who disagreed with him.

As the sands of her reign trickled away, Victoria possessed an intellectual soul mate in Lord Salisbury. Though the two were as oil and water—in their qualities of mind, he an intellectual of the first order, she the believer in the commonsensical approach—both felt regard and respect for the other. At those frequent times when Salisbury's ministerial duty obliged him to attend on the sovereign at one or another of her residences, Victoria always received this last of her chief ministers with a respect she had in her life accorded extremely few men. The regard shared by sovereign and this subject for class prerogative was meant, in the end, not to preserve the comforts of their own class, but instead, both deeply believed, to protect all those below who depended on their betters to look out for them.

# Wednesday,
# January 16

❖   1   ❖

W hatever Victoria's faults, lying about in bed all day wasn't one of them. Yet this morning the Queen's maids couldn't for the first time in anyone's memory rouse their mistress. Reid had been keeping close watch on his patient, and when she didn't ask for him early this Wednesday morning, he uneasily did something he had never done before. The doctor went to Victoria's bedroom.

It was the first time the physician had seen the monarch in bed. Victoria was lying in the great canopied bed of sculpted walnut burl, curled up in a fetal position on her right side, toward the photo of Albert that hung over the headboard. That Reid had never before this moment seen the Queen in her bed was a remarkable fact for the man who for more than twenty years had been her closest medical attendant. But it hadn't been her physician who gave her all the midnight medications whose dosages Reid had carefully worked out. Instead, it was Victoria's maids who were the administrators of these comforting draughts. The doctor was shocked at how small and vulnerable she seemed, this woman who ruled nearly a quarter of the world's people. He noted she was breathing normally, and looked to be in no immediate distress. But he couldn't help wondering if she knew he was even in the room. The monarch's "dressers"—the only people in the world privy to the truly intimate Victoria—assured the doctor that she was too drowsy to notice him. Still, Victoria's fear of the stethoscope, as well as her general loathing of being touched by any of her medical attendants, made Reid's job of checking her heart as delicate a task as ever.

With Victoria sequestered behind her bedroom's massive carved-oak doors, the business of the monarchy was beginning to fray, like the filaments of an old lightbulb. The fact was that the highest workings of the British government could not proceed normally without the direct and daily participation of the sovereign. This situation was, of course, largely a result of the Queen's own style as developed over the decades, rather than a fundamental requirement of the constitution. While it was true that no act of Parliament could become law without Victoria's signature, beyond this nothing further from the Queen was absolutely required. The ministers didn't *have* to hear Victoria's views on pending legislation; the Queen insisted they do. Her ministers *could* have governed without consulting Victoria; the Queen insisted they do nothing of the sort. Boxes stuffed with state documents, ranging from treaties to pardons to communiqués with the Crown's diplomats in every quarter of the globe didn't *have* to be sent to Victoria's residence of the moment before their contents could be acted on; the sovereign insisted her advice on their contents be considered before a single paper was sent on to its destination.

With the illnesses of age closing in over the Queen like a gently folding chrysalis, her court and family were forced to recognize what had before been unthinkable. This morning, Reid would finally take it on himself to let Victoria's family know what he believed was coming. With the courage born of conviction, Reid went to the suites of the Queen's two daughters—Helena and Beatrice—to inform them that their mother's general weakening had made her long-term outlook perilous. In medical terms, he told them her condition was a kind of "cerebral degeneration," an illness from which there was little hope of recovery.

After leaving the princesses, the physician wrote to the Prince of Wales—the man whose position would be monumentally affected by Victoria's passing—to convey the same news. He also informed the Prince's heir and second in line for the throne, the Duke of York. In this torrent of telegrams, so too was Sir Richard Douglas Powell, the Queen's heart and lung specialist, notified. Finally, Reid formally advised Frederick "Fritz" Ponsonby— Bigge's lieutenant as assistant private secretary and the son of Sir Henry Ponsonby—of his patient's condition, giving a frightening gravity to what he had been broadly hinting at for some days. Together, Reid, Powell and Ponsonby began telephoning and telegraphing in cipher the ominous news to other central players in what was becoming a darkening drama.

In the midst of the morning's quickening mood of apprehension, a private cable arrived at the Osborne wireless office from Germany. Its news would rob Victoria of the little connection with sensibility she maintained. The telegram informed her that her beloved eldest child, Vicky, long ill with spinal cancer, lay dying at her English-style castle in the hills north of Frankfurt.

When these desperate tidings were delivered to the weakened monarch, Victoria must have let her mind float back more than six decades to the days when Albert was delirious with joy at the newborn princess he called Pussy. So bright and full of promise, this daughter was ordained to carry the power of her mother and the brilliance of her father into some great marital alliance which would go far to ensure the peace of Europe. Instead, her daughter's life was one long ago broken, its promise devastated almost as if in a Greek tragedy. The beloved daughter, one who had suffered misfortunes as wrenching as any known to her widespread family, was now succumbing to a disease for which no cure existed.

❖ 2 ❖

The birth of Victoria Adelaide Mary Louisa, the Princess Royal (the title an honorific given to the monarch's eldest daughter and bestowed by her mother shortly after birth), was fantasized by her parents to be the harbinger of a lasting, peaceful union between Briton and German, the two preeminent European Anglo-Saxon peoples. Instead, this Princess would come to stand as a symbol for the growing discord between two proud nations, a disharmony that would a few short years after her death mutilate the dream world her parents had so hopefully conceived. Vicky, the pet name by which her family knew her, became instead one of the most tragic characters in the history of Anglo-German relations. From a place where she might have cultivated great good, all her adult life she instead perpetrated incalculable harm.

"Oh Madam," gasped the accoucheur in a near-apologetic tone, "it is a princess!" The new mother, sodden with sweat from a twelve-hour labor, grimly but swiftly responded, "Never mind—the next will be a prince." Though the Queen was intensely aware of her constitutional burden to produce an heir—a *male* heir being immeasurably preferable to the other kind—Victoria and Albert would soon plant their first child on a pedestal under which all eight of her future siblings would long lie in shadow.

It was not surprising that Albert swiftly envisioned his daughter serving as the linchpin in an alliance between his native and his adopted countries. In 1841, the not-yet-united Germans were straining against petty regional bonds that had kept them from achieving anything like the triumphs of Victoria's kingdom. Albert clearly conceded that whatever future Germany might have, that future would be controlled by Prussia. A despotically militaristic nation already flexing its muscles against any Austrian claims as leader of a greater Germany, Prussia's bloated army guaranteed for its Hohenzollern rulers a chokehold on the dozens of petty principalities and middling kingdoms that made up the loosely organized German alliance. But Albert believed that if the strong-arm Prussians could be civilized under a constitutional monarchy and united with Great Britain in an international "moral" bulwark against any threat to the peace—despotic Russia the obvious preeminent menace—his patrimony would usher in a golden era such as the planet had never known.

Vicky's place in that future would come in the venerable institution of an arranged dynastic marriage. At the princess's birth, the scion of the Hohenzollern dynasty was the nine-year-old Prince Frederick William of Prussia. Nephew of the childless King Frederick William IV and second heir, the boy—called Fritz—was preceded only by his father, William, the King's brother. It was generally understood that young Fritz would in all likelihood succeed in a "reasonable" time to the Prussian throne, his father, after all, having been born in 1797. Were he to succeed with Vicky as his consort, and with Vicky thoroughly steeped in Albert's liberal virtues, miracles, Victoria and Albert trusted, might be wrought.

To burnish this golden vision, Vicky was indeed developing into a child of marked intelligence. The rapport between father and daughter soon became intense, resulting into an intimacy between adult and child highly unusual for the age. Though anxious that his vision for Vicky's future be borne into reality, Albert was torn by the prospect of losing the daughter he loved to another man and to another country.

Just as Vicky held so much promise, so too was Prince Frederick William hewn from a different oak than those common to the militaristic dynasty into which he was born. His mother, Princess Augusta of Saxe-Weimar, had grown into young womanhood in a court and state renowned for its liberal values. Though after her marriage she failed to abate her husband's and her new country's reaction—a reaction forged in great measure from generations of Prussian fears of being crushed between the French on one side and the Russians on the other—Augusta's innate tolerance clearly molded and softened her son's character.

Vicky and Fritz were first put in each other's company in 1851. The British Princess Royal was ten, her prospective Prussian match a fair-haired and handsome twenty when the young man's parents were invited by Victoria and Albert to England. Notwithstanding the disdain in which Fritz's father held British liberalism and his conviction that reaction remained the only effective way to govern Prussia, the son came away from the visit to Victoria's court with the seeds of new—and decidedly liberal—ideas.

Vicky was kept in the dark by her parents about a hoped-for match with Fritz, though the boy himself was plainly intrigued by the English Princess Royal's grown-up poise. Realizing the enormity of her value in the wider European royal marriage market, Fritz quickly determined to have her for himself. Surprisingly, his parents raised few objections to the match, but he feared that his less sympathetic uncle, King Frederick William, still might throw insuperable obstacles to any departure from the Prussian tradition that its princes take their brides solely from fellow German courts.

Britain's increasingly friendly relations with France proved to be the key that unlocked the King's reluctance to accept the daughter of the relatively progressive English court into the House of Hohenzollern. Though France was also Britain's most ancient enemy, Victoria and Albert had grown exceptionally attached to the ambitious French Emperor, Louis Napoleon, and to his wife Eugénie. Frederick William, consumed by growing mental illness, still recognized that an Anglo-Prussian alliance between the two states' royal houses would be a worthwhile counter to an Anglo-French alliance that might well make Prussia its main target.

With his family's permission to ask for Vicky's hand, in 1855 Fritz set out for Balmoral and the warm welcome he knew awaited him. The only uncertainty in the thickening romance remained Vicky herself. But the Princess Royal, now just fourteen but a girl fast maturing into a sophisticated-seeming young woman, well understood her father's dreams for her, and rekindling the still flickering spark for Fritz proved easy enough for someone who could all too clearly envision a glorious future as Queen of Prussia alongside a dynamic King. After winning acceptance of his offer of marriage, Fritz spent most of the remainder of his stay at Balmoral being indoctrinated by his future father-in-law in the utility of constitutional monarchy presiding over a liberal, non-despotic government. As for the Queen, whatever her beloved Albert saw as good, she accepted fully, and welcomed Fritz into her family with every good wish at her command.

In the spring of 1858, the now seventeen-year-old British Princess Royal married the heir to the Prussian throne in the Chapel Royal of London's St. James's Palace. (As to Fritz's parents' suggestion the wedding be held in Berlin—the groom was, after all, heir to the Prussian throne, a station considerably higher than that of his wife-to-be—Vicky's mother fired off a letter declaring that "whatever the usual practices of Prussian princes it is not every day that one marries the eldest daughter of the Queen of England.") When she arrived in the Prussian capital with her new husband, Vicky immediately began her education into the rigors of Prussian royalism—the palaces without bathrooms, the draperies that were never opened lest sunshine pierce the gloomy chambers, the new relatives who, already suspicious of Vicky's Englishness, refused to bend an inch into friendliness. In Berlin, royal wives were expected to merge into the gloomy background of gloomy palaces and even gloomier etiquette. They were not expected to forward views of any sort, except perhaps on motherhood; politics especially was their husbands' province.

The character traits that would lead to Vicky's eventual undoing almost immediately came to the fore: when in her husband's world, everything English would be volubly and inarguably better; when back in England, in her mother's world, all that was German was superior to anything English. It was a pattern from which she would never deviate. If she was marginalized for it in England, she was there, at least, forgiven. But in her new homeland, Vicky would be vilified until her dying day.

Still her mother would press her for the next four decades to follow the moral and political precepts of the Prince Consort. From the days of her honeymoon, the diplomatic bag brought a stream of letters from her parents—daily from the Queen, weekly from her father—both outspokenly advising Vicky to retain her own self and her own character rather than try to conform with the standards of her new surroundings. That these dictates would always be alien to her husband's country set the stage for the tragedy that would enfold her relationship with the first child born to her and Fritz.

From the start, Vicky suffered intensely from homesickness for what after her marriage seemed an irretrievably sunny English world. Her only happiness quickly proved to be her husband, and within a short time, a child was expected. At its birth, on January 27, 1859, a medical accident occurred that would have enormous consequences for the baby, and—in a very real way—for the world. At the time of the delivery, the child was being carried by its mother in what was then the highly dangerous breech position. At the arduous delivery, no anesthesia was given. As a result of the Princess's obvious suffering and to lessen the risk to their patient, the doctors wanted to get the ordeal over with as quickly as possible. In their haste, the infant's neck and left arm were wrenched when forceps were clumsily applied, medical fumbling that resulted in the crushing of the left arm, which was, in fact, almost pulled out of its socket. Further, the baby—a boy—was long moments out of the womb before breathing began. At first, it appeared that everything might turn out all right, but within three days it was apparent that muscles had been crushed and the injured arm was paralyzed, the nerves in the Prince's limb damaged beyond any hope of regeneration. William, as the infant was named, would grow up with a stunted and useless left arm, at adulthood several inches shorter than its counterpart.

Two years after the new heir was born, Vicky's brusque and reactionary father-in-law finally came to the throne, at the age of sixty-four. A decade later—in 1871—following three short, sharp wars of aggrandizement, the German states united under a Prussia that would call every shot that mattered. King William hesitated to add to his Prussian kingship the title of German Emperor ("Kaiser")—deeming the latter little more than downmarket window-dressing—but Fritz goaded his father into accepting the crown of a unified Germany, the son's motive a desire for a strong Germany as well as the vision of himself within a few years at the helm of that new nation. His father's Chancellor, Otto von Bismarck, voiced his surprise at Fritz's eagerness for the change. "The Crown Prince is as stupid and vain as any man," Bismarck acidly commented about a young Prince he already regarded as a threat. "He has been made crazy . . . by all this Kaiser madness."

In the event, Prussia did not become German. Germany became Prussian. The new state's political fabric rested almost exclusively on the foundation of reaction, footings the new Emperor's Chancellor would turn into a kind of national religion. But the liberal hope remained, as it seemed that Fritz and Vicky would reign on their own very soon, with the power to implement Prince Albert's policy of moderation, perhaps even truly constitutionalizing the German monarchy. Instead, two things got in the couple's way. One was the new King William's extraordinary good health. The second was Bismarck, the King's first minister, the father of the modern German state and, together with Napoleon, one of the two giants of nineteenth-century European politics. As to the relative ranking between William's health and Bismarck's existence, it was the latter that would do the most to ensure Fritz's historical obscurity.

Now Crown Prince and Crown Princess, Fritz and Vicky happily contemplated visions of soon-to-be political power, but it was a happiness ominously impaired by their son's stunted arm. Wanting a perfect heir for a husband she considered a perfect father, Vicky was bitterly disappointed at young William's ever more obvious deformity, as if the boy's shortcoming took away from her own sense of self-perfection. She vowed not to let the near-useless arm hold her son back in any way, but in her zeal withheld from the boy the succor that might have made him less sensitive to his impairment. Vicky gradually came to understand William would— *could*—never be another Albert, the father she admired with unchecked extravagance. It was a realization the mother inevitably and in countless ways communicated to her son, and in which her husband acquiesced. William would grow emotionally distant from both parents, and, menacingly, look for approval elsewhere.

He found it in three places, the first two of which could not have been more antithetical to the ideals Vicky and Fritz espoused. One was at his grandfather's knee, the King anxious that his heir's heir not be polluted by the liberal political claptrap to which he knew his parents subjected him at home. Another was at a different knee, that of the man who was the King's mentor, bully-in-residence, servant, intellectual superior, and ideological soul mate —Otto von Bismarck. And the third was at Windsor, from his forceful grandmother. Ironically, Queen Victoria had warned her daughter against trying too hard to turn the boy into something he wasn't. "I am sure you watch over your dear boy with care but I often think too great care, and too much constant watching leads to the very dangers hereafter which one wishes to avoid." It was some of the best advice Victoria would give her daughter, but it was almost entirely ignored. As for her impact on her grandson, Victoria was the recipient of William's lavish admiration, even if he misjudged her place in Britain's constitutional scheme of government.

Because their views differed so greatly from standard Prussian conservatism, Vicky and Fritz grew increasingly isolated from the court. The aristocracy, the bureaucracy, and the army—the latter Fritz's career—all looked on the heir with suspicion that as Emperor he would unravel the strong military and illiberal monarchy that kept the new Germany safe from the sort of rabble-rousing that had since 1789 continually disordered the French. Furthermore, the Crown Prince and his wife's admiration for all things English—exclaimed loudly, often, and with extraordinary lack of tact—clashed headlong with the new nationalism building to a head in Germany. These royal difficulties were being mirrored in German feelings of inferiority at British strength, and were increasingly fostering unhealthy suspicions between the two most powerful nations on earth.

Yet another factor was cutting Fritz off from his patrimony. In a society as patriarchal as Wilhelmine Germany, the Crown Prince seemed to be manipulated by a domineering wife who took orders straight from her omnipotent mother, the woman the Germans called the Widow of Windsor. The Prince's image as an appendage of *die Engländerin*—a nationwide title of derision for Vicky— made Fritz a poor candidate to espouse progressive political views in Germany. Not only did their future subjects come to view the couple with contempt, but so too did their eldest son. And all the while Bismarck was making sure that the Emperor's son was kept as far as possible from any involvement in the running of the German state.

Besides the tragedy of estrangement from a son who was himself destined for the throne, Vicky and her husband had to endure a King who lived to within a fortnight of his ninety-first birthday. Long-since senile, William had completely fallen under his Chancellor's control, a truly Machiavellian figure of astounding political skills. Otto von Bismarck was a *Junker*—a landed aristocrat—from old and reactionary Brandenburg, which lay east of the Elbe. He took note of world opinion but never allowed it to stop him from achieving his goal of strengthening Prussia and Germany at Europe's expense. Yet he was not a *German* nationalist, and did not look upon post-1871 Germany as the basis of the nation's strength. It was Prussia that mattered to the Iron Chancellor: the parts of the new nation outside of old Prussia's borders were mistrusted and largely unworthy, tainted by notions of parliamentarianism and susceptible to the same irresponsible liberal and democratic rubbish springing from England and France. Unhampered by principle, the only boundaries on Bismarck's aims were those that he thought best for his state; the practice of *Realpolitik* was a religion to *this*

Chancellor. In the exercise of this religion, he held the Crown Prince and Crown Princess as Antichrists, their influence over their son to be reduced to as little as possible. To Bismarck, it wouldn't be "speeches and majority votes" by which the great questions of the day would be decided, but rather by "blood and iron." Bismarck was a very personal nemesis to the Crown Princess. As William grew older, it wasn't his own shortcomings to which his mother would ascribe his failing. Instead, always the blame lay at Bismarck's feet as well as those of the old King, men who, according to Vicky, "used her son as a tool and instrument against his parents."

The completion of Vicky's ruination in Germany came with the debacle involving her husband's fatal illness. Shortly before his mother-in-law was to celebrate the Jubilee marking a half-century of rule, the Crown Prince began to notice a hoarseness in his voice. No relief for it could be found in any of the palliatives his doctors gave him. The old Emperor was finally beginning to fail—he was being given daily morphine injections for excruciating kidney and bladder pains—and the aging Crown Prince's health, glowing up to now, gave cause for concern. In winter 1887, Fritz's private physician called a throat specialist to the New Palace in Potsdam to examine the heir.

The specialist, a German, found a swelling on the patient's left vocal cord, and diagnosed it as a "polypoid thickening." After attempts to remove it with a white-hot electric-wire snare, procedures which were all but unendurable for Fritz, the physician recommended that the nodule be surgically removed by splitting open the larynx from the outside. The recommendation was no doubt prompted by the German doctors' growing suspicion that the condition involved a malignancy. But this surgical procedure —the only treatment that stood any chance of saving the Prince from certain death if the growth were indeed a cancer—would have meant the loss of Fritz's voice, not to mention the very great probability that he would lose his life as well. A further consideration muddying the medical concerns was Vicky's overwhelming desire to attend, in the company of her husband, her mother's approaching Jubilee, a goal she knew would be impossible if Fritz were subjected to a major operation. Impelling the Crown Princess was the certainty that if Fritz and she didn't attend, their eldest son would represent the German Emperor in the festivities, a scenario Vicky wanted at all costs to avoid.

When Vicky was informed of the planned surgery, she panicked. She knew her husband would come out of it voiceless at best, and therefore unquestionably ineffective as a monarch. The German specialists suggested a consultation with Dr. Morell Mackenzie, a socially prominent and German-speaking English throat specialist, and Vicky quickly agreed to it. Even so, she knew the danger that lay in bringing an outsider—especially an Englishman—in on the case: should anything go wrong in treating Fritz, the foreigner would undoubtedly be blamed and, since she had agreed to it, she would herself bear the worst of such criticism.

The plans for the German operation nevertheless went forward. Fritz was prepared for surgery in the New Palace. A couch was scrubbed with carbolic acid, and two rooms had been turned into an operating-recovery suite. But on the very eve of the procedure, Mackenzie dramatically arrived. After inspecting the patient, he self-assuredly counseled a delay so he might first remove a small piece of the patient's vocal cord to study the growth. Mackenzie grandly informed the panicky Vicky he could cure her husband without an operation. She rejoiced in the possibility that her husband might at least retain the use of his voice. Meanwhile, the German doctors continued to advocate the radical operation to cut the growth out once and for all (they were by now almost certain it was cancer). But the royal couple completely fell for the English physician's less drastic approach. Mackenzie's non-surgical scheme to treat Fritz's ailment became the path that was followed throughout the remainder of the gruesome course of the Crown Prince's illness.

A few weeks later Vicky and Fritz arrived in England to help the Queen celebrate the most lavish public ceremony of her reign since the coronation almost fifty years earlier. In the procession from Buckingham Palace to Westminster Abbey, the German Crown Prince towered above his fellow royalties, dressed in white uniform with the gleaming breastplate and eagle-topped helmet of a Pomeranian Cuirassier; the cornflower blue sash of the Garter lay against the silver of his breastplate, and in his left hand a baton signified the rank of field marshal. For this shining moment in his mother-in-law's kingdom, the price Fritz had possibly paid—albeit a price unknown to him at the time—was life itself.

While Vicky and Fritz remained in England after the round of Jubilee ceremonies, the Crown Prince was constantly attended by Mackenzie. The doctor wrote to the Queen to tell her of her son-in-law's progress under his palliative though still-painful treatment: ". . . from a condition in which there was a great and immediate danger to life the case has changed to one of a slight chronic inflammation or rather congestion, the cure of which is humanly speaking only a *question of time*."

Mackenzie's misassessment of the Crown Prince's illness meant only temporary relief for Fritz, and even the English doctor soon came to recognize the condition as a malignant carcinoma. Victoria's own doctor, James Reid, urged that the growth be treated for what it was, and that it be excised without any further equivocation. He passionately appealed to the Queen to convince her daughter and son-in-law that a Crown Prince "with an impaired or even no voice would be infinitely better than no Crown Prince at all." Still, after all the merits of both courses of treatment had been placed before them in writing, Fritz and Vicky continued to put their faith in Mackenzie, and supported his cautious course of treatment that avoided major surgery. Fritz continued to be subjected to horrifying agonies as doctors took one sample of the growth after another, and time after time peeled away at it with hot-wire snares and forceps introduced through the mouth of the fully awake patient.

After lengthy periods of recuperation at Osborne and Balmoral, the Crown Prince finally acceded to his father's minister's demands that he return home. But almost immediately after their arrival back in Germany, the weakened prince and his wife set off again, first, for the Tyrol, and, when the mountain air in the autumn proved too rigorous, to Baveno, in Italy. There at the end of October the cancer gnawing away at the tissues in Fritz's throat began the final assault on its victim. Increased hoarseness was within days followed by, ironically, an almost complete loss of his voice. A still warmer climate was sought, and the royal party moved further south, to San Remo, there to take up residence in a villa set amid the olive trees and soothing sun of the Italian Riviera. Mackenzie finally had to admit his own certainties to the couple that he did, indeed, believe the cause of Fritz's illness was cancer. With a heroic calmness, the Crown Prince accepted the physician's death sentence, and replied in the few measured words he was able to get out. He whispered: "I have lately been fearing something of this sort." The understatement was monstrous. He continued, kindly: "I thank you, Sir Morell, for being so frank with me." Having at last accepted his fate, Crown Prince Frederick William knew he could do little other than simply wait out what few months—or perhaps even weeks—of life he had left.

When the news broke in Germany that the Crown Prince's English doctor had acceded to a diagnosis of terminal cancer, the slander directed at Mackenzie was predictably furious, but not nearly so furious as that leveled at the Crown Princess. Vicky was characterized as the villain of the affair, not the German doctors who had in the first place invited Mackenzie to consult with them on the Crown Prince's condition. Furthermore, the danger of the operation the German doctors had first proposed was grossly minimalized. There is today general medical agreement that the procedure proposed in the spring of 1887 could very likely have killed Fritz. And, if by some godsend, he had pulled through, it would have left him unable to speak, a condition in which he would in all probability have been "persuaded" to renounce his rights of succession in favor of his son.

It was this latter course that was now touted as the one that Fritz should follow. The enfeebled Emperor signed an order giving his grandson William the power to sign documents for him should he not be able to do so himself. No one bothered even to tell Fritz of his son's new authority until the official documents were drawn up and sent to the Crown Prince and William concurrently. Their effect on both Fritz and Vicky was shattering. "So they already look upon me as dead," the dying man murmured to his wife. The mitigating circumstance that he was in Italy and thus unavailable to his father's ministers was overshadowed by the brusqueness of the decree and the knowledge that it was promulgated before he was consulted. Still Fritz stood his ground against a son clearly anxious to snatch the inheritance for which his father had waited so long, and, in recent months, in such agonizing condition, to receive.

The long-awaited death of the aged Emperor finally came on March 9, 1888. When Queen Victoria heard the news, she wrote in her diary, "Poor old Emperor, he was always very kind to me." Nonetheless, fully aware that he had been under Bismarck's heel since 1871, she added, "but for some years, alas, he was made a tool for no good."

When all the majesty and power and influence of the imperial German throne finally passed to Fritz after such a formidably protracted wait, it amounted to little more than bitter dust. The mortally ill Emperor understood that he had to return to Berlin or else appoint his son regent, and thus journeyed back to his capital, in a blinding snowstorm, in a blur of physical torment. There he publicly assumed the style Frederick III. Hardly able to breathe, now without the power to speak, his general's uniform collar hiding the excruciatingly painful steel cannula sticking out of his windpipe, the only joy the ravaged man had left in his heart was the satisfaction that his doctors had gotten him through long enough for his wife of thirty years to live out the rest of her life with the style and titles of Majesty, and Empress, and Queen. He knew full well that without Vicky's encouragement, he would never have made it this far.

Thus began a reign that history has all but forgotten. For ninety-nine days, Fritz would try to secure his wife's safe and comfortable future, while Vicky never stopped hoping that her husband would somehow survive long enough to alter Germany's increasingly belligerent course. And the excited William fumed while he waited impatiently for his father to die so he himself could finally come into the glory destiny had set out for him. The Empress wrote to her mother that "people in general consider us a *mere passing shadow*, soon to be replaced by *reality* in the shape of *William!!* . . . Shall we not have to leave all the work undone which we have so long and so carefully been preparing?" It was not just a case of Vicky letting her imagination carry her away: nearly the entire court deserted Frederick III as it gathered around the bombastic new Crown Prince.

The end of Frederick III's phantom reign came very soon, from broncho-pneumonia. (A postmortem showed that his larynx was a single gangrenous ulcer.) It was June 15, 1888. While Fritz passed the searing last moments of his life in the New Palace rooms where he had been born and which had been his and Vicky's home for decades, his energetic son ordered that a regiment of Hussars surround the palace to prevent any possibility of his parents' papers being smuggled out. The moment he heard of his father's death and thereby his own succession, a regiment of troops that were now officially his to command double-sealed the cordon the Hussars had already erected. The forty-seven-year-old Vicky became, literally, her son's prisoner, a status which she was to maintain, more or less fully realized, for the remainder of her life. Though his grandmother repeatedly wrote to the new head of the House of Hohenzollern imploring that he help and respect his mother, William was by this time hopelessly alienated from a mother he—and, most especially, his closest advisers—considered far too English and not nearly enough German.

Vicky's next thirteen years were years without influence, years during which the title Fritz fought so tenaciously to bestow upon her would prove to be without value. Her movements were circumscribed by her son's whims and paranoia. Having given up on any hope of ameliorating William's more outrageous stupidities, she would likely have settled permanently in England had it been politically possible to do so. Vicky would borrow one page from her mother's book for her own years in the wilds: like the widowed Queen, so, too, would the widowed Empress assume as a uniform the black weeds signifying her status. But in place of the white pompomed cap of the mother, the daughter's would, like the rest of her clothing, be entirely black.

If anything positive came of Vicky's tragedy, it was to draw her closer to her mother. For years, the Queen believed her imperial daughter had become too grand, too intellectual. When Fritz died, Victoria's misgivings about Vicky evaporated overnight; now mother and daughter were two widows who could understand and sympathize with the other's plight as no one else could do. The Queen wrote her grandson again, asking that he "bear with poor Mama if she is sometimes irritated and excited. She does not mean it so; think what months of agony and suspense with broken and sleepless nights she has gone through . . ." William respected and feared his grandmother, but her request that he bear with his mother was ignored. The only sympathy William would show would be to his official rather than his filial duties.

The English Princess Royal had come to Germany four decades earlier with a will to understand the ways and mores of her new home. Her writings showed enormous pride in Germany and its accomplishments. This intelligent and tenacious woman tried hard to acquire the spirit—if not the way of life—of her adopted country. But she failed miserably to convince her husband's countrymen of such commitment. Lacking tact, Vicky spent her entire adult life trying to live by her father's moral precepts. The tragedy was that she had to do so in a country where those precepts were as alien as the Koran.

A grace note followed Fritz's death, one that demonstrated his mother-in-law's love and admiration for the man she had hoped might become a second Frederick the Great. The Queen sent for Fritz's favorite charger, an eighteen-hand-high stallion he had ridden as German Crown Prince in Victoria's Jubilee procession. The beast was stabled, in great luxury, at Windsor. Queen Victoria commanded that no rider was ever to cross its back again.

❖ 3 ❖

While uneasiness about the failing Queen rippled outward from Reid and Bigge through the wider circles of the Household and staff, the mechanisms of Osborne itself continued to move with their long-accustomed perfection. Though the Queen had allowed mostly insignificant changes over the years, had Albert walked into Osborne in January 1901, little would have shown of the four decades that passed since he left it.

Osborne, the house, was split primarily between the Pavilion and the far larger adjoining block, with that block itself divided into so-called Main and Household wings joined by the long Grand Corridor. Even as the geography of the house was thus sharply apportioned, so were the inhabitants: there was the immediate Royal Family in the Pavilion, and there was everyone else of any rank at all, from the junior members of the Royal Family and highest visiting ministers of state to minor clerical officials, in the Main and Household wings. The remainder of Osborne— more a parallel universe than a separate world—consisted of the outbuildings and cellars and tucked-away cubbyholes that housed a serving army ranging from the heights where Housekeeper and the Chief Butler ruled to the depths where scullery maids and stable hands passed their austere existences. Moreover, the whole mass had been designed by the Prince Consort—with Albert's unshakable sense of propriety—so that it was almost impossible for any of the lower orders to see into the Pavilion's windows. Victoria was adamant that her servants not be able to peek at her. (In fact, all domestic servants with the need to enter the royal presence were under unyielding orders not to so much as glance at their royal mistress; infringement of this law was accounted a mortal sin in the royal catalog of such matters.)

The very heart of the Osborne complex, the Pavilion was an entirely detached, strictly off-limits-to-everyone-but-the-Royal-Family, box-shaped, porte-cochere-fronted, Portland-cement-rendered-to-imitate-Bath-stone mansion. Victoria thought it was the most wonderful thing in the world. She probably thought this mostly because Albert had supervised its design, but also because it really wasn't a palace, at least not in the way she took the measure of such things. The Pavilion consisted of three stories: a mausoleum-like main floor, a simple and charming bedroom floor, and an even simpler nursery floor atop the first two. By royal standards, the whole thing didn't amount to overly much.

The top-heavy entrance hall was in a sheltered nook roughly where the three wings of the complex joined. Its walls were painted a faux marble, typical of the economy measures that went into Osborne's construction and decoration. Immediately inside the great entrance doors a small, recently added elevator sat perpetually ready for the Queen's exclusive use. The lift was hand-operated by an attendant stationed in the basement, the Queen's slow rides taken in privacy; its walls were lined with a linoleum-like covering called Lincrusta, and a bench hung from the sidewall so the Queen could sit during her journeys between floors.

The central staircase was a gloomy affair, in part because no natural side light was admitted, the only illumination coming from a skylight far overhead. Furthermore, the stairs overwhelmed the relatively compact space they occupied, the sense of disproportion fostered by a huge allegorical painting by William Dyce, *Neptune Resigning the Empire of the Seas to Britannia*, which covered the wall of the first landing. The Queen quite liked it, but the painting, in which Neptune's attendants appear unclad, shocked many visitors to Osborne with its abundant nudity.

At the heart of the Pavilion was the Drawing Room, where the Queen and her court gathered. With its garishly embellished walls and ceilings, it drew from Lord Rosebery, the Prime Minister during 1894–95, the comment that he thought it was the ugliest drawing room in the world "until I saw the one at Balmoral," an extreme but not an exceptional opinion.

The traditional rule that no one could sit in the Queen's presence was a dictum Victoria believed helped sustain her dignity as sovereign, but the Drawing Room was so designed that the rule could be bent during the long, bleak after-dinner hours the Queen and her court spent there. At the end of the Drawing Room overlooking the east terrace, the room angled around through a "screen" of double columns, to a billiard room. The latter theoretically counted as a part of the Drawing Room and thus its occupants remained in the Queen's "presence." There the gentlemen of the Household not only were able to get in a little recreation after dinner, but because the Queen was sitting around the corner and thus out of actual view, its occupants could *sit*. Players faced a hard time at their billiards, though; the room was packed with so many statues that it was difficult to back up far enough to aim one's shot. Ladies didn't play billiards, didn't even enter a billiards room, and were thus obliged to spend these evenings on their rapidly tiring feet.

The only other rooms of significance on the main floor were the Dining Room, generously provided with huge panes of sheet-glass by Albert and Cubitt—an expensive luxury in the mid–nineteenth century—and the so-called Horn Room, the latter filled with furniture made almost entirely of stag antlers Albert had picked up somewhere in Germany on one of his furniture-gathering trips.

Only a tiny handful of people outside the immediate Royal Family ever saw the bedroom floor. This was the private world Victoria and Albert created for themselves, the least grand of any of their personal suites of rooms in the residences they used, and the rooms in which their hours off display from the Household and guests—even, in large part, from their children—were lived. The only servants allowed to share the bedroom floor were the body attendants to the royal couple, for whom small private apartments down the hall from Victoria and Albert's rooms were tucked into the odd recess. Albert's valet had once slept in the Prince's wardrobe room, nearby to his work, and Victoria's dressers were now almost as close to their mistress, being assigned rooms in the flag tower at the corner of the Pavilion.

The four principal rooms on this floor included a dressing room for Albert, another for Victoria, a sitting room–office shared by the couple, and a bedroom which—highly unusual for people of their rank—they also shared. Next to Albert's dressing room was placed a small bathroom, decorated in a robin's-egg blue and fitted with a tub and, inside a cabinet at the end of the tub, a shower, this last an uncommon possession anywhere in the world at the time Osborne was built. The tub was constructed without spigots, bathwater instead rising through a grill of perforations in the contraption's bottom, its controls operated by Albert's Swiss valet, Carl, who filled his master's bath every evening. Many of the Prince Consort's own paintings hung on the room's walls. As to his own efforts at art, Albert unfortunately didn't draw human eyes very well, which gave his canvases an inhuman flavor that nonetheless seems in keeping with the Prince's sense of otherworldliness.

The Prince's dressing room served triple duty as a private sitting room, as a study, and as the place where Albert changed his clothes four or five times a day. These changes started at 7:00 A.M., when he stepped into his long white drawers with the feet sewn on, to the last change into his dressing gown late in the evening. The Consort kept his French harmonium (on which he was a practiced player) in one corner, opposite where Cubitt built into the wall an ultra-modern water closet enclosure, replacing the chamber pot that was at the time a near-universal toilet arrangement, even in the houses of the great. A fireplace was always lit on chilly days with the sweet-smelling beech logs that the Queen insisted be used in the private apartments of all her residences.

Albert kept all sorts of mementos on his rolltop desk. An amber ball that had belonged to his grandfather and had been in the old gentleman's hand when he died sat next to an inkstand in the shape of a curling stone made of Balmoral granite, the two overlooking a marble paperweight, carved with a snake attacking an owl and which had been a childhood present from his grandmother.

Far the most valuable of the room's decorations were the early Italian pictures that Albert was then buying at relatively low prices, decades ahead of the vogue. Mantegnas, Bellinis and Verrocchios covered much of the small room's walls. (These paintings were, because of their immense value, moved to Buckingham Palace after Victoria's death.) When Albert died, his dressing and bath rooms became, like practically everything else associated with him, mortuarial icons for his grieving widow. For the forty years of her widowhood, the rooms were maintained as close as humanly possible to their state when the Prince Consort had last used them: after his death, each was photographed as Albert left it, and the maids were required to replace each item precisely in its same spot after having cleaned it.

Victoria's cluttered sitting room, Osborne's real nerve center, was nearly square, except where a curving bay of three tall French doors gave onto a shaded balcony overlooking the lawns and, in the distance, the Solent. Rather than grand, it was cozy, and might have belonged to any of her more affluent subjects with similar middle-class tastes. Instead of the silk damask that paneled the walls in her study at Windsor, here simple green paint was made to do. Upholstered in green and red flowered chintz, the furniture was middle rather than upper class: a card table with four chairs, small book cases, an ivory-inlaid piano, and the adjoining pair of matching brass-galleried tables that long served as the Queen and Prince Consort's work desks and whose photo-topped surfaces didn't change by so much as an altered inkwell for half a century. Prominent on the Queen's desk—the one on the right-hand side—was a stand filled with black-bordered writing paper, stamped with the ubiquitous royal cipher—*VRI,* for *Victoria, Regina et Imperatrix*—

"Queen and Empress." Beneath a stand holding the correspondence and dispatch boxes from which the Queen was never free
(largely by her own choice), a wealth of framed portraits, minia-
tures and statuettes and bric-a-brac associated with family members
were situated where she could lovingly look upon them and be
reminded of the sweet past. A music box nearby played part of the
chorus from *Tannhäuser*, and next to it stood a plaster statuette
representing her randy brother-in-law, Ernest of Saxe-Coburg-
Gotha; on a nearby wall was a framed program of the concert given
by the royal children on the Queen's thirty-fifth birthday. Over the
tables hung a triple-chained ormolu-and-china lamp, which gave
the room its primary illumination at night. Three buttons on Victoria's desk summoned her dresser Skerrett, a page, or Rudolf Löh-
lein, a Coburger who was first Albert's personal attendant and after
the Prince's death became Victoria's factotum. The electricity for
the bells was provided by the chemical action of a simple primary-
cell battery.

Further embellishing the room was a glut of fascinating litter:
candlesticks with tips shaded by dainty enamel butterflies, ebonized
clocks, miniature chairs, book carousels, dried flowers whose provenance was the fields and hedgerows of the island estate, more
pictures painted by such talented hands as Winterhalter and Angeli
and such unskilled hands as those of the Queen's grandchildren.
A marble head-and-shoulders bust of Albert looked down from a
tall pedestal to the left of the mantel, before which a chaplet of
fresh flowers was laid daily in commemoration of the Prince.

Between her sitting room and bedroom was the Queen's dressing room. The sole remarkable feature in this small corner chamber
was the plumbing arrangements. A pair of mirror-fronted doors
hid a large wooden-fronted tub, and, in a smaller closet to the left,
a shower. In the narrow passage giving onto her bedroom a toilet
was installed, with easy access from dressing room or bedroom. On
the wall hung a portrait of her favorite dog Sharp, a companion
that had been the most unusual of creatures—a ferocious collie.

In the last of Victoria's private rooms—her bedroom—would
be enacted the drama that filled the final days of her reign. This
chamber was a virtual gallery-memorial to the Queen's dead relatives in its decor and objets d'art. The salmon-pink chamber was

commanded by the great walnut-testered bed against the wall that faced the bay window. Over the fireplace hung Gustav Jäger's *The Entombment of Christ*, a gloomy oil commissioned by Albert in 1845. A somewhat more cheerful statue of the Queen's mother from her Frogmore Mausoleum lightened the room, as did a photograph of the Temporary Sarcophagus of the Prince Consort. By the bed's side, Albert had had a small device implanted which allowed the room's occupants to lock the door without having to get out of bed, a practical luxury ensuring privacy from importunate children, servants, or, one supposes, even lost ministers. Over Albert's side of the bed, the widowed Queen had hung a deathbed portrait of her husband, which with his overnight watch pocket formed a permanent part of the headboard.

The top floor of the Pavilion, originally meant for Victoria's own children while still toddlers—when they got older the young princes and princesses moved to separate suites in the Main Wing —had by 1901 turned into quarters for the children of the Queen's youngest daughter, Princess Beatrice (who lived over the Durbar Room in the new wing). There the Battenberg children romped, learned, and slept in the same nursery suite their mother and her eight siblings had once romped, learned and slept in. The cleanliness and airiness of the suite helped see to it that the royal children who lived here survived in a time when, as noted earlier, the infant mortality rate in less fortunate parts of the Queen's kingdom had reached astonishing heights.

❖   4   ❖

As the Victorian monarchy had, in the words of one of the era's Prime Ministers, become like one of the "great departments of state," so too did the sovereign's Medical Household become one of her own most important bureaucracies. By the time of her final illness, the Medical Household constituted a formidable battery of the most renowned and skilled medical practitioners in the kingdom. It was headed by physicians-in-ordinary, doctors who formed its nucleus and represented the consultants and the general practitioners directly attendant on the Queen. Senior among them was the head of the Medical Department; the ranking surgeon was called the sergeant surgeon, an ancient office that had served generations of English monarchs through their medical travails. In January 1901, the sergeant surgeon was Lord Lister, who as Mr. James Lister (surgeons in England were always addressed as Mister) had pioneered research on blood poisoning. In 1901, the three physicians-in-ordinary were Drs. Sir James Reid, Sir Richard Douglas Powell, and Sir Edward Sieveking. Reid was, in effect, Victoria's "private" physician, the closest of any of the Medical Department members to the monarch, and the one who was for two decades at Victoria's bidding almost without respite.

Subordinate to the physicians-in-ordinary were what were called physicians-in-extraordinary. This level formed a backup cadre of doctors who could treat the Queen on an emergency basis if none of the principal physicians was available (this scenario admittedly rare); one of them, Dr. Thomas Barlow, served as the official Physician to the Household. Retired Physicians-in-Ordinary generally became Physicians-in-Extraordinary as a reward for good service, thus composing what might be called royal physicians emeriti. Of the dozens of doctors who had served as ordinaries or extraordinaries during Victoria's long reign, fifty-seven had been presidents of their respective royal colleges, and forty-two had been members of the Royal Society, including two Society presidents—Lord Lister and Sir Benjamin Brodie.

A curiously named branch of the Medical Household was the Apothecary division. Though this category had centuries earlier started out as the court's druggists, in modern terms, the apothecaries had mutated into general practitioners. The lesser among them served the Household, up to but excluding the Royal Family, while the lavishly styled Apothecary to the Person could treat Blood Royal as well as blood blue.

Finally, there were the ancillary professionals: the surgeon oculist, who saw to royal eyes, the surgeon dentist—ditto to teeth—and the combined chemist and druggist, in January 1901 one Peter Wyatt Squire, Esquire. (Relations with dentists were, incidentally, difficult for Victoria; the monarch had always suffered from bad teeth, and hated the dentures made for her.) In the past, a Royal Accoucheur was on staff, but no such specialist was required at this point in Victoria's reign.

Though Victoria was grateful to her physicians for their skills, she by no means considered them the social equivalent of her senior Household, or, for that matter, even of the officer class of the uniformed services. According to one biographer, she treated doctors with "meticulous respect as regards fees and titles, but though she liked them far better than, say, cavalry officers, she never regarded them as the officers' social equals." As Dr. Reid's biographer suggests, this reserve towards the physicians in her Household was perhaps predicated on discomfort over the intimate tasks that such men had by necessity to perform. Writing with her usual candor to Vicky, the Queen called such bodily involvement "disgusting."

Whatever his social standing, for his services James Reid was well compensated by the standards of the time, though his responsibility to keep the sovereign both alive and comfortable was an onerous one. His salary came to £400 a year. It was less than what he might have knocked down in a Harley Street practice, but at court he faced few expenses; he was housed and fed at the Queen's expense, in luxurious if often banal circumstances and surroundings. There was a downside to the job, namely being treated like an adolescent by his employer. His first written instruction from the Queen upon his hiring gave him a taste of the sort of life he would lead. "Let Dr. Reid go out from quarter to 11 to one, unless the Queen [Victoria habitually wrote of herself in the third person] sends before to see him, and from 5 till *near* 8. If he wishes on any particular occasion to go out sooner he shd. ask. These are the regular hours. But I may send *before* to say he is not to go out before I [and, obviously, as often slipped right back into the first person] have seen him shd. I not feel well or want anything. This every Doctor in attendance has done and must be prepared to do."

Reid's rise was remarkable. Hired in 1881 to the relatively lowly status of resident medical attendant on the Queen, his original contract specified that he wasn't to be considered a member of the Royal Household, although he was to "take breakfast and luncheon with the Ladies and Gentlemen in Waiting." (The contract just as clearly stated that he wasn't to be considered a "servant," either.) His own self-realization that, although the *social* inferior of the tight coterie with whom he lived and worked, he was undoubtedly their intellectual superior was what Michaela Reid believed gave him the self-confidence to get on so successfully in his new job. In an exceptionally short time, he rose to undisputed preeminence in the royal medical establishment, so trusted by the Queen that it was he whom Victoria empowered to carry out the most intimate details of her eventual burial.

There was a bad patch for poor Reid when he decided to marry. Victoria always felt strongly against her servants marrying, especially the higher ones (she thought of her lords and ladies as essentially "servants," just as she did all those who worked for her). Viewing such marriage as a kind of personal affront, she came to equate it with disloyalty bordering on treason. So it was with James Reid. When at nearly fifty he resolved to wed the socially well-connected Susan Baring, Victoria erupted in fury, Reid's happiness or lack of happiness utterly immaterial where her convenience was concerned. To express her indignation, and to set house rules for the newlyweds' future social station and degree of independence, she fired off the following memorandum:

> I think it absolutely necessary that Sir J. Reid and Miss Baring know exactly what their position will be when they are married. . . . He must continue living in the house *wherever* we are. . . . He must always, as now, come round after breakfast to see what I should want, and then be back before luncheon. He must also in the afternoon, before he goes out, do the same. . . . Sir James should always ask if he wishes to go out for longer, or to dine out, returning by eleven or half past eleven. His wife should not come to his room here [at Windsor], nor to the Corridor, where some of the Royal Children live. . . . she might occasionally come to his room but this must not interfere with his other duties. It is absolutely necessary that they should be fully aware of these conditions so that they cannot complain afterwards.

The marriage went ahead, in spite of this astonishing screed from his monarch and patient.

❖ 5 ❖

The worn-out Queen lay in her bed this afternoon. Perhaps she passed the hours calling up memories of when she and Albert seemed to possess the keys to the kingdom. If so, that reverie must now have seemed hollow indeed. Her troubled but dear Affie gone only a few months past. Jane Churchill, the friend and companion of a half century and more, in her own grave since she was found dead in her bed at Osborne this past Christmas morning. Now Vicky, too, dying an agonizing death without even the warmth of her eldest son to help sustain her through the last days. Victoria couldn't have been faulted for thinking she had simply lasted too long. The trials and losses she was enduring seemed to simply be beyond what anyone should bear. Unable to eat, unable to sleep, torn by countless small pains of great age, now she couldn't even force herself to do that which she had done, every day, without fail, since June 1837. She couldn't do her duty.

Dr. Reid hadn't seen the Queen since he looked in on her this morning. It was the first time he could remember that Victoria had remained in her bed the entire day. The royal dressers finally were summoned by the Queen's bedside bell to help her rise around six o'clock, long after the last rays of the weak winter sun had sunk over the island's westernmost reach. After having her nearly waist-long hair pinned up by a body servant, the Queen ordered that she be wheeled into the sitting room next door to her bedroom. She finally called for Reid at seven-thirty. The doctor found her "dazed, confused and aphasic," the latter a condition that implied Victoria's speech patterns were disoriented, the malfunction affecting the left, or dominant, side of the brain for the right-handed Queen.

Sir Francis Laking, Physician-in-Ordinary and Surgeon Apothecary to the Prince of Wales, who trusted him implicitly, had been sent down to the island earlier in the month to do what he could for the monarch. Reid, though, didn't share the Prince's high opinion of his doctor, considering Laking's skills insufficient for the Queen's requirements. Victoria had herself refused to see her son's doctor the month before, when Bertie had asked him to visit the island. But Laking, who was some years older than Reid, had nonetheless arrived again at Osborne on the 5th of January, considering his visit a double kindness in that he believed he would be giving Reid a few days' relief from the strain of caring for Victoria virtually single-handedly.

It didn't surprise Reid when Laking told him that evening as the two men were going into dinner in the Household Dining Room, that he had found Victoria "all right." Laking casually informed Reid that he had earlier spent three-quarters of an hour with the monarch, discussing a large variety of topics, and he thought she didn't appear "too bad," a judgment Reid found ill-informed. The younger man suspected the nature of the show Victoria had put on for the outsider, a physician whose allegiance was directed primarily not to herself, but to the Prince of Wales. A woman of enormous strength of will, the sovereign had evidently commanded the strength to convince Laking—and through him, everyone he would talk to, particularly Bertie—that she was just fine. Reid was certain those forty-five minutes of putting on a play for Laking must have cost her dearly, the exact price the physician was pretty sure he would discover when he himself next saw Victoria.

His intuition was stunningly close to the mark. Ten minutes after leaving Laking, Reid was in his mistress's sitting room again, having been sent for through the maids. There he found a woman as expended and confused as the one he had seen earlier in the evening, and almost immediately she returned to her bedroom. Reid now felt certain that the end was approaching, the simple fact of the sovereign's great age a reality which justified slight hope that any significant delivery might be forthcoming. He sat down and wrote a precise assessment of Victoria's condition to the man who would be most directly affected by the monarch's demise. His message would be delivered to Marlborough House that evening.

## CHAPTER IV

# Thursday,
# January 17

❖ 1 ❖

B aron Hermann von Eckardstein had been chargé of the German embassy in London since illness had incapacitated the seventy-year-old ambassador, Count Paul von Hatzfeldt. This Thursday evening, Eckardstein was returning to his London club from a midweek visit at Chatsworth, the Derbyshire palace of the Duke of Devonshire. At the club, the baron—who was married to the only child and heiress of Sir Blundell Maple, the empire's richest furniture manufacturer and a name long a byword for British quality and middle-class respectability—met an acquaintance, an official in the Queen's Household. The courtier gravely confided to the distinguished-looking Eckardstein that the Queen's illness was such that death could come at any moment. The diplomat knew the official to be trustworthy, and he immediately wired his master with the news. His master was not only the Queen's eldest grandchild, but was also the most potent monarch in the world.

❖  2  ❖

Earlier this day, Reid had gone over to the Pavilion to look in on the Queen. Judging from the sight of the shriveled bundle lying in the bed, he realized that overnight his patient's condition had substantially worsened. He reported in his journal that though Victoria had most likely passed a quiet night unaware of her deterioration, this morning she wasn't able to understand what he was saying. Her aphasia was likely the result of an unfelt overnight stroke, the Queen's drooping right cheek seeming to confirm the unpleasant assessment. Knowing her to be on the verge of falling into a coma, Reid made a professional judgment that she wouldn't last more than a few days. He concluded that the time had arrived to begin alerting an even wider circle of people to the state of the sovereign's health.

Having already wired the Prince of Wales the prior evening, Reid's first mission this morning was to meet again with the princesses who were already at Osborne, the Queen's daughters Helena—invariably called "Lenchen" in the family—and Beatrice. After gently describing their mother's condition to the two middle-aged women, the doctor obtained their formal leave to send for the eminent London heart and lung specialist, Sir Richard Douglas Powell. Powell, a baronet, had once been assistant to Sir William Jenner, the latter the principal physician to Victoria whom Reid had replaced twelve years earlier; Powell retained his largely honorary appointment as physician-in-ordinary to the Queen, and Reid was anxious to have the respected diagnostician's views on the Queen's condition. When Powell received the wire from Osborne, he immediately caught a cab for Waterloo Station and took the first train for Southampton with a connection by ferry to the Isle of Wight.

Sir James already had Laking at Osborne, of course, a fellow physician in whom he could confide about Victoria's condition. But Reid's lack of confidence in Sir Francis's medical judgments made the former uneasy. Fritz Ponsonby shared Reid's low opinion of Laking, once having gone so far as to refer to the Prince of Wales's doctor as a "charlatan." Like Reid and Powell, Laking held an appointment in the Royal Household's Medical Department, in his case formally surgeon apothecary to the Queen and Household. On his visit to the Queen in December, Laking had advised the Queen that it would be a good idea if she got over her "squeamishness" about food and took a "little whisky" with her milk, as well as a "stimulant." Such cavalier advice clearly did not set well with Reid. Since at least December, Victoria herself had been uneasy about seeing Laking, wanting *all* her medical problems to be personally attended to by her own chief physician.

Laking's presence provoked from Susan Reid a degree of animosity, antagonism likely influenced by her husband's opinion. Susan wrote that "Laking's visit at Osborne is a great fraud! and does not relieve Jamie of any of his work! . . . The Queen will not see him! at least not about her health, and she can hardly bear Jamie out of her sight! . . . The only difference Laking's visit has made is that Jamie was able to dine [at home] twice." Reid himself subtly noted his own disappointment with the Prince's physician in his own diary entry for the 17th: "Laking . . . said he would like to stay another day to 'help' me."

So in spite of his colleague's "assistance," Reid found that he was as busy with the Queen as ever. Though the monarch wanted no other doctor, Reid remained exceedingly anxious for Powell to arrive, hoping almost against medical logic that the trusted specialist might be able to advise some course of treatment that would get the Queen through her crisis.

Today went very much as yesterday for Victoria. Again, she remained in her bed the entire morning and afternoon, not allowing her women to help her up and into clothes until early evening. When finally settled in her wheelchair, Victoria was pushed into her sitting room, where on a normal day she would have plunged into a sizable pile of government dispatches and parliamentary papers to read and digest, and then sign. Reid made sure no such exertions faced Victoria now, her condition—both physical and mental—making such effort impossible. When her daughters came in to see her, the Queen weakly asked if "people were worried" about her, as her movements hadn't been reported in the *Court Circular* for the last two days, the Queen clearly having been apprised of this one document. Beatrice said the weather had been so bad that everyone would "understand" her being housebound, which faulty reasoning Victoria responded to with characteristic skepticism, saying "people know I always go out in the rain!"

What made people "know" this and much else about her activities was the practice of circulating an announcement of the chief public activities of the members of the Royal Family, a routine first devised as George III's way of making certain the news that was spread about him and his family was accurate; few things angered King George as much as the false reports put abroad concerning royal activities. Since this new *Court Circular* was vetted by the palace before being released to the newspapers, it soon gained the stature of reliable information, and thus became a trusted record.

Queen Victoria was convinced that no activities that her family might engage in would be too trivial to interest the public, and the *Court Circular* became her vehicle to keep the country informed of all that concerned its sovereign (even with its stilted language: the Queen did not have a "happy birthday," but rather an "auspicious return of her natal day," and guests were not invited to "dine," but were "graciously invited to partake of a collation"). Now that rumors about serious problems with the Queen's health were beginning to cause alarm, Reid felt it was time the *Court Circular* include an accurate, if muted, statement about Victoria's condition. He also wanted to prepare a still largely unsuspecting public for the shock he knew would be coming very soon.

With Bigge's help, the physician drafted a terse paragraph for the following day's *Circular*, mentioning among other things that the cardiac specialist, Powell, had been sent for to consult about the Queen's health. Understanding the sensitivity of the monarch's condition at Marlborough House, the two men first sent the draft to the Prince of Wales's secretary. The surprising reply came back from Sir Francis Knollys that "under no circumstances" should the *Court Circular* include information about the Queen's health, the Prince evidently wanting to alert the world to his mother's condition in his own way and in his own time, especially wishing to make personally sure of the seriousness of her condition before raising *any* public alarm. Accordingly, Bigge and Reid were obliged to abandon for the time being any notice of their own that Victoria's health was rapidly failing. The *Court Cir-*

*cular* that appeared in the *Times* for the 17th mentioned only minor activities at Marlborough House and York House, the latter the Duke of York's home. But for the first time in memory, no mention of the monarch's own residence was made.

As always, the sovereign's mind still caught small details, particularly those concerning death, the subject that absorbed her more than any other. The Right Reverend Mandell Creighton, Bishop of London, had died only a few days earlier, his funeral having been held just this morning; Randall Davidson, clerk of the closet to the Queen and Bishop of Winchester, had represented the sovereign at Creighton's service at St. Paul's Cathedral in London. Long obsessed with funereal minutiae, Victoria became fixed on the notion that the funeral had been conducted with "unseemly haste," pointing out to Reid when he came up to see her again that it was "very odd" and "so foreign" that the burial was held so soon after the bishop's passing. Victoria remained coherent enough to go on with the advice that Reid shouldn't be overworked on her behalf, the Queen convinced "[you are] the only one that understands me" and thus must not be made ill when he might be needed at any moment in an emergency.

About seven-thirty in the evening, Powell finally arrived. Because of the Queen's fiat that no one but Reid treat her, Reid was worried she might refuse to let Powell even examine her. But when he told her, in the most offhand way possible, that the heart specialist had "arrived in the island" for a visit with himself, and "as he was in the house," he could look in on Her Majesty, Victoria's easy and eager agreement took her physician by surprise, and seemed further evidence that her health was altering her personality. What Powell saw on examining the Queen left him as certain as his colleague was that her brain functions had degenerated dangerously. Able to do little other than to respond in a dazed fashion to the questions Powell put to her, Victoria didn't even put up a pretense of her usual robustness, a shield she had always been able to conjure out of some inner reservoir. Though Powell didn't think the Queen's condition hopeless, neither did he delude himself about its seriousness.

❖   3   ❖

At the same time the medical men were examining Victoria in her second-floor bedroom at Osborne, the first indication to the Kaiser that his grandmother was dangerously ill was being received at the Royal Palace in the heart of Berlin. When on Friday morning William learned of the British monarch's condition, the willful German ruler knew exactly what he had to do. He swiftly determined on a pilgrimage to Osborne, a trip that would show to a restive Europe the extraordinary ties of kinship and respect between the rulers of the world's two preeminent powers.

Frederick William Victor Albert—called by the second of his names, a decision settled on from infancy—would become by the time of his abdication from the German throne in 1918 one of the most influential figures of the twentieth century, in a perverse way one of its creators. The world his actions did so much to shape was not the result of genius, nor of vision, nor even of true malignancy. It was the consequence of an almost limitless hubris that he brought to life through the unassailability of his position in a deeply flawed political system. The bill for the avalanche set off by Emperor William II would bankrupt the new century and set the stage for a catastrophe of unimaginably greater horror.

"The Emperor is like a balloon: If one did not hold him fast on a string, he would go no one knows whither." In a few words, Otto von Bismarck captured perfectly the essence of the man who was for a long generation Germany's mercurial master. Entangled between two worlds, two families, and two diametrically opposed facets to his personality, for forty years William was both the pride and bane of Queen Victoria's life.

The factors that made William's life a continual balancing act between farce and disaster had their roots in a fusion of components: heredity, education, his unique position, his ministers. But it was the influence of his parents that more than any other agent set the young prince on a collision course with history. The glories Victoria and Albert envisioned for Vicky on her marriage, so too did Vicky and Fritz hope someday their eldest son would inherit: that he would be the glue to bond Britain with Germany, that the two nations would jointly lead Europe toward a permanent peace.

This vision shared by both grandparents and parents ran headlong into roadblocks at every step of William's life.

As William grew into manhood, the one family member he clung to and admired was his grandmother, and it was the grandmother who warned William's mother of the dangers of Vicky's constant hectoring and disparagement of William. Victoria fully returned the love her eldest grandchild lavished on her, a love abetted by the knowledge of the almost transcendental burden Albert had bequeathed the boy. Contrary to the warmth between grandmother and grandson, the impressions William made on his English family were too often unfavorable, and, occasionally, even disastrous. The earliest mischievousness was petty, but it set the pattern. On the young Prince's first trip to England, for his uncle Bertie's wedding, he rattled the congregation at St. George's Chapel by noisily hurling the dirk from his Highlands costume across the stone; later, he spitefully bit the legs of two of his young uncles when they intervened to compel their headstrong nephew to behave. Victoria quickly understood that William's lawless streak was ominously inappropriate for a boy destined for the future that faced him. When as a five-year-old he threw a tantrum over the indignity of being put in the back seat during an Osborne carriage ride with his grandmother, Victoria wrote of her alarm over such "a tinge of pride" in one so young. The fact that he always signed his letters to his grandmother "William Prince of Prussia" further worried the Queen, even leading her to suspect this trivial but potentially dangerous egotism was the result of the Prussian Chancellor's influence.

By the time William's father died, the new young Kaiser's estrangement from his mother had long been all but complete. Though Bismarck openly loathed Vicky, William himself simply ignored her, turning his attentions elsewhere—too often to the affairs of his neighbors' governments. All Vicky could do was complain to her mother: "I still believe that since he is your grandson and dear Papa's, the antediluvian ideas of the Hohenzollerns will be modified by a broader and more humane spirit, but unfortunately he is at the mercy of a military clique." When William sacked Bismarck two years after his accession, one of the only two people who could effectively tame his unquenchable bravado disappeared.

In terms of his own national identity, William suffered throughout his life from a deep split between his German and his English sides. His closest friend, Philipp Eulenburg (who would soon after Victoria's death become estranged from the Emperor as the result of a sex scandal), wrote about this duality: "It sounds ghastly to a German ear when I say: the German emperor is not a German at all, but actually an Englishman." But Eulenburg was only half right: William never resolved whether he wanted more to assume the boldness of a Prussian monarch or the amicability of an English gentleman-king, an irresolution that was one of the profoundest causes of his tragedy. His inability to decide which half of his heritage would play the dominant theme in his life meant that British politicians would come to resent his obsessive interest in their country, while his own ministers and minions were equally unable to sympathize with this closeness to England, forgetting that besides being the scion of a long line of Prussian kings, he was also the eldest of the English Queen's forty grandchildren. Mistrusted and misunderstood on both sides of his heritage, William's impulse was to engage in a sort of bonhomie designed to impress both British and Germans but which finally ended up convincing all of his unworthiness.

The greatest symbol of European power in the nineteenth century was colonies—the chunks of territory in the undeveloped or "barbarian" world by whose acquisition the states of Europe ranked their realization of Great Power status. Many European countries retained large, sometimes vast, colonial empires at the end of the century: France, Spain, the Netherlands, Belgium, even little Denmark, all clung tightly to their collections of non-European populations. Yet Great Britain stood far above the others, its empire one on which virtually every schoolchild knew "the sun never set" and which was the envy of every German from the Kaiser down.

The security of Victoria's empire rested on one constant and thus far unconquerable pillar: the Royal Navy. For any of the thousands witnessing the 1897 Diamond Jubilee naval review at Spithead—the panorama of the great Portsmouth naval roadstead in the Solent ornamented the view from Osborne—the might of the Royal Navy and the safety of the empire seemed beyond any possible threat. As the monarch watched from the stern of her yacht *Victoria and Albert*, dozens of men-of-war and hundreds of their support vessels passed in front of Victoria's admiring gaze. Buttressing her admiration was the fact that fully half of the world's merchant fleet sailed under the Union Jack. Britain could not aspire, and never had aspired, to preeminence on land, a status it had allowed other European states to assume in neatly balanced measure. Its fundamental defense policy was instead to abide supreme on the world's seas, ensuring its status as a mercantile island-nation without peer, and to cultivate through diplomacy a balance of power whose goal was the peace not only of Britain, but of Europe and the world beyond.

Germany had until recently little impinged on Britain's calm in establishing a permanent Pax Britannica. The British considered the Germans misguided, a people who had sadly failed to establish a constitutional system along the lines developed by themselves, and held little fear of German industrial competition. The British further regarded their Continental cousins as fundamentally vulgar, a condescension that infuriated Germans, particularly the prickly Prussians. But with the rise of Bismarck's Prussia, the comfortable status quo became increasingly threatened as Germany aspired to a position of dominance that first concerned, then alarmed, and now seriously frightened the British.

It wasn't only Germany's growing strength that frightened the politicians in Whitehall. The new German loathing of Britain had begun to settle into a serious pathology. Though Germany was perfectly willing to become a typical colonial oppressor, Germans hypocritically and ever more openly considered their British competitors little more than robber barons intent on ransacking the world's wealth while leaving an aggrieved Germany mere crumbs to grovel after. Adding to Berlin's sense of mistrust, German politicians suspected Britain would eventually join a Franco-Russian alliance, encircling Germany and holding potentially lethal consequences. The Boer War acted as the catalyst that finally turned inward German wariness outward, allowing William's subjects to undisguisedly vent their rage at what they saw as British obstruction of legitimate German aspirations. The culminating factor that brought together all these dangerously volatile elements was the Kaiser.

Though Britain might allow Germany a great deal of latitude in the matter of European land forces—a freedom it would have been hard to deny the Continent's strongest economy—it was the increasing willingness of the Kaiser's government to upset the naval status quo that frightened the British and finally put Whitehall up in arms. And unambiguously urging Germany to strengthen its naval capabilities was the Emperor. If William's Prussian predecessors had brought the nation glory in the saddles and on the caissons of its armies, why, he thought, could he not bring luster to himself and his country with the creation of a modern navy? By doing so, British mockery would, William reasoned, be stilled and the Royal Navy would be forced to share its supremacy. And when London got used to the new equation, the two nations would rule the world together—at last as *equals.*

William, of course, saw his vision of such an Anglo-German domination of the world as something to benefit both Berlin and London. But Victoria's ministers were aghast at what was behind it: great new naval behemoths sliding down the ways of Germany's mammoth shipyards. Though Berlin continued to offer assurances that its headlong rush to naval parity with Britain was defensive, and (as far as Britain and its empire were concerned) benign, the British believed there could be no reason for Germany's shipbuilding than to eventually *overtake* the world's only naval superpower —namely themselves.

The result of this mutual misunderstanding was an arms race between the two countries that devoured gigantic expenditures of public monies. Though the outcome could still only be dimly perceived at the end of the century, the consequences of this marathon between the two states pointed most logically to war. Bismarck had always been able to keep Russia and France—his two flanking enemies—from forming an alliance. But with William's jettisoning of the Iron Chancellor in 1890, Bismarck's less-skillful successors —Caprivi, Hohenlohe, Bülow—weren't able to maintain Bismarck's balance. Nor, tragically, was William the astute diplomat his first Chancellor had been. To safeguard themselves from what they saw by the end of the century as a potentially lethal German threat, Russia and France eventually formed a mutual-protection entente against Germany—Russia benefiting from French money, France from Russia's counterbalancing presence and near-limitless manpower. In addition, the Tsar's ministers believed William's mutual defense treaty with Austria-Hungary, whose aspirations in the Balkans ran headlong into what Russia thought were its "historical" claims in that tinderbox region, left them no choice. The end result for Germany was the nightmare Bismarck dreaded: the Reich was now flanked by allied Franco-Russian foes, his brilliant foreign policy strategy for the enrichment of Prussia/Germany at Europe's expense melting away like snow in spring.

Mistrust then became the single most important factor leading to a catastrophic twentieth-century war. Germany's determination to join the colonial big leagues could only happen at the cost of antagonizing Britain. As for Britain, it was seeing the gleam on its own sword begin to dim—if ever so faintly. Its navy was undeniably huge, but much of it was still wood and powered by wind. Its colonial grip was still strong, but now it was bogged down in a miserable little war in South Africa. And off in the distance, the ever-cockier American colossus was beginning to look as though it just might soon be able to compete with its European forefathers on an even footing.

# Friday,
# January 18

### ❖  1  ❖

Reid could do little more now than watch, wait, keep the Queen comfortable, and make sure her family was aware of the shifts and currents in the monarch's worsening condition. After checking in on Victoria this morning, the physician recorded in his journal that she had passed a "fair night," her condition little changed from yesterday. But his foremost concern remained her drowsiness and weakness. The Queen slept all day, and when she finally roused late in the afternoon, she was confused and unable to describe what was distressing her. The right side of her face had noticeably sunk, evidently from yesterday's stroke; the left side was also "drooping" a bit, in Reid's expert estimation. Victoria was still unable to eat anything of substance, the patented preparation called Benger's Food being about all she could get down. The physician suspected the Queen was in fact slowly starving to death, but there was little he could do for her, other than make sure she was comfortable and trying to get her to take nourishment. On this Friday afternoon, Reid made a bold decision—despite the certain knowledge it would irritate the Queen's daughters. He would write and let the Kaiser know what was happening at Osborne.

Bully and buffoon that Reid knew the German monarch could

be when feeling the necessity to assert himself, William remained the Queen's only grandchild whose rank matched her own. The British monarch had long ago made it clear to her principal physician that should her health deteriorate to a life-threatening point, she wanted the Kaiser informed. Having no way of knowing that Eckardstein had already wired his master of Victoria's perilous health, Reid went to his room to write out the telegram he would send to Berlin.

❖  2  ❖

In January 1701, bolstered with the authority of the Holy Roman Emperor's compliance, the Elector Frederick III of Brandenburg upgraded himself to Frederick I, King in Prussia (the title would later change to King *of* Prussia). Frederick was able to carry off this bit of royal legerdemain for two reasons: the first was that Prussia lay outside the boundaries of the Holy Roman Empire and thus his authority would technically not infringe on that empire, the second because this son of the Great Elector wanted it so. The signal sent to his fellow monarchs in Europe by Frederick's advancement was clear. Prussia had become a Great Power through the military miracles wrought by its muscular army, a reality that deserved recognition in the form of an upgraded dignity for its rulers. Frederick accordingly crowned himself at Königsberg, the city that stood as the heart of old Prussia, and in doing so deliberately rejected any priestly involvement. On the same day he founded the Order of the Black Eagle, Prussia's equivalent of the Garter, one celebrating not knightly gallantry but, far closer to the new King's heart, military prowess.

Over the next two hundred years, the power of the unrefined but pugnacious kingdom grew steadily until by 1901 its army had become Europe's most potent land force, its economy the Continent's strongest. To mark this transformation, Frederick's descendant William II decided to stage a gigantic commemorative celebration, taking his grandmother's recent Diamond Jubilee as the model for his own festivities. William's authority derived firstly from his role as German Emperor. But in his own capital, and—

especially—among his own class of *Junker* nobles, he remained first and foremost King of Prussia, the status in which every member of his family took the greatest pride.

Under normal conditions, Victoria herself might have been invited by her grandson to help solemnize the bicentenary spree in person, though for her to have accepted would have been highly out of character, even as a favor to the most prominent of her descendants. In the event, the Queen deputed the Duke of Connaught—her favorite son, Arthur—to represent her at the festivities; she knew her grandson was closer to Arthur than to Bertie, and reckoned William would likely appreciate the absence of the limelight-stealing Prince of Wales. The Kaiser planned the occasion to be his apotheosis, the proudest moment in his reign. People in every corner of the empire were wild with anticipation. It was unthinkable in the Emperor's mind that anything could mar this celebration of Prussian triumph.

❖  3  ❖

One of the best things to come of mothering five daughters was that Victoria was sure that one of them would remain as the comfort and crutch of her later years. For Victoria, these "later" years started on December 14, 1861, when she was still only forty-two years old. By then, the eldest of the five—Vicky—had already been married off to her German prince. The next oldest, Alice, was betrothed to Prince Louis of Hesse, the second German liaison Albert had been instrumental in cementing for his daughters. (Two of her four sons were still at home when their father died, but Victoria never expected they should assume the role of companion to their mother.) With the two eldest girls gone, that left three daughters at home—Helena ("Lenchen"), Louise, and "baby" Beatrice.

In the years following the cataclysm of December 1861, Victoria evidently resolved that a second marriage was inconceivable, her union with Albert having been in her settled view the consummate exemplar that must not in any way be diminished. For the kind of companionship that for royalty can only come from within the family circle, she would have to make do with what was already at hand, namely the three maiden princesses.

After the death of the Prince Consort, it hurt Victoria deeply to endure those children enjoying the kind of adult romantic and physical happiness that she, determined to preserve Albert's uniqueness, denied herself. The Queen professed to want, in her own idiosyncratic way, that all her children should be happy. But with Bertie's and Alice's marriages coming so soon after Albert's death, it is understandable that she would make their weddings more funereal than connubial in tone, at both ceremonies mono-maniacally insisting that any "happy" feelings be kept to the absolute minimum appropriate to occasions the monarch charac-terized as "religious rather than pleasurable." As to her younger children's lives, any display of enjoyment or childish giddiness was almost certain to make their mother feel as though it were an act of personal disloyalty. This attitude did not endure for mere years, but stretched on for decades.

The trio of daughters who remained after Vicky and Alice de-parted for Germany were oddly dissimilar. Each bore a personality at wide variance from that of each of her sisters, and having grown up in the peculiar and protected atmosphere of a royal Victorian palace meant that each found the outside world a difficult place in which to function. The oldest of the three was Helena, fifteen when her father died. "Lenchen," as her parents called her from the German diminutive for her real name and the name by which she would be known within the family circle for her entire life, was the child cast by Victoria in her inimitable candor as the least suc-cessful of her nine offspring. "Poor dear Lenchen, though most useful and active and clever and amiable, does not improve in looks and has great difficulty with her figure and her want of calm, quiet, graceful manners." In these remarkably unsparing words the mother summed up a daughter who would pass her life as little more than a cipher, though admittedly a cipher writ large. Plain and overly fond of food—a fondness that made her quest for a husband a challenging one—what could be said in esteem of this introverted princess is that she was trustworthy.

In 1865, the nineteen-year-old Lenchen made her bid to es-cape a suffocating life of endless rounds passing between Windsor,

Balmoral, and Osborne in the sepulchral company of her perpetually mourning mother. While in Germany visiting with her sister Vicky, she met and was smitten with Prince Christian of the minor duchy of Schleswig-Holstein-Sonderburg-Augustenburg, fifteen years her senior, and a man completely free of ambition or purpose. The princess's mother was certainly aware of Christian's limitations, but the prince agreed to come live in England, thus gratifying the Queen who could comfort herself that she wasn't really "losing" a daughter. Lenchen and her German duly married, and, styling themselves Prince and Princess Christian, settled down first at Frogmore House, later at Cumberland Lodge, both houses snugly located on the grounds of Windsor Castle. Victoria employed her son-in-law in light duties, principally as "Ranger" of Windsor Castle's private park, stipulating he wasn't to have "anything to do" with the shooting arrangement, which she seriously meant to maintain under her own supervision. As it turned out, Christian should have forsworn shooting expeditions altogether. One day Prince Arthur mistook his white-bearded brother-in-law for a low-flying pheasant and shot out Christian's eye. The German managed some satisfaction from his injury, soon collecting an enviable set of glass eyes to fill his empty socket, an assortment that included a bloodshot model for use on days when he was feeling under the weather.

Princess Christian was to cause her mother significant concern over a touchy issue: a more-than-casual user of opium and laudanum, Lenchen's unfortunate habit threatened to scandalize the court. Both the Queen and Prince Christian confided in Dr. Reid about the problem, especially in the wake of some of the princess's more embarrassing drug-highs. Though she was long able to wheedle the drugs out of her physicians to alleviate what Reid referred to as her "imaginary ailments," Reid stopped any more such prescriptions in 1896 when Lenchen seemed on the verge of losing control of her habit.

The Christians begot a middle-sized Victorian family, five children, all but the youngest living to adulthood. It was very likely the shock of the death in late December 1900 of the eldest, Prince Christian Victor—nicknamed "Christl"—that sent his grandmother into the decline that marked the beginning of the end for her. Despite a lackluster marriage, Lenchen managed to find some purpose in life, her main outlet in improving the abysmal quality of Victorian nursing institutions; she founded the Princess Christian Nursing Home in the town of Windsor, an institution that survived as the chief remembrance of her life.

If Helena was the least prepossessing in personality of the trio—a description in which most members of the Royal Family and Household would have concurred—her next younger sister, Louise, was always the "most beautiful" in the collected family hagiography. Louise wasn't really all that much better looking than her sisters—her inheritance of the conspicuously bulging Hanoverian eyes saw to that; it was merely that she didn't have all that far to go to merit the description. The only child to bear the name of Albert's mother and the first too young ever to have been tutored personally by the Prince Consort, Louise shone in two areas: artisticness and waspishness, neither of which was particularly suited to or required of a Victorian-era princess.

Just as stifled as Lenchen, Louise yearned to elude the gloom of her mother's house. Too frisky to be bridled by a German princeling for a husband, Louise instead fell madly in love with a Scottish aristocrat. The Marquess of Lorne, heir to his father's duchy of Argyll and one of the richest men in Victoria's kingdom, was with his golden hair and wisp of a Highland burr Louise's romantic ideal. Irrespective of the fact that his ancestors had been kings when the Hohenzollerns were, in Lorne's word, "parvenus," the prospect of a royal princess marrying one of her mother's subjects sent a shiver throughout Victoria's kingdom. No daughter of an English monarch had married a subject since Henry VII's daughter Mary wed the Duke of Suffolk in 1515. There were some who worried whether such a union might even be illegal, but Victoria's response to this particular concern was one of contempt. "Times have changed," opined the Queen sensibly. Besides, the sovereign was anxious that some "new and healthy" blood strengthen the precariously inbred royal caste.

Being unmistakably her mother's daughter in her sense of station, Louise found the transition from princess-in-a-palace to wife-of-a-lord—albeit a very rich lord—difficult to negotiate. Life at Inverary Castle, Lorne's seat in Scotland, was onerous for Louise.

Accustomed to a status that ranked above just about everyone, at Inverary she became, according to her new in-laws, a "mischief-maker" who was continually creating a "perfect pandemonium." Wanting to dine apart from her husband's live-in relatives, one of those she snubbed sniffed that it was "absurd talking of two dinners in a private house." The Lornes would leave Inverary to go to the governor-generalship in Canada in 1878, there to represent the Scottish peer's mother-in-law. In a sleigh accident in Ottawa the princess was dragged by her hair and scalp, an ordeal that resulted in her ear being torn off.

The marriage soon disintegrated, Louise finding her solace in solo travel rather than in the dreariness of an indifferent husband. Unfortunately, the couple produced no heirs, a situation which occasioned the princess's receiving hundreds of letters from busybodies offering to share their personal solutions to her fertility difficulties. As for the Queen's wish to put some fresh blood into her line, it was, unhappily, dashed. Particularly unpopular with her mother's ladies-in-waiting because of her waspish tongue, Princess Louise nonetheless turned out to be far the most artistically talented of the Queen's children, her forte sculpture.

Louise formed a warm and sympathetic friendship with James Reid some years after he came into the royal service as the Queen's principal physician. He had once given the princess a sprig of heather he had collected on a walk in the Balmoral countryside, and the gesture led to a warm companionship that would last for the remainder of Reid's life, the pair looking to one another for counsel on many issues.

The third of the trio was the last of Victoria's children, Beatrice Mary Victoria Feodore. Other than giving birth to a future Spanish Queen (who would, incidentally, carry the family's hemophilia gene to her own children), "Baby Bee" is best remembered for committing after her mother's death one of the new century's most bizarre acts of cultural vandalism, an injury that historians would regret every day since Victoria's death. Charged in her mother's will to act as her literary executor and thus to edit her journals, Beatrice assiduously obeyed Victoria's instructions to excise anything that might "cause pain" to those mentioned in them. Continuing until her death in 1931, the princess would copy out her mother's words into notebooks, often bowdlerizing the content, and destroy the originals as she went along. This she did in spite of the Royal Family's pleas that the historical importance of Queen Victoria's most intimate writings far outweighed Beatrice's duty to her late mother's wishes.

Four years old when the Prince Consort died (in later years she adamantly maintained she could clearly remember her father), it would be this shyest of her daughters who would more than any of her siblings be tied to the aging Queen. From virtually the moment of Albert's death, Victoria resolved that young Beatrice would eventually be the foremost comfort and crutch of her widowhood. "The Queen can only pray," the almost-demented monarch wrote at the time, "that this flower of the flock never . . . may leave her, but be the prop, comfort and companion of her widowed mother to old age." In fairness to the mother, Victoria surely didn't think her widowhood would last as long it did when she wrote those words. But as the girl grew into womanhood, treated like a child by everyone in the Queen's homes and consequently behaving like one, the lengths to which her mother went to ensure Beatrice not be bitten by the marriage bug were often preposterous. Any guest at the Queen's table who, when Beatrice was present, in any way mentioned "marriage" over the meal could expect a sharp look from Victoria and later a curt message telling the offender not to make the same mistake again. Irrespective of her mother's frantic efforts to keep her from any thought of matrimony, Beatrice was said to have gone "all soft" over the Prince Imperial, the son of the ex-Empress Eugénie. The young man's death in 1879 put an end to the mild flirtation, but not to Beatrice's hankerings.

As yearning for marriage and escape had come to her sisters, so it hit Beatrice—hard. The object of her mature desire—Beatrice was twenty-seven when smitten—was Prince Henry (known in the family as "Liko"), the youngest of the three scintillating Battenberg brothers. The dashing princes were the offspring of a morganatic marriage between Prince Alexander of Hesse and his Polish lover, Countess Julia Haucke; when the countess was created Princess of Battenberg, the promotion gave the boys just enough royal status to be allowed to marry into the reigning families of Europe.

Which they did, to what many held an excessive degree. The year before Beatrice caught the eye of *her* Battenberg, Prince Henry, sister Alice's daughter Victoria married Prince Louis, the oldest of the Hessian siblings. The middle brother, Alexander, enjoyed an affaire de coeur with the daughter of Beatrice's sister Vicky, but the Kaiser (the unfortunate princess's brother) scotched any thought of such a base marriage in his own family. Stiffening William's resistance was the fact that Alexander had in the meantime been elected (by Europe's powers) sovereign Prince of Bulgaria. For the Kaiser to allow his sister to marry a parvenu, one the Tsar happened to intensely dislike because he wouldn't run Bulgaria as a satellite of St. Petersburg, would have upset the Tsar, whom William was cultivating at the moment and whom he therefore strove to please in whatever little way he could.

Prince Henry Battenberg was, compared to the usual run of German princes available to Protestant princesses, gorgeous. Shortish but all muscle, graced with a rakehell mustache and possessing looks that jumped right off the page, especially when the prince was dressed in his tight white buckskin army breeches, there was little wonder Beatrice should have been smitten. And her Henry fully reciprocated Beatrice's attentions, though whether it was because of the princess's modest charms or because his prospective mother-in-law was the doyenne of European royalty is hard to say. In any event, it was that very mother-in-law who would soon prove to be the wrench in the happy young couple's marital prospects.

In late 1884, Beatrice informed the thunderstruck Queen that she and Henry wanted to marry. If the determined princess was expecting a certain measure of resistance, she was horrified at the monarch's reception. Always the dutiful servant to her mother—the principal reason Victoria wished not to part with the now fully adult daughter—the monarch simply couldn't understand where she had failed Beatrice. For months, the two refused to speak to each other, the Queen passing tart little notes to the princess at the breakfast table, the princess too terrified of her mother to simply have it out with her and explain that she, like her sisters—and, for that matter, like the Queen herself—deserved the opportunity of married happiness and children.

Eventually, Victoria gave in, probably greatly astonished at this heretofore shy daughter's spunk in not blinking first. Victoria did append one condition to her permission to wed: the couple must live with her, so Beatrice could remain on call in her station as her mother's chief *lectrice* and factotum. Beatrice eagerly agreed, and so (of course) did Henry, who had little else going except for his commission in the Prussian army. For the prince, there was also the bright prospect of an upgrade from Serene Highness to *Royal* Highness, thus putting the second of the quartet of brothers on a par with the best of the rest of Europe.

After their July 1885 wedding at Osborne's Whippingham Church, Beatrice and Henry settled down with Victoria, where the reality of the matter was that, once again, the sovereign hadn't lost a daughter but gained a son. The couple speedily got to the task of raising a family: three sons and a daughter were quickly born, the lone daughter destined one day, as mentioned earlier, to become Queen of Spain. (Incidentally, 32 years separated Victoria's first grandchild, William of Prussia, from her last, Maurice of Battenberg; the deaths of these forty grandchildren would be separated by an incredible 115 years. The first to die, Prince Sigismund of Prussia, did so in 1866, while the last—Princess Alice of Albany—passed away in 1981.) The Battenberg family's presence at Osborne was particularly gratifying to the Queen. She ordered that the old nursery quarters on the Pavilion's top floor be turned into a special suite for Beatrice and Henry's children, and in her final years nothing made her quite so happy as the sounds of the rambunctious Battenberg children banging around all day directly overhead; the Queen told her friends that "I love these darlings almost as much as their own parents do." Beatrice and Henry were provided with quarters of their own in the new Durbar Wing, giving them a modicum of physical separation from the mistress of the estate. A victim of rheumatism since childhood, Beatrice must have found the often chilly conditions at Osborne infelicitous, conditions her mother actually liked and thus maintained with little regard to the wishes, needs, comforts or discomforts of others.

Through the years, the debonair Henry kept his mother-in-law amused, even inducing her to relax her stand against tobacco smoke in Osborne—an injunction which even Bertie had never been successful in getting his mother to relax. (At Windsor, Victoria remained adamant against any move to allow smoking anywhere except in the billiard room—and even there only after eleven at night.) Princess Beatrice might have remained happy in her marriage if her husband hadn't after a few years got bored out of his mind with the repetitious and arid round of Windsor, Balmoral and Osborne, all the while without any real job to do. The Queen made him governor of the Isle of Wight, an encomium about as exciting as the morose dinners he was forced to endure every evening at the monarch's table. Unfortunately for Henry, his sister-in-law took an inappropriate shine to him, Louise by now all but totally estranged from her Scottish consort, and wholly entranced with Liko's compact set of muscles. Unable to keep her eyes off Beatrice's husband during her visits to her mother, tensions between the Queen's two youngest daughters soon reached a steamily tense impasse.

In 1895, Prince Henry decided he couldn't take his surreal habitat any longer, and persuaded the Queen to allow him to go off to Africa to fight in the trumped-up little Ashanti affair, where British imperialism had gone off the deep end. Since Beatrice thought her husband's absence might well be for the best, the Queen obligingly gave her permission for Henry to go away to Africa, letting things cool off at home, domestically speaking. Sadly, Henry caught malaria as soon as he got to his West African posting, and, in January 1896, succumbed to it. Since the journey home was long and the equatorial sun hot, the delicate problem of how to get the monarch's son-in-law back to England in a suitable condition gave pause. The palace wired instructions that the prince was to be dressed in his Ashanti uniform, with a locket containing his wife's hair placed around his neck. On board the ship, a tank was rigged out of old biscuit tins, this container filled with rum, and the deceased preserved in it (the intestines were removed and put overboard).

The stunned and widowed Beatrice returned full-time to her old job, after the appropriate period of mourning. More than ever, she was subsumed in the role of the Queen's most intimate private secretary, an office Victoria was happy to keep in her family (although she allowed the Honorable Harriet Phipps, who had been in the Queen's service since 1862, to share in Beatrice's duties). Beatrice read the contents of her mother's dispatch boxes to the all-but-blind Queen, and acted as the primary link between the monarch and her Household, an undertaking her real private secretaries soon came to resent for the Queen's implied greater trust in her daughter than in them. Most critically, Beatrice's rudimentary formal education gave the Queen's officials cause to worry that important technical points concerning government affairs might not be adequately explained to the Queen by her daughter.

❖ 4 ❖

Two of the three Petticoats had already made their feelings clear to Reid. They didn't want their nephew William to even *think* of coming to Osborne from Berlin. Together, Lenchen and Beatrice informed the doctor that the Kaiser "must be stopped at all hazards." It was by no means clear at this point that the Queen's illness was incontrovertibly mortal—at least not to observers other than the most intimate of her physicians—and Victoria's two daughters, who undisguisedly loathed William, believed that his perpetually volatile presence would only upset their mother. Louise hadn't yet arrived on the island, but Lenchen and Beatrice knew that she too would join her sisters in whatever efforts were needed to keep their nephew away from his weakening grandmother. Adding to their apprehension was the prospect that the German Empress might come along. Augusta Victoria—"Dona" to the family—was a creature both bovine and timid, who didn't speak English at all well, and who treated William as though he were her overseer rather than her husband. On visits to England, Dona drove the Queen to distraction with her loud and monosyllabic utterances of "*Ja*" in response to every remark addressed at her. The Petticoats would have neither her nor the Kaiser making a difficult situation even more difficult.

The news that Victoria was sinking reached William from at least three sources. On Thursday evening, Eckardstein, in his role as chief German diplomat in London, had sent a wire officially notifying his master. This morning, the German monarch received

Reid's message (which the doctor might not have sent had he known the depth of feelings of the Queen's daughters). Also this morning, Bertie wired his brother Arthur, in attendance at the Prussian bicentenary, and the latter broke what he believed was unknown news to his imperial nephew. Whoever it was who first told him, the effect on William had been electric: he decided instantly, without regard to his ministers' wishes or to his own expected presence at the imminent state festivities, to cancel all his engagements and hasten to his grandmother's side.

The Duke of Connaught well knew what his sisters' reaction would be to William's intentions. He had already received an unsubtle telegram from Lenchen and Beatrice begging him to keep William at home. As soon as he met with the Kaiser this morning, Arthur broadly hinted to his nephew that it might happen that, noble though his intentions were, the Kaiser wouldn't receive the warmest of welcomes at Osborne, what with all the hubbub there. William, his mind already firmly made up, ignored the advice, insisting that his place "as the eldest grandson" was at his grandmother's side. Rightly perceiving that his impetuous nephew wouldn't be put off, the duke wired London requesting a cruiser be sent to Flushing to ferry the Kaiser across the Channel. The Admiralty obligingly ordered the *Minerva* to meet the imperial party.

❖   5   ❖

As Reid had expected, the Queen spent the whole day in bed again. He was happy that Laking had decided to return to London, still convinced that the Prince of Wales's doctor was more a hindrance than a help. He heard from Laking later that evening, though, with the news that the Prince planned to go down to Sandringham for the weekend, a sign that either Laking didn't share his own evaluation of the seriousness of the Queen's condition, or that Bertie felt his presence at Osborne would only serve to excite public attention to his mother's condition.

Victoria herself finally was wheeled out of her bedroom into the adjoining sitting room at about half past eight in the evening, and Reid went in to see her fifteen minutes later. About the most he could report in his journal that night was that at least she hadn't appeared to be in a "vegetative state." He did, though, judge her mental processes to have worsened since the prior day. Victoria expressed concern whether her heir was in the house, evidence to her physician and her Household that she herself believed her condition to be terminal. When the sovereign pressed Reid on the matter of Bertie's presence, he asked her if she wanted the Prince summoned to the island. The monarch wearily responded, "I do not advise it at present."

Meanwhile, Arthur Bigge, Victoria's private secretary, put his own call through to the Prince at Marlborough House. Bigge had been overwhelmed with inquiries about the Queen, the news that she was seriously ill beginning to percolate through the country like a floodtide. What the harassed courtier sought from the Prince was permission to release some kind of statement over Marlborough House's authority, one that would at least give the country an accurate indication as to Victoria's health. At last, Bertie himself finally seemed to realize that a statement had to be made. Wearily, he told Bigge to have an appropriate bulletin go out over Reid's name.

# Saturday,
# January 19

❖ 1 ❖

The bulletin the Prince authorized was released from Osborne House this morning, and though the wording was designed to avert alarm, it struck the civilized world with the shock of a thunderclap. There was no question now among the public that Queen Victoria was seriously ill, her condition confirmed in the restrained but unprecedented admission of the official *Court Circular:* "The Queen has not been in her usual health and is unable for the present to take her customary drives." The gingerly phrased bulletin went on in what was for the Victorian court highly unusual detail. "The Queen during the past year has had a great strain upon her powers, which has rather told upon her Majesty's nervous system. It has, therefore, been thought advisable by her Majesty's physicians that the Queen should be kept perfectly quiet in the house and should abstain for the present from transacting business." Though the words were far from an admission of immediate danger to the monarch's life, the uniqueness of the announcement was meant, as many grasped, to prepare for what was likely in the offing.

At the same time the news was posted in the window fronts of the dozens of daily newspapers that served the capital, it was also tacked to the bulletin boards of the palatial clubs that lined Pall

Mall from Green Park to Trafalgar Square. The members of Parliament who utilized the clubs as their workaday living rooms forgot all about the now-mundane-seeming political problems as they pursued authoritative embellishment on the thin threads of the court bulletin. In response to the tinny sound of telephone bells ringing at Buckingham Palace and Marlborough House, the royal operators were authorized to say only that "we have no information."

The realization that Victoria might actually die struck with as much of a shock as would the news of an overwhelming disaster to British arms. Rumors as to the specifics of the Queen's illness had for several days been circulating with increasing urgency through the higher echelons of London's social and government elite. Many surmised the problem to be something along the unthreatening lines of a "slight indisposition," the Queen's subjects simply not ready to imagine a world without her, regardless of the unalterable reality that Victoria was nearly eighty-two. This morning's court bulletin generated a foreboding that a familiar world was about to change forever.

❖ 2 ❖

Though Victoria was the woman at the eye of the approaching whirlwind in England's constitutional life, her son and heir was the *man* there. Immeasurably more than anyone else, Albert Edward, Prince of Wales and Duke of Cornwall, would be transformed by the death of the Queen. For nearly six decades, Bertie had abided, restlessly, just outside the epicenter of the British monarchy, eclipsed by his mother's deep and omnipresent shadow. Now he was about to step over the unsharable boundary from subject to sovereign, into what Victoria called—rightly for 1901 —the "greatest position there is." But by the time his turn to reign finally arrived (he had been Heir Apparent longer than any of his predecessors), a significant question persisted as to whether the aging prince was up to the task.

Had Bertie been born to other parents, the chances are remote that his life would have created waves still reverberating nearly a century after his death. He was innocent of the keen intelligence of his elder sister Vicky, of the passion of Alice or the mechanical ability of Alfred, the artistic ability of Louise, or the musical ability of Leopold. His principal gift was instead a sweetness, a characteristic that as he grew into manhood transformed itself into a grace and social acumen that meshed gloriously with the essential and expected requirements of the position to which he was born.

His mother's wish, devout though it was, that Bertie grow into a carbon copy of his cerebral father was quickly seen to be a pipe-dream. Nevertheless, every effort was made to ensure such an outcome. From the beginning, Victoria, Albert and their German *éminence grise*, Baron Stockmar, charted a course that, had it achieved its ambitious goals, would have yielded in Albert Edward a paragon of princely virtues. But the clay wasn't there to be worked. Each year that passed only brought Bertie's parents worry, then despair, and finally a conviction that the boy would be a disappointment of heroic proportions. They saw only that which their son could not grasp—the standard attributes of classical learning. They ignored those qualities which might have been nurtured—Bertie's affection and abilities to gracefully socialize. In consequence, the Queen and her Consort withheld from their son the approbation that might have unearthed what intellectual abilities there were to mine.

A ludicrous brouhaha of late 1861 was to have devastating effects on the fraying threads of Bertie's bonds with his mother. When that fall his parents discovered him in an affair with an actress, a guileless indiscretion Victoria and Albert grossly and foolishly blew out of proportion, the father confronted his still-adolescent son at Cambridge. While in the university town, Albert caught a chill in the late autumn rains. On his return to Windsor, weakened by a growing stomach cancer and now a cold, the Prince contracted typhoid fever, a disease that most likely had spread through the castle's antiquated drains. His condition was either misdiagnosed or else downplayed by sycophantic physicians anxious to assuage the worried Queen, with the result that possible lifesaving treatment was undercut. Drained of the stamina to fight his illness, Albert quietly succumbed. Bitterly blaming her son's transgressions rather than the fever or the doctors' malfeasance, the Queen allowed the incident to poison the relationship between mother and heir for the rest of Victoria's life.

For the next forty years, the regime the sovereign established between herself and her eldest son was practically purpose-designed to ensure the Prince would find employment for his talents away from the Queen and the apprenticeship she might have given him. Though Bertie would beg each of his mother's first ministers for access to information, for the chance to perform significant labor, for an opening to use his skills in a way that would support the hermit Queen, Victoria vetoed all such aspirations. As the years passed, the Prince's behavior, in no small part the consequence of the Queen's rejection, gave Victoria ever stronger "proof" that the harsh judgment she rendered on her son was justified.

His mother hoped that his 1863 marriage to the beautiful Danish princess Alexandra would give Bertie's life the stability to keep his behavior on a firm footing. But Bertie's eagerness to partake of the most beautiful women in the world was legendary by the time middle-age overtook him. His inamoratas included many of the lushest actresses, professional beauties, peeresses, and *grandes horizontales* of half a dozen countries. Scandals erupted at regular intervals, providing new lows in public approval for the Prince with each fresh revelation of Bertie's inferiority in comparison to the hardworking, albeit largely invisible, monarch. That the mother was to any degree responsible for Bertie's failings was little commented upon, except by those of her ministers who risked Her Majesty's wrath by even suggesting that what talents the Heir did possess might be more usefully employed.

Sir Henry Ponsonby, Victoria's private secretary until his death in 1895, made clear his opinion of the Prince in a letter he wrote in 1872 to his wife:

> Nothing can be more genial and pleasant than he is for a few minutes. But he does not endure. He cannot keep up the interest for any length of time and I don't think he will ever settle down to business. . . . To get the P. of W. to enter into a subject or decide on it is most difficult. They have to catch snap answers from him as he goes out shooting, etc. Then he runs off on his lark to Trouville where of course business is impossible. . . .

Sir Henry's son, Fritz Ponsonby, would later assess the Prince of Wales's character in words that made those of his father seem almost praise. ". . . [I]t was all *façade*, the most engaging, decorative but quite misleading *façade*. There was practically nothing behind. His wonderful social tact could not always be a sufficient screen for his official ignorance. When he died, the chorus of exaggerated praise engineered by those who had been deluded by his friendly charm, turned criticism for a while against the Queen for not having enlisted his services more. But in her day Queen Victoria knew better." Loyalty to the Queen might have accounted in some degree for these biting words, but the judgment was one that would have been shared by many who knew the Prince—and the Queen—best.

Such was his stunted life that Bertie's frustrations often turned to malice, this dark side of his personality largely hidden to the public but all too often in evidence to his Household and friends. One of the least consequential manifestations of the Prince's insensitivity revolved around his obsession with dress and decoration. The stories of his cutting remarks to those he thought inappropriately attired or who incorrectly wore some ribbon or medal are legion: asking a friend with turned-up trouser cuffs if he were "going rattin'," or remarking to a lady seated next to him at dinner that the Princess (his wife) had taken the trouble to wear a tiara— "Why haven't you?" Few could successfully respond to these comments, but one who outmaneuvered the Prince was the Marquess of Salisbury. When in response to Bertie's comment that the Prime Minister was wearing the wrong trousers at some function, Salisbury poisonously apologized by saying, "I'm afraid my mind must have been occupied by some subject of less importance."

In the last years of Bertie's wait for the throne, the Honorable Mrs. George Keppel, a handsome and stately woman who was dexterous enough to act as a discreet intermediary for the Prince, had succeeded to the position of chief mistress. The daughter of Admiral Sir William Edmondstone and married to the third son of the seventh Earl of Albemarle, Alice Keppel and her husband had first entertained the Prince in 1898. She was then twenty-nine and still in the flush an English-rose beauty, although already a remarkably plump flush. The fifty-seven-year-old Bertie and Alice, instantly attracted to each other, became a recognized couple almost immediately, the Prince overwhelmed by his new lover's vivacity and cleverness. She was able through her tact and *joie de vivre* to make the Prince bright when he would have been bored, and with her good nature to make him happy when he was frustrated. Princess Alexandra even allowed Mrs. Keppel into her friendship, the Princess appreciating the check Mrs. Keppel had on her husband's less-desirable behavior. Abroad, she was received like royalty, whether with or without her Prince, while in England only three of its great nobles—the Duke of Norfolk, the Duke of Portland, and Lord Salisbury—remained so resolutely moral in their standards of hospitality as to deny entrée to Mrs. Keppel. All others welcomed this paragon of royal mistresshood, and so successful was she that it was said she hadn't an enemy in the kingdom.

In his life, Bertie's success in the last of his paramours was exceeded only by his success in the choice of the woman who was his wife. Princess Alexandra sprang from a background—her father was Heir Presumptive to the Danish throne—about as near to "normal" as a nineteenth-century European princess could have. Denmark was a small and unimportant kingdom, and its Royal Family had neither the means nor the inclination to live life on a lavish scale, which meant that the Royal Family assimilated many of the bourgeois values of their peaceful countrymen. Alexandra's engagement to the Prince of Wales had most enthusiastically been vetted by Prince Albert, this in spite of the "risk" such a marriage was seen to pose to Anglo-Prussian relations. Prussia had just finished its brutal annexation of the two tacitly Danish duchies of Schleswig and Holstein. Alexandra's family attributed this loss directly to Bismarck, and, by extension, to the Prussian crown. Repercussions from this Prusso-Danish war continued to poison the two countries' relations, but such were the Princess's virtues that Albert overlooked the dangers inherent in an Anglo-Danish alliance. After his death, Victoria permitted the matrimonial alliance to proceed in spite of her mourning, the Queen wishing her late husband's dictates be fulfilled. Indeed, she herself had been smitten by Alexandra's charm during an "on approval" visit by the Princess to Windsor.

During the earliest years of marriage, Bertie found in Alexandra all the female companionship he needed. The young Princess of

Wales was one of the most beautiful public women in the world and, except for her politically annoying habit of badgering the Queen to intercede on Denmark's side in the tussle over her father's troublesome duchies, pleased her mother-in-law greatly. Six children came of the union (the sixth died when only a day old), providing two male heirs for the succession. The firstborn, a future Prince of Wales and second in succession to the throne after his father, proved an embarrassment almost from the beginning. Prince Albert Edward—"Eddy"—was "lethargic," the word many historians apply to him, growing into a young man who was curious about little more than raising hell and skirts. To try to instill a sense of responsibility in him, something she saw to be in ominous short supply in her grandson, Victoria created the Prince Duke of Clarence and Avondale, the ungainly double-title one more example of the generally unfortunate tone of Eddy's life. After much energy was expended in an attempt to marry him off —the family hoping that a wife might keep him on the straight and narrow (just as Victoria had earlier hoped Alexandra would tranquilize Bertie)—Eddy finally became engaged to his cousin, Princess May of Teck. Six weeks before the planned wedding, the combination of influenza and pneumonia (some reports included syphilis) killed him. Almost everyone, except his immediate family but not excluding the Queen, agreed that the British throne had likely been done a signal service by Eddy's removal from the succession. Nonetheless, Queen Victoria was heartbroken at his death, the young man having been, after all, her grandchild, whom she had loved. As for Alexandra, she followed much the same course her mother-in-law adopted when the Prince Consort died: Eddy's rooms were kept as living museums, the Princess often visiting the darkened chambers to see that the Union Jacks covering the beds were always spread neatly.

The second son, Prince George, inherited both his brother's birthright and Eddy's fiancée. A year and a half after the Duke of Clarence and Avondale expired, George and May were married. While it was true that George wasn't the rake his elder brother had been, neither were his intellectual horizons particularly far-reaching; only his naval career, which had to be prematurely discontinued when he became his grandmother's second heir, had captured whatever imagination he possessed. Very much a paradigm of his time and class, he shot birds and other little animals with a gusto that almost came to a form of animal genocide. His wife May, who slowly became known to the public as Mary (her real name), was primarily interested in the Royal Family's history (not surprising, since she was the great-granddaughter of King George III) and acquiring every conceivable object connected with its history.

Alexandra's last three surviving children were daughters, one plainer than the next, a condition not compensated for by any particular intellectual curiosity. Louise was for a while—ominous realization as it was to all concerned—third heir to Victoria after her father and brother. The situation was happily corrected when George and May were blessed with their first child in 1894. Louise, choosing like her namesake aunt a Scottish nobleman, married the Duke of Fife and settled down to a life as near to obscure as any British princess could hope for. Victoria, in the running as the least lovable of all the Queen's granddaughters, never married, remaining what was, in effect, a glorified maid to her mother for the rest of her life, a lifespan which didn't greatly exceed that of her mother. Maud did better, marrying a handsome but prospectless Danish prince who nonetheless ended up as King of Norway, which of course made Maud that country's Queen. Never was there the least doubt that it was her sons whom Alexandra loved best, matter-of-factly relegating the daughters to the more distant recesses of her consideration.

While pregnant with her third child, Alexandra took ill with rheumatic fever, which worsened the otosclerosis that had come via her mother's gene pool. The rheumatic fever also ended up giving the Princess a limp, which prompted the ladies of her Marlborough House court to take up something called the Alexandra Glide, in imitation of their mistress's hobble. The otosclerosis got continually worse, until by mid-life Alexandra was all but deaf, a notable social impediment for the wife of the heir to the throne. The health problems tended to keep her at home while her husband was off with his fast set and mistresses, which, ironically, pleased the Queen, who got to have Alexandra's company all that much more.

By the time the prospect of the throne had cast its shadow over Bertie, he and his wife had long since worked out an "understanding." Alexandra wouldn't fuss about the revolving-door mistresses—as long as Bertie remained discreet—and Bertie would do little things to make sure that his wife always knew he "loved her best." Without the importuning of a media corps with which their great-granddaughter would one day have to wrestle, this arrangement worked out fine. Of course, the Queen knew all about Bertie's philandering, giving her all the justification she needed to make sure her heir was kept as far away as possible from any real share in her constitutional prerogatives. That this would ensure his ill-preparedness for the inevitable day his "turn" would arrive was, to all indications, immaterial to his self-centered mother.

Yet for all Bertie's needs to find contentment in other women's beds, it was Alexandra's embrace that he always wanted waiting for him, and for which he was genuinely anxious lest it be withheld. Perhaps this explains in great part the willingness with which the Princess of Wales so generously overlooked the indiscretions and infidelities of her husband, indeed welcoming the best of his women, most notably Lillie Langtry and Alice Keppel, into her home, and even into a degree of familiarity. The conventions of the time and class in which the couple lived lent themselves to such "understandings," but unlike other couples who maintained little more than a facade of marriage, the Waleses enjoyed a relationship of genuine love over the half century of their marriage.

❖   3   ❖

Today was a red-letter day for Victoria. She reached 81 years, 240 days, replacing her grandfather George III as the oldest monarch in English history. But the crown she had worn so long and, in considerable measure, so admirably, now seemed in her weakness a responsibility incapable of being sustained. Where her Tudor ancestor Elizabeth had been enjoined by the conventions and requirements of her time to be a worthy *king*, Victoria had worked only to be a conscientious monarch. Removed from the decisions her predecessors had to make to ensure the seaworthiness of the ship of state, as well as attending to a considerable share of its navigation, Victoria had only to maintain her self-imposed obligation of oversight.

Victoria's six and a half decades of involvement meant that her chief ministers were accustomed to hearing her opinions and, whenever those opinions weren't in conflict with settled government policy, acting in accordance. This exposure assured Victoria the undeniable influence of being heard, which is, of course a kind of power. But it shouldn't be imagined that in January 1901 the British government was paralyzed because of its monarch's inability to function effectively.

Since the Magna Carta, Englishmen had developed a unique government in which, by the beginning of the twentieth century, the monarch was wholly dispensable yet at the same time deeply involved in its functioning. The sovereign had become immaterial in the sense that the shape of the law was in any way dependent on his or her personal wishes, except insofar as the Prime Minister wished to accommodate some particular wish or notion or prejudice of the monarch, such wishes and notions and prejudices that had only a marginal effect on the major social trends of the day, patterns set by the larger society through its elected representatives. Yet the sovereign remained an indispensable part of the rituals the nation's elected governors established to administer society: Laws remained mere bills until the monarch's signature made them enforceable. Commissions of every officer in Her Majesty's forces required Her Majesty's personal signature before the recipients could fulfill their duties. Warrants of every nature required the Queen's acquisition, including, as Walter Bagehot famously pointed out, that which would require her own death if both houses of Parliament were to demand it. It was here, in the thicket of constitutional minutiae, that lay Her Majesty's government's dilemma in the matter of Victoria's indisposition.

Victoria's near-total freedom from illness over her long reign had lent both the country and the government the notion that she was something more than mortal. Now, overnight, the prospect of a regency had to be faced. A historical precedence of such a regency involved Victoria's uncle George IV, who had served as regent for his mad father for the last decade of George III's life. With the present sovereign's incapacity, the prospect for a repeat of that experience was beginning to cause apprehension in the cabinet. Until a parliamentary declaration of a formal regency, no one could act for the Queen—including even the Heir Apparent. Salisbury would very soon have to decide whether to recall the recessed House of Commons to have its members approve the government's contingency plans in the event of the Queen's continuing inability to function.

❖   4   ❖

Prompted by Reid's increasingly urgent tone concerning the Queen's condition, Bertie gave up his plans for Sandringham and left London for Osborne around noon. In the company of his sister Louise, he boarded the royal yacht *Osborne* at Portsmouth just as the last desolate rays of a dim January sun were setting on the Solent. It had been raining all day, and the nasty whiplash of a southeast gale still swept the waterway, sending the vessel diving through deep swells and high waves. The little steamer's master, Captain Holford, was anxious to make the journey as comfortable as possible for his royal passengers, but he was in a rush; he had already been informed that the Princess of Wales would be arriving at Portsmouth from Sandringham on the royal train later this evening, and he had little time to make the turnaround at Cowes' Royal Pier to get back to the mainland.

In spite of his ministers' deep vexation at the prospect of the Kaiser rushing off to Osborne—Chancellor Bülow suggested it might be better to wait and see how the Queen's illness progressed—William departed Berlin's Potsdam Station this afternoon on the first leg of the journey to his grandmother's bedside. All day, on orders from the Palace, the German Imperial Railways had been holding a special train at Potsdam Station, which lay a few blocks to the west of the Royal Palace; the locomotive, with its Krupp-built engine, sat majestically at the platform, straining under a continuous head of steam. With the Duke of Connaught on board, the Kaiser's luxurious train now headed for the little

Dutch seaport of Flushing. There the Kaiser's aides had already reserved cabins on the Dover mail boat: the weather was so wretched on the Channel that the party had no alternative to commercial travel—the Royal Navy's *Minerva* was delayed by the weather and wouldn't be able to get there in time to ferry the German Emperor to England in its protective embrace.

As the train sped across the flat plains of Prussia and Saxony and into the snow-covered hills of the Rhineland, an atmosphere of diversion filled the compartment holding the royal passengers. In view of the private nature of his journey, the Kaiser's suite was remarkably compact: only three aides-de-camp were in attendance—Generals von Scholl and von Kessel and Commander von Krumme, as well as the imperial physician, Dr. von Leuthold; the Duke of Connaught was accompanied by three military aides of his own. William wore the uniform of the 1st Dragoon Guards, his grandmother's Prussian regiment, his uncle outfitted in his full Prussian kit as colonel of the Ziethen Guards.

All along the route from Berlin the train received telegrams from William's aunts—Lenchen, Louise and Beatrice—urging that the Kaiser break off his journey; the Petticoats explained that the Queen "couldn't stand any shocks." William held his ground, wiring back that "I have duly informed the Prince of Wales, begging him at the same time that *no notice* whatever is to be taken of me in my capacity as Emperor and that I come as a grandson," a sort of promise of good behavior. He added that "what I do is my duty, the more so as it is this unparalleled Grandmama, as none ever existed before." Though genuinely distressed, the German monarch still exhibited his usual bonhomie, even telling his travel companions that "Uncle Arthur is so downhearted that we must cheer him up." On arrival at Flushing, William disregarded the rough weather that had stopped the *Minerva*, not thinking twice about setting out on the little mail boat. William had *always* loved England, and he meant to have the best time he could—savoring the anticipation even on this trip across a raging North Sea.

❖ 5 ❖

Reid wasn't having a very good time at all. First, he knew the Queen's daughters were in a frenzy at the prospect of their German nephew charging into Osborne like some great Teutonic bull. Reid thought it was he who was responsible for the situation, still not knowing that both Eckardstein and the Duke of Connaught had also informed the Kaiser of the Queen's condition. The physician was thus expecting a "pretty row" from the Petticoats when they found out *he* was the cause of their nephew flying to his Grandmama's side. (Reid wouldn't find out until a report in *The Daily Telegraph* on the following Monday that his telegram had apparently not been seen by the Kaiser, lying unopened at the Royal Palace in Berlin and thought to have been merely another congratulatory message on the festivities of the Prussian kingdom.) Trying to put thoughts of the Kaiser out of his head, the physician was pleased that he had seen a bit of improvement this afternoon in the Queen's ability to tell what was going on around her. Yet if the Kaiser were to arrive unexpectedly at Osborne, she might interpret his visit as a sure sign that everyone thought she was dying, which might actually further her doing so.

Again with the Prince of Wales's permission, Reid and Powell issued a second bulletin at six this evening. "The Queen's strength has been fairly maintained throughout the day, and there are indications of slight improvement in the symptoms this evening." Considering that six hours earlier their release said that "the Queen is suffering from great physical prostration accompanied by symptoms that cause anxiety," the doctors could now reasonably expect that anxiety might be allayed—at least for a time. After authorizing the new dispatch, Reid went up to see his patient again. He found Victoria "coherent," though still able to talk only with difficulty. When she feebly asked, "Am I better? I have been very ill," the physician gently replied, "Yes, Your Majesty has been very ill but you are better now."

Indeed Victoria felt strong enough to talk a bit longer with her doctor. The Queen expressed concern to Reid about his "overworking." She told him "you must be very tired, but you must not break down, you ought to have help." Reid assured the monarch he was getting all the help he needed from Powell. That seemed to mollify the Queen. She went on to say that she had heard positive news from South Africa earlier in the day—probably from Princess Beatrice reading telegrams to her—and then turned to her own condition, saying she thought the Prince of Wales ought to be told of the state of her health. Reid said that he had already informed the Prince of "all that I think Your Majesty would wish me to tell him." Victoria expressed a desire to see her son, but added she didn't think he should stay at Osborne, unaware that Bertie had just arrived at the house and planned to remain as long as he was needed.

The little exchange of information gave Reid fresh hope, even that she might still somehow pull through this illness. But his raised spirits were soon frustrated. When with Powell he went to her bedroom later in the evening, the Queen asked everyone but Reid to leave the room. Weakly, she turned to her doctor, now somehow seeming aware of the gravity of her condition. "I should like to live a little longer, as I still have a few things to settle. I have arranged most things, but there are still some left, and I want to live a little longer." Reid would do everything he could to satisfy what he knew might well be his mistress's last command.

Though Bertie expressed relief at Reid's assurances that the monarch's condition over the afternoon had changed a bit for the better, the Prince agreed with the physician that it might be best if his presence in the house were kept from his mother. Ever restless, Bertie felt a bit irritated at what now seemed to him a rather unnecessary call for him to come to the island; clearly Reid was yet to make it unequivocally clear to the Prince that, in his medical opinion, the end of the Queen's life was drawing near. But knowing that his presence tended to inflame the public's perception of the Queen's state of health, Bertie thought that he might even have been "made a fool of," an irritation he quickly expressed to his sisters. When Reid later heard of this skepticism, he realized he would soon have to make the Prince of Wales unmistakably aware of the truth of Victoria's condition. Together with Dr. Powell, Reid went to see the Prince, the two men to discuss with the soon-to-be sovereign the seriousness of Victoria's prognosis.

As to the Kaiser's impending arrival in England, Bertie—now

fully apprised of all the doctors knew of Victoria's illness—agreed with his sisters that their nephew should at least be kept away from Osborne. The Prince wholly shared his family's intense dislike of the Kaiser. He understood he would have to go back to London in the morning to ceremonially welcome the Kaiser to England, but he told Reid he would do everything in his power to keep William at Buckingham Palace and away from the Queen. Reid probably wondered how even the Prince of Wales meant to convince the Kaiser not to come to Osborne after William had broken off the massive celebrations in Berlin and rushed to England. The Prince thought the best course was to say the doctors had forbade "absolutely" any disturbances of the Queen, even keeping her eldest son from seeing her. To maintain his own honor in the subterfuge, the plan meant that Bertie would turn down Reid's offer to let him peek in on his mother from her bedroom doorway: if he could assure William that not even he himself had seen the monarch, his nephew might just understand and stay in London —for the time being.

Eckardstein was deeply anxious to meet his master's boat, due to arrive tomorrow morning at Port Victoria, down the Thames estuary from London. During his just-concluded visit with the Duke of Devonshire at Chatsworth, his host and Joseph Chamberlain, two of the most powerful men in the British government, had raised a momentous subject with the diplomat. It concerned their views of a possible Anglo-German alliance, such a union a dream that filled the Anglophilic Eckardstein with hopes that the increasing tensions between his own nation and the one he had come to love might be converted into a permanent partnership. Eckardstein planned to report fully on these glad tidings the moment he was alone with the Kaiser.

❖  6  ❖

Bishop Randall Davidson was just as excited about his part in the fateful events at Osborne. The prelate possessed the uncommon gift of being able to please the Queen, the reason he would soon become a key participant in the drama of her final illness. Davidson had been appointed dean of Windsor in 1883, and he had preached many sermons at St. George's that his chief parishioner found to her liking. He was graced with an outgoing personality and a lack of either the obsequiousness or the pomposity often present in those who addressed the Queen from the pulpit, and Victoria had always felt comfortable in Davidson's presence. When she promoted him to the episcopate in 1891 and made him, first, Bishop of Rochester, and for the last six years Bishop of Winchester, he became an exception to her famous dislike of bishops, men who, in her view, "never remained what they were before."

Ironically, Davidson's relationship with the Queen had, in terms of the young prelate's future prospects, gotten off to an exceedingly dangerous start. In a discussion she had initiated with him at the time of their first meeting, he dared to tell Victoria that she shouldn't publish any more revelations about her private life —the overly frank *More Leaves* from her private journal had just been published, and the Queen fancied herself a successful writer, ignoring the obvious reality that *anything* she wrote would become an automatic and instant best-seller. When Davidson commented freely on her private plans, Victoria was furious at the presumption. But after reflection—reflection being one of the sovereign's best and most useful personality traits—she realized the young dean's advice had been correct and to have ignored it might have led to a personal fiasco. The relationship between sovereign and cleric thereafter grew exceedingly close. In his new appointment at Winchester, one of the most important sees in England (together with London and Durham, one of the trio of bishoprics taking automatic precedence over all the other bishops of the Church of England), Davidson was happily near at hand to the Queen during her stays at Osborne. He was often invited to the island to tend to her spiritual needs, having retained the honorary position of clerk of the closet in the monarch's Ecclesiastical Household.

On this Saturday afternoon, the fifty-two-year-old cleric was relaxing at his official residence, Farnham Castle, planted squarely in the hop-growing country on the outskirts of Winchester. While preparing the notes for the sermon he was scheduled to preach the next morning at Holloway College, the solitude of his study was interrupted by his housekeeper handing him a cipher telegram. It was from Sir Arthur Bigge at Osborne. Taking some few moments to decode the message (Bigge had encoded it incorrectly), the bishop learned the Queen's health was in a dangerous state and that her immediate family had been called to the island. Davidson understood his presence at Osborne was being tacitly requested. He decided to go immediately to his Queen, and wired Bigge of his plans.

Sending word to Holloway that he wouldn't be preaching the next morning, he then dispatched a wire to Launcelot Smith, the vicar at St. Mary's Church in Cowes. Davidson asked if Smith could meet him at the ferry landing on the island. Arriving late at Southampton from Winchester, he luckily caught the last boat of the night across the Solent. On a miserable night, the soaked bishop found already gathered on the ferry a large contingent of journalists and telegraph clerks, part of the army of newspaper people that was beginning to home in on the island, there to wait out what their editors sensed would soon be the story of the new century.

When Davidson finally arrived at Cowes an hour before midnight, a letter from Bigge was waiting for him at the ferry landing. The Queen's principal assistant was sorry that Osborne was already filled to overflowing, but that the last bulletin from Reid gave everyone hope that the Queen's condition was turning a bit for the better. Davidson asked the anxious Reverend Mr. Smith if he might spend the night with him in the vicarage. Mr. Smith was clearly honored to put up his bishop.

# Sunday,
# January 20

### ❖ 1 ❖

The skies that had been like blackened steel all day Saturday had turned this morning to a brilliant blue. It was rare that anyplace in England—not excluding this "garden" island—should revel in such sunshine in January, and in the company of such splendor even the biting winds were forgiven their sting. The lawns Albert had laid out for his family's pleasures were this morning covered with a silvery hoarfrost, melting slowly under the rising sun. In the distance, the cruiser *Australia* sped along the metallic Solent, the coastline of Hampshire rising on the horizon in the view from the Queen's bedroom window. Yet in spite of such beauty outside the house, all inside was full of apprehension that its familiar cadences were about to change forever.

This morning's official bulletin from Reid and Powell—now a routine part of the physicians' day—was meant to diminish the fears of anxious millions, its wording gentle and noncommittal. "The Queen has passed a somewhat restless night. There is no material change in her condition since the last report." The worried Reid knew the tone was optimistic where little optimism was warranted.

Fatigued and desperately wanting to rest, Reid had been at his sovereign's bedside throughout yet another entire night. He judged her to be sinking rapidly, her restlessness much worse, and her now almost-total inability to take any nourishment weakening her by the hour. He and Powell had ordered oxygen tanks during the night, hoping that the monarch might take some comfort from the restorative contents of the newfangled canisters.

There was one problem Reid knew had to be attended to immediately, at least if he and Powell and the women attendants were to properly nurse the Queen in her remaining time. The double bed she slept on—the same one she and Albert had shared in what now seemed another age—equaled the dimensions of a good-sized raft, while its four-foot eleven-inch occupant, her amplitude shrunken by weeks of malnourishment, lay nearly swallowed up in it. It was hard to reach the Queen, to gently turn her to make her more comfortable, to try to medicate her. Reid decided to move her into a bed that would make the task of nursing Victoria more manageable.

Calling attendants to erect a screen around the Queen and thus ensure privacy, Reid then had the components of a small single bed, one precisely fitting the physician's specifications, brought in. After reassembling the pieces, the screen was removed, and Reid and the Queen's personal attendants—four dressers now functioning in the role of nurses—pulled it next to the larger bed. Together they gingerly lifted the Queen over onto the small cot. They found it difficult not to jostle her more than was absolutely necessary, but her only apparent awareness of the transfer was an occasional look of discomfort on her face. The cot with the monarch was then wheeled into the corner; the screen again put up, and with some effort the men moved the larger bed over toward the fireplace. Then the Queen and her cot were finally centered where the big bed had formerly stood.

With his mother being rearranged in her bedroom, downstairs the Prince of Wales was getting ready to forsake the private comforts of Osborne for the rigors of a return to London. Protocol demanded he personally receive his imperial nephew into his mother's kingdom, disagreeable as the prospect of such a meeting seemed at this difficult time. Bertie still hoped he could keep William in London, and was more determined than ever to convince the Kaiser that if the Queen saw her imperial grandson it would certainly tip her off that the end was considered to be near.

With the last-minute pleas of his sisters to keep their nephew away from Osborne still ringing in his ears, Bertie kissed his wife good-bye and went to his carriage in the Pavilion's forecourt shortly after noon. The Prince boarded the *Alberta* to hasten across the unseasonably bright Solent, and in Portsmouth a special train was waiting to speed him the eighty miles to Victoria Station.

Though no official announcement had been made of the Heir Apparent's return to the capital, reporters—"pressmen," as they were then called—in the island had wired the information to London, ensuring that a large crowd would be gathered at Victoria to meet the royal train. At the head of the throng was the reception committee—the Earl of Clarendon, the Queen's Lord Chamberlain, and the Earl of Pembroke, her Lord Steward. Not wanting to miss the opportunity to mingle in such distinguished company, William Forbes, the general manager of the London, Brighton and South Coast Railway proudly accompanied the two earls to the Prince's carriage as it pulled alongside an awaiting red carpet.

As soon as Bertie alighted onto the platform, the officials solicitously inquired as to the Queen's state. "You see they have let me come away," the Prince smilingly replied, knowing full well his words would be reported and thereby assuage the anxiety spreading throughout the country. The carriage bearing the royal party immediately set off at a trot for nearby Buckingham Palace, where, amid the bric-a-brac–clogged rooms that had been little used for four decades, Bertie would nervously pass the two hours until his nephew's imperial train was due at Charing Cross. At the palace, he changed into the uniform of the Prussian 1st Dragoon Guards, ceremonial garb he knew William would appreciate.

❖ 2 ❖

The Royal Zeeland Steamship Company's mail packet *Engeland*, bearing the German All-Highest and his English uncle, had in the still-black hours of the morning sailed out of the harbor at Flushing into a choppy North Sea. Unusual for a vessel bearing the Kaiser, not a single German naval ship guarded it. William apparently took no notice of the security breach, and remained in the good spirits that characterized the journey from Berlin. He was now anxious to get to the place where he could assume another and much-loved persona out of the closetful he juggled with seasoned dexterousness. This time it would be a very great favorite: that of the English gentleman who happened to be the ranking male in his sovereign grandmother's vast family. In any event, he thought, there was no time to mourn, as morose Uncle Arthur still needed cheering.

Waiting to greet the Kaiser at Port Victoria was Baron von Eckardstein, there to inform his sovereign of the promising Chatsworth discussions. Eckardstein happily envisioned being personally instrumental in easing the tensions between official Berlin and official London, and was anxious to let the All-Highest know of this diplomatic opening.

When William strode down the gangplank, Eckardstein gravely bowed, the Kaiser immediately thanking his envoy for letting him know of the seriousness of the Queen's illness. William told Eckardstein that over the entire journey from Berlin he had been peppered with telegrams from Osborne, missives from his aunts telling him his presence wasn't necessary. The excited Kaiser assured the envoy he could "never while I live forgive myself" if the end were to come and he wasn't there to witness it.

On the train ride into Charing Cross, Eckardstein finally briefed the Emperor on his conversations with Chamberlain and the Duke of Devonshire, telling William how "delighted" he was that two such prominent British ministers—their cabinet positions as Lord President of the Council and Secretary of State for the Colonies only hinted at their real influence in the government—had put forth the prospect of an Anglo-German alliance. To his London chief-of-mission, William quickly expressed full agreement with the goals of Chatsworth, for what he grandly termed "the protection of their mutual interests and for the preservation of the peace of the world."

Whatever William really thought about such a future for the two nations, his ministers in Berlin held thoroughly negative views on any such entente. Baron von Holstein, the influential but shadowy head of the Foreign Ministry's political department and the bureaucrat to whom Eckardstein had transmitted the details of the discussions, had immediately wired the diplomat with orders that he should personally beg the Kaiser not to discuss these matters with any British ministers on his visit, the Anglophobic Holstein knowing the Emperor would encounter many such officials in England. When, in his obedience to Holstein's orders, Eckardstein tactfully murmured to the Emperor that "it would be best" if such advice from Berlin were adhered to, William sensibly promised to talk only about "Anglo-German relations generally." Nonetheless, he sent a telegram to Chancellor Bülow: "So 'they come' it seems—just as we expected—this is what we have waited for." But the Kaiser's chief minister, who was in perfect agreement with Holstein, resolved to ignore any British overtures for an alliance.

Though only a subdued announcement had been released that the Kaiser was arriving in the capital—the trip was strictly a private one, and therefore most of the usual formalities associated with an imperial visit had been dispensed with—the forecourt at Charing Cross station had nonetheless begun to fill with curious spectators late in the afternoon. Most of the spectators seemed in restrained spirits, sadly aware that the Kaiser's arrival very likely signaled their sovereign's imminent death. The stationmaster had allowed the earliest arrivals among the crowd to go onto the platform so they could see the Kaiser's train up close, but when it became apparent that a substantial throng was beginning to bear down on the station to witness the Queen's grandson enter London, officials decided to close the platform to any more onlookers.

No guard of honor waited at the station—again due to the private nature of the visit—but neither was the Kaiser's arrival anything remotely like an ordinary one. All other traffic was stopped, the carriageways were sanded to ensure the royal brougham and team a better footing as it entered the station, and a scarlet carpet was laid where the Kaiser's coach would stop on the platform. An unusually strong security force from Scotland Yard was dispersed throughout the main hall to provide protection for the many dignitaries, a not-unjustified precaution in an era of anarchist murders and assassinations.

Just before the train bearing the imperial party steamed into the shed, a carriage arrived carrying one of Victoria's sons-in-law and three of her grandchildren—Lenchen's husband and sons, the Princes Christian and Albert of Schleswig-Holstein, and the Duke of Connaught's son, Prince Arthur of Connaught. The Duke of York's carriage followed close behind. When the entire reception committee was assembled, Bertie's own carriage pulled into the arrival hall to an excited murmur from the crowd. With the military precision that marked such royal movements, the Kaiser's train pulled to a screeching stop within seconds after the Prince of Wales got into position on the platform. William and Uncle Arthur were clearly seen standing in the center saloon, waiting to disembark.

The moment the train halted, Bertie leaped across the space into the car holding his kinsmen, and immediately kissed William on both cheeks. The Emperor had changed from his uniform, and was now dressed in ordinary civilian clothes topped by a hard felt hat, the mufti making him look far less ferocious than usual. All the assembled princes hugged, and finally the Kaiser and Prince of Wales presented their attendants to each other. Bertie, William and Arthur, lifting their hats to acknowledge the silent salutes of the crowd both inside and outside the station, climbed into their carriage, and set off at a brisk clip, across Trafalgar Square and down the Mall, for the palace.

From his nephew's quickly voiced anxiety to see the Queen, Bertie knew it was hopeless to try to keep William in London. Besides, the Emperor's relationship to the British monarch gave him an undeniable right to be present at the monarch's bedside, regardless of the high feelings it would cause with the rest of the family. The Kaiser seemed gratefully aware of the respect of the crowd as the carriage sped along at the trot. One plainly dressed man stepped out of the silent and densely packed mass of people, and coming up to the side of the carriage and baring his head, simply said, "Thank you, Kaiser." Bertie leaned over and diplomatically whispered to his nephew, "That is what they all think, and they will never forget this coming of yours."

The Prince dropped William at Buckingham Palace to allow him and his party time to refresh themselves. For security considerations it had been decided that the royal party should wait until the next morning before going down to Osborne, though a special train was being held in readiness at Victoria in case the Prince of

Wales decided to ignore the advice. Bertie returned to his own residence at Marlborough House, later to return to the palace to join the Kaiser for an intimate family dinner. A small crowd of seasoned royalty-watchers chased alongside the royal carriage as it carried the Heir back down the Mall, many doing so in the mistaken belief that it contained the Kaiser as well as the Prince.

❖   3   ❖

If the atmosphere at Osborne wasn't gloomy enough already, today marked the fifth anniversary of the death of the still much-missed Prince Henry of Battenberg. Few rituals carried such force at the Queen's residences as that proper obsequies be paid to commemorate the deaths in her family. The Queen herself could not today be expected to pay the normal tribute to her son-in-law's memory, but the rest of the family knew better than to neglect their matriarch's traditions.

Thus at noon the swelling collection of the sovereign's progeny descended on the beautiful little Whippingham chapel, the church that served the estate, there to remember Henry. His death from fever on the Ashanti campaign may have lacked real heroism, but the Prince's resolve to serve his Queen and adopted country had earned him genuine admiration throughout the kingdom. The widow, Princess Beatrice, appointed by her mother to follow Henry in the largely ceremonial post of governor of the island, led her sisters and brothers-in-law and a swarm of nieces and nephews into the homey and snug church that her father had fashioned so many years ago. Bishop Davidson offered to say a few words, an overture Princess Beatrice gratefully accepted.

❖   4   ❖

All over Britain—in fact, all over the world—other congregations this Sunday were also focused on the Royal Family. At the Queen's own "parish"—St. George's Chapel, Windsor— Canon Dalton offered special prayers for the mistress of the castle.

As the parishioners filed out after the service, many eyes looked toward the Round Tower, where the waving Union Jack seemed to lend reassurance that the Queen still lived.

In St. Paul's Cathedral, Canon Holland spoke a few special words to the congregation before launching into his prepared sermon: "Today I . . . beseech your earnest prayers for her who for so many years has been a mother to our nation. So long as we can remember anything her name and her presence have been felt in every beat of our hearts and pulse of our blood . . ." The preacher concluded by commanding his flock to "pray for all those around and near and dear to her. You will pray for the whole nation forlorn and bereaved in the hour of its need."

The tone at Westminster Cathedral, the historic scene of Victoria's coronation, was apprehensive: "May we all say that we meet here today under the shadow of a great fear, and an overwhelming sense of anxiety as a nation, which must send us on our knees in humble and heartfelt prayer to God?" Throughout the kingdom, something indeed like a wave of fear was sweeping thousands of homes. The fear was of the loss of the familiar, the loss of the deep and wide foundation to her nation that Victoria had represented for longer than most could remember.

Nor was it only Christian congregations who this weekend concerned themselves with the soul of the Queen. Jews, who had advanced far in the country's life over the course of this monarch's reign, turned out in large numbers at the kingdom's synagogues. In London's Lauderdale Road temple, Dr. Moses Gaster, chief rabbi of the country's Sephardic communities, ordered the opening of the ark so special prayers for the recovery of the Queen could be recited in front of the holiest artifact of Judaism. So, too, did Islam remember in the Bedford Place mosque, where worshipers had gathered to celebrate the end of Ramadan, solemn prayers being directed to Allah for the recovery of "the Sovereign of the greatest number of the True Believers in the world."

The *Times* was flooded with dispatches regarding the monarch from its correspondents all over the world. From Calcutta came word of intense anxiety in the native community as to the Queen's condition. Canadians were reported to be "grief stricken," with subdued crowds gathered around newspaper office windows in every major city, engrossed in the bulletins from Osborne. An item in the *Times* filed from Capetown said that the dean of the city's cathedral characterized the Queen's illness as "the worst news received during the past unhappy twelvemonth, and regarded at the moment as a national crisis."

From Paris, where high emotions against British policy reflected French disapproval for the conduct of the Queen's soldiers in South Africa, came a sampling of the attitude toward Britain characteristic of the French press. The *Times* reported that many papers were "fearful" in case any "respectful courtesy" in their stories about the Queen be misinterpreted as "servility." The *Liberté* walked a fine line by commenting on the mood in Britain that "for a race which is proverbially phlegmatic it must be acknowledged that on this occasion the English display a warmth of feeling which shows the depth of their affection for their Sovereign."

In Pretoria and Johannesburg and Blomfontein, all over the velds and desolate scrublands of the South African plateau, there was little talk of anything but what the death of the Queen would bring. Vilified by the Boers as a "dissolute old harridan," the followers of Kruger hoped her passing would shake the spirit out of their foe. To the Boers, fighting for what they perceived as an inalienable right to cast the southern part of the continent in the image of their censorious God, Victoria represented dead mothers and children in the British concentration camps, burnt-out farms, the land threatened by a vast and menacing black tide.

Now that the British fighting forces were clearly in the strategic and tactical ascendancy in Africa, their fears had subsided since the calamities of the last year. And they knew their sovereign stood with them in this godforsaken place, not in body but certainly in spirit. Among her fighting troops a palpable apprehension could be felt, a fear that a world without Victoria could not be so happy.

❖  5  ❖

With Bertie off in London greeting the formidable Kaiser, tensions at Osborne had loosened a bit. Reid noted in his diary this evening that the Queen was taking food somewhat better than had been the case over the last few days, but also recorded that she was still "apathetic and aphasic, and hardly ever intelligible." He found himself as busy telephoning the Prince of Wales in London with hourly reports on the Queen's condition as he did actually caring for his patient. By sunset, the tone of the physician's reports had, sadly, deteriorated. Victoria, unable to swallow any food whatsoever, had become unconscious early in the evening; her condition, in Reid's view, verged on the hopeless, so much so that he told her daughters and Princess Alexandra they could go and watch over the Queen without worrying about doing her any harm.

The doctor wanted yet another physician to join him and Powell, and he knew Sir Thomas Barlow, physician-in-extraordinary to the Queen, would be the most helpful. Reid trusted Barlow, an old friend, and was anxious for his advice. He telegraphed Barlow, asking him to take the 7:55 A.M. train down from London Monday morning. Afterward, fearing this might be too late, he again sent a wire to his friend, asking if he could possibly get the 5:40 A.M. train. Clearly, Reid was prepared for the end at almost any moment.

The physician was apprehensive about sending for Barlow, knowing that Victoria didn't want any "strange" doctors called in at the end, her lifelong aversion to outsiders well-known to him. Reid was, in fact, acting against precise instructions his mistress had given him three years ago. Victoria had written out her wishes as to what should be done in case of her own serious illness. She equivocated not by so much as a single syllable. In the first place, she *commanded*—specifically using that word—that no outside doctors were to be summoned. Though the memo was written for Sir William Jenner, her then-doctor now long dead, she clearly expected Reid to follow the document to the letter. As she herself wrote, ". . . it is *on the express understanding* that *her wishes expressed* in this memorandum should be *strictly adhered to*, and *in no way departed from.*"

As to any nursing requirements, at the time the instructions were drafted John Brown was designated, because of the "strength, care, handiness and gentleness [that] make him invaluable at *all* times," to fulfill a kind of chief caretaker role. No one else would be allowed to lift her or carry her, though her dressers—her faithful "female attendants"—were to act as Brown's assistants. With the death of the controversial Scot, the Queen wanted Reid to know that it was to be *only* her dressers who were to render nursing services, other than for medical procedures and examinations Reid and her other personal doctors would be required to carry out.

Jenner—and now Reid—was expected to inform Bertie and Alexandra of the contents of these instructions when the time came, but it was to be made clear to the Waleses that neither they nor anyone else were to alter a single jot of what the Queen wanted done when her death approached. Victoria further demanded that no minister of state interfere. Perhaps more than anything else, she wanted to be put fully in the picture as to her condition and her prognosis, *whatever* they should be.

Late this afternoon, Reid and Powell sent out another bulletin on Victoria's condition. Though the Prince of Wales had been notified by the two that he should return to Osborne with all haste, perhaps not even waiting until the morning, the words they chose were again meant to allay the country's uneasiness, and were purposely—if not quite justifiably—soothing: "Osborne, 4:30 P.M. Her Majesty's strength has been fairly maintained throughout the day. Although no fresh developments have taken place, the symptoms continue to cause anxiety." Though he had tried not to equivocate regarding her condition in response to her own inquiries, Reid still tried, in the gentlest way possible, to dispel the Queen's fears, if only to keep her from further dangerous agitation. When yesterday she asked, "Am I better?" the doctor replied, ". . . You *are* now better"—justifying the less-than-half-truth to himself on the premise that she might indeed pull through. Today, he knew hope was gone.

After the service at Whippingham Church for Prince Henry, Randall Davidson was handed a message from the Queen's daughters. Knowing how close their mother had been to the handsome and eloquent young preacher during his days at Windsor, they asked him to come up to the Pavilion, where they were sure the entire family would find his presence reassuring. Throughout the afternoon, Davidson fell into intimate conversations with many members of the family, imperial and royal and serene highnesses now gathering from every corner of Europe. Princess Beatrice later excused herself for a while to prepare a special message for the Isle of Wight in her capacity as governor. Believing that the islanders deserved a direct word of the Queen's condition, Beatrice kept her bulletin brief but designed it to prepare the people for the worst: "The condition of the Queen is very grave but not entirely without hope." The news was conveyed via the *County Press*, the island's local newspaper.

At six, Davidson returned to Whippingham to preach at another service, finally returning to town after an exhausting day. But shortly after midnight, having just gotten into bed, a royal carriage clopped up to the door of the vicarage. The driver told Davidson he was urgently wanted at Osborne, the Queen having taken a turn for the worse and his ministerial services needed at possibly any moment. After rushing up the hill and through the estate's gates —in front of which a small cluster of journalists stamped their feet in the cold air of this starlit night—the gathered family surprised the prelate with the news that their mother had seemed to have come round a bit. Nevertheless, Davidson was given a room in the Household Wing, where, just in case, he would still be near at hand.

While Davidson settled down in the Household Wing, Reid and Powell were observing their near-comatose patient. Despite the family's hope that her slight stirrings constituted a rally, the men could see that the Queen was sinking rapidly. The two stayed up with her all night, administering oxygen and expecting that she might die very quickly now. At midnight, they issued yet another medical bulletin, the final one for the day. "The Queen's condition has late this evening become more serious, with increase of weakness and diminished power of taking nourishment." All over the country, British men and women who read it expected tomorrow morning's news from Osborne would announce that Victoria's struggle had ended.

### ❖ 6 ❖

With the day closing on Britain, still-bustling New York was deeply immersed in the drama playing out on the other side of the Atlantic. This morning the Sunday *New York Times* dedicated a third of its front page to the story. "QUEEN VICTORIA AT DEATH'S DOOR"—"VIRTUAL REGENCY EXISTS"—"QUEEN REFUSED TO SEEK MEDICAL ADVICE WHEN HER ENTOURAGE BEGGED HER TO DO SO"—the latter headlines characteristic of the sort of melodramatic reporting in the United States whenever the British Royal Family was concerned. Nonetheless, it was true that Victoria's affliction absorbed the American public's curiosity to the seeming exclusion of all other matters. As dispatches came in from their London bureaus, the big papers were posting them instantly in their display windows, as often as once an hour throughout the night. The *New York Advertiser* was of the opinion that Queen Victoria's death would "partly discompose the whole British social and political order." The *New York Times* correspondent reported that most Americans felt Britain was "in danger of an irreparable loss." The New York Stock Exchange had the prior day closed its half-day Saturday session with a marked loss in international stocks, caused, many said, by traders hearing the unsettling news from the Isle of Wight.

No event had so stirred Washington since the mortally wounded President Garfield had twenty years earlier lain between life and death for weeks. The capital's newspapers had kept their staffs on duty this Sabbath, ready to get out extra editions should the worst be telegraphed from London. President McKinley, sick with influenza, left orders with his personal secretary that he was to be notified instantly if any change in the monarch's condition was reported from the British embassy. When earlier in the day the President first heard that the Queen was dying, he turned to his companions and remarked with a sense of genuine wonder, "Why gentlemen, she began to reign before we were born."

## CHAPTER VIII

# *Monday, January 21*

## ❖ 1 ❖

For the second night in a row, Reid and Powell had been up continuously with the Queen, again administering oxygen to her and spelling each other throughout the long hours. Reid found some faint reason for optimism, when toward dawn Victoria's condition improved enough for her to swallow a bit better, and even speak haltingly to her doctors. But she had gotten very little sleep over the past night, or for that matter over the past several nights. Combined with near-starvation from her inability to eat, this sleeplessness was contributing heavily to her weakened state. Unless her body could get the rest it needed, Reid knew there was no chance the monarch was going to survive.

In the diary where he was carefully recording these historic events, Reid commented with a touch of bitterness about the conspicuous absence of the Queen's daughters over the last night. He pointed out that although neither he nor Powell had called for the princesses, neither did they come at any time during the night to ask about their mother's condition. Though throughout the physician's written recollections of his years with Queen Victoria his attitudes toward her daughters is ambivalent, there is a case to be made for the princesses' timidity where their mother was concerned.

Victoria demanded almost airtight privacy in regards to entry to her bedroom; this included her family and, God forbid, anyone unknown to her—meaning servants or doctors. As we've seen, even her principal physician had never been truly intimate in the patient-physician sense with his sovereign, never even having tended her undressed until her final days. All her life, Victoria allowed only a tiny coterie of dressers—women in the most literal sense handmaidens to the Queen—to administer to her after she retired for the evening. None of her daughters (let alone her sons!) saw her in her bedroom after their own childhoods, and none were allowed to enter the room in these final days, not even to do so little a thing as help her take her medicines. It was Mrs. Tuck, the Queen's Chief Dresser (a woman who had, incidentally, once suffered a nervous breakdown in the Queen's exacting service), who acted as Reid's chief nurse.

The Queen did ask Reid for one "outsider" to visit Osborne House's innermost sanctum this morning. Shortly before noon, in a fleeting moment of lucidity, she suddenly appealed to the physician whether she might have her lapdog Turi to keep her company. Reid immediately sent for Victoria's favorite Pomeranian, having to wait until someone went to fetch it from the gardens where it had been exercising. When it was carried into the bedroom, Reid placed it on the bed with the Queen, who stroked the happy little creature and seemed pleased for the small diversion. Turi, who had been brought home from a holiday in Italy, remained—restlessly—with his mistress for about an hour before he was gently taken away.

At mid-morning, Dr. Barlow arrived. A professor of clinical medicine at the University Clinic Hospital in London and recently advanced to the dignity of baronet, Sir Thomas Barlow was trusted implicitly by Reid, and he and Powell were relieved to have the distinguished physician help them shoulder the responsibility of administering to the nation's most august patient.

Ready for a break from the strain of keeping the sovereign alive, Reid sent a hurried note to his wife Susan, who was staying on the estate at May Cottage. Using the nickname by which he and his wife privately referred to the Queen, he told Susan that "Bipps was very bad last night, and we thought she was going to bat [i.e., die]: but she rallied and is rather better again! but is almost unconscious. Come up to the bicycle house about 12:45 and I'll come to you." But Reid's wife didn't feel like coping with the royal crowd at the Pavilion, and notified her husband that she would stay away for the time being.

An hour before noon, Reid and Powell, the pair now joined by Barlow, issued the first medical bulletin of the day.

> The Queen has rallied slightly since midnight.
>
> Her Majesty has taken some more food and has had some refreshing sleep. There is no further loss of strength.
>
> The symptoms that give rise to most anxiety are those which point to a local obstruction in the brain circulation.

❖ 2 ❖

In London's Victoria Station, the special train that all last night had been waiting under steam for the Prince of Wales was finally about to receive its distinguished passengers. Leaving Buckingham Palace at an ungodly hour for royal movements, the royal party reached Victoria Station at 8:00 A.M.; accompanying William and Bertie were the Connaughts and the Duke of York. Prince George was feeling the strain nearly as much as his father was, not only because he knew he was about to become Heir to the Throne, but because the thirty-five-year-old naval officer was also suffering from a formidably bad cold.

While Forbes, the railway manager, nervously waited, the Prince of Wales and his family were briefly held up by the ubiquitous necessities of protocol as they entered the carriage on the royal train. Bertie obligingly bowed to his imperial nephew—the latter a monarch, which he wasn't, yet—bidding the younger man to enter first. William, who rarely yielded precedence to anyone, declined to take it, evidently mindful of the "strictly private" nature of his visit and anxious to show public respect to an uncle about to join him in the rarified circle of sovereigns. Bertie persistently declined, until finally the Kaiser jumped across the gap between platform and carriage. With Prince and Kaiser, Uncle Arthur and his wife, Prince George, and a passel of aides-de-camp, equerries and secretaries all aboard, the gleaming black and gold train pulled out of Victoria bound for Portsmouth and connection to the Isle of Wight. The company immediately progressed into the dining saloon for a large breakfast to sustain them for the ordeal that would soon greet them on the island.

The city the royal party was leaving was this morning awakening to a ghostly anxiety about the Queen. Many among the millions of Londoners were certain they would face the first day without the royal presence on which their collective consciousness had for so long been fixed. In the Mansion House, the Lord Mayor's official residence in the City, dispatches from Osborne were being periodically received from the Home Secretary's representative. Outside, wealthy stockbrokers and destitute street vendors alike anxiously scanned for the official word which would be affixed to the soot-blackened stones of the palatial residence. The clerks inside found themselves flooded with wires and telephoned inquiries from provincial mayors and Scottish provosts, all anxious to learn some scrap of official information that was not yet reported in the newspapers.

A considerable crowd had gathered in front of Buckingham Palace, there to await in the wintry air the bulletins officials placed on the gates; the noon dispatch was the first new information since Sunday's reports from Osborne. Copies of the same news were quickly posted at St. James's Palace as well as at nearby Marlborough House. At each of these points, crowds pressed forward to read the terse statements, the implied seriousness of the monarch's condition instantly reflected in somber faces that turned and went back to whatever business they had to attend.

From Whitehall and Downing Street and the polished porticoes of Belgravia and Mayfair and St. James's, from all over the more fortunate precincts of the capital, carriages bearing the possessors of British power and wealth and privilege arrived at Buckingham Palace to allow their occupants to sign its sympathy book. Page after page soon filled this Monday morning, all with neatly scribed names of those who felt closer to their Queen for having done this small duty. Many of these same carriages now drove to the smart West End precincts where their owners would call in on their tailors and dressmakers, there to order new accoutrements of the official mourning that was so central to proper and prosperous Victorian society.

After the workday ended, there was little but emptiness and silence in the streets, a condition particularly arresting in wealthy Pall Mall and in the normally exuberant Oxford Street. Only in the Strand could there be found something approaching the crowds common to a typical evening. It was a first night at the Globe Theatre, where *Sweet Nell of Old Drury* had just been brought in triumph to London from the provinces. The old playhouse was crowded to welcome the popular stars, its outdoor lights shining through the fog of the winter evening. Still, the theatergoers couldn't totally forget what was happening at Osborne. When the applause died down at the end of the play, "God Save the Queen" was sung with an unaccustomed fervor by audience and players alike. As the Globe and the other theaters quickly emptied at the evening's end, the Strand and Piccadilly and Leicester Square joined the rest of the vast metropolis in the gloom of the national deathwatch.

❖ 3 ❖

Two hours after leaving Victoria Station—precisely on schedule—the royal train silently glided into the Harbour Station at Portsmouth. Once aboard the *Alberta*, the Kaiser, the Duke of York and the Duke of Connaught stood chatting on the bridge (Bertie remained in the yacht's saloon), under the Royal Standard flying overhead in the bright, sunny weather that was favoring the Solent for a second day in a row. Waiting at the island's pier were carriages with pair-horses and postilions that had been sent down from the royal stables, along with a crowd of two hundred or three hundred spectators eager to get a glimpse of the distinguished passengers.

When the carriages rolled into the grounds through the Queen's entrance, the correspondent from the *Times* was seeking out whatever sources he might find at the Gate House; the *Times* was then, much as it still is, the newspaper of record in the kingdom, but its representative had little more of substance to report than his competitors did. With the world now fully aware that the Queen's life was drawing to a close, the number of reporters arriving on the island had grown substantially. Gleaning any bit of intelligence about what was happening inside the estate's gates was the highest obligation of the day for the newspapermen, many of whom represented foreign papers. For most, the watching and waiting were monotonous in the extreme. Unless some action was going on at the gates, the majority of the reporters sought refuge from the chill at the Prince of Wales Public House across the street from the entrance. In it they found a roaring fire and a simple meal of cheese and bread as they scribbled their daily dispatches.

The exact nature of Victoria's illness was still unknown to all but a very few of her medical establishment and her closest relatives, the end of the Victorian age not being one in which people believed the public had a "right" to know the details of a royal person's illness. As for the illness of a king, delicacy would have prevented the specifics from being bandied about, while those concerning the illness of a queen were seen as even less fit to be shared with the public. In the case of so private a woman as Victoria, extreme guardedness surrounded the facts of what exactly was wrong with her. Old age, or "senile decay"—a state of physical deterioration rather than a specific medical disorder—was the public's only indication of their sovereign's ordeal. The attempt to gain further knowledge of Victoria's illness—at least as far as propriety permitted—sharpened every reporter's ambitions.

❖   4   ❖

In Kronberg, where lay another eminent patient, Vicky's physicians were doubtful that the Dowager Empress could survive her dying mother. A somber medical announcement in the German newspapers made it clear how desperately ill Vicky was: "It is with sincere regret that we announce that the Empress Frederick's condition has become materially worse. There has been a serious development of the disease from which she is suffering and her physical pain is intense." To lay to rest any question of whether the Kaiser's mother would be joining her family at Osborne, the bulletin continued, with startling frankness, "All idea of any journey in pursuit of health has been definitely abandoned, and it is in the highest degree improbable that she will ever leave Kronberg."

The news from England of her mother undoubtedly worsened Vicky's already unbearable condition; the pain from the cancer that was eating her spine away was beyond any real relief despite the morphine her doctors were freely administering to her. Nevertheless, Vicky begged for some way to be found to get her to Osborne, and the physicians were hard-pressed to convince her of the impossibility of such a journey. They assured the haggard Empress that any such attempt would probably kill her before she even arrived in England.

Upon leaving Berlin, William had asked his wife to go to Kronberg during his absence. Vicky and Dona's relationship had long been strained, but the Dowager Empress was nonetheless happy to have the younger Empress at her side. Joining the women was Vicky's son Henry with his wife Irene (the latter also Vicky's niece through Princess Alice). In the Taunus fog, Queen Victoria's daughter could do little other than wait, in an agony of both mind and body, to hear of her mother's fate.

❖   5   ❖

One of the many idiosyncrasies of the British system of government has it that the demise of the Crown—that is to say, the death of the sovereign—is the only contingency upon which Parliament is required to meet without summons. Until the members of both houses swear allegiance to the new monarch, no action can take place in the nation's legislature. With the members having been in recess for three weeks, the Right Honorable William Gully, who was M.P. for the city of Carlisle and who also served as Speaker of the House, came to London this morning to confer with Lord Salisbury's ministers as to what course should be taken in the immediate event of the Queen's death.

Arthur Balfour, First Lord of the Treasury and Leader of the

House of Commons in the place of his uncle the Prime Minister, canceled his plans to go to Edinburgh to carry out long-standing engagements. Instead, he stayed in his residence in Downing Street for the word that he knew might come at any moment directing him to proceed at once to Osborne. There he anticipated an emergency meeting of the new monarch's Privy Council would have to proclaim the new King's accession. On the June day in 1837 when Princess Victoria succeeded her uncle, the Privy Council met to sign the proclamation while William IV's body was still warm, preceding the assembling of Parliament by two hours. Now with the Queen at Osborne and the House in recess, the waters were clouded for Balfour. Nonetheless, he intended to see that the kingdom's constitutional demands were carried out as quickly as possible. Special trains and steamers were being held in readiness all over Britain in case it became necessary to speed the Councillors to the Queen's island.

❖   6   ❖

It wasn't only in the corridors of government where an atmosphere of dread had descended. Everywhere, from the palaces of the nobility to the dwellings of the humble, public functions and private gatherings were being called off. The morning and evening papers carried long columns of cancellations from across the country, listing events from the lord mayor's reception in Leeds, to the Chamber of Commerce's annual banquet in Swansea, to the Primrose League Ball in Wolverhampton. At Crathie, outside the Queen's home at Balmoral, where Victoria had figured as an honored neighbor to many in the district, the shock was palpable. In Dublin, a rumor that the Queen had died swept the city, the judges in the law courts prepared to adjourn their courts until word came that Victoria was still alive. An ongoing house party at Chatsworth was called to a halt by the Duke and Duchess of Devonshire; after the last of her guests had gone, the duchess decided to come up to London herself to join her husband, who as a member of the cabinet was sticking close to Downing Street. As elsewhere in Britain, routine events in London were put off until further notice:

canceled were the Lincoln's Inn Grand Day dinner, the dinner of the Carpenters' Company honoring General Buller, the banquet of the Empire Lodge of Freemasons, the reception for the mayor and mayoress of Fulham, Sir Charles Warren's inspection of boys of the Church Lads' Brigade. Dozens of columns of such tidings filled the newspapers.

Reuters was reporting on the expressions of sorrow and sympathy for the Queen's illness cascading in from all over the world. Churches in Jamaica were said to be packed to overflowing with people praying for her. The commander-in-chief in Gibraltar ordered the garrison band not to play any music in public. From Australia, feelings of grief were described as "universal." The mayor of Ottawa notified his city that the Queen's death would be announced by the tolling of the bell in the town hall, at which time every church bell in the city would begin to peal.

French papers were, as they had been for days, glutted with reports of the royal drama. The afternoon journals were now being rushed out in the morning, so anxious were Frenchmen to learn details of Victoria's illness. The Chamber of Deputies announced that when the worst news reached Paris, it would immediately terminate its sitting "as a token of mourning and sympathy with Great Britain." Crowds gathered around the Crédit Lyonnais and the other great banks, the only places where tape machines existed, to see what effect the illness was having on the Bourse. Phone lines from the exchange to London were held open all day; the excitement among the brokers was portrayed as "indescribable," and when word came through shortly before closing that a small improvement in the Queen's condition was announced, share prices instantly rose.

As much as Frenchmen were by genes and breeding contemptuous of their neighbors across the Channel, for a multitude of reasons Queen Victoria had nonetheless become for them a symbol of general European prosperity and well-being, of a century without a world war, the monarch's personality and endurance endowing her with a "kind of halo of magical charm." Commenting on what could be expected under the reign of her son, *Le Temps* noted forebodingly that "His Royal Highness has already nearly sixty years of life behind him, and says that it will be difficult for him to follow the example of his mother." Only the *Libre Parole* cast a discordant, Anglophobic note by printing a personal attack on the Queen, scorn which Reuters predicted the French government "will not improbably be called to explain."

Court balls planned for this Monday evening in Vienna and Athens, Brussels and St. Petersburg were canceled; from the Hofburg in the Austrian capital, Emperor Francis Joseph made inquiries as to his sister sovereign's state of health. Pope Leo XIII requested that the Duke of Norfolk, the premier Catholic peer in the United Kingdom, keep him directly informed as to Victoria's condition. Crowds thronged around the Casino in Monte Carlo to read the latest bulletins; all members of the principality's English community withdrew from the International Pigeon Shooting Competition scheduled for the afternoon as a token of regret at their monarch's illness.

In Washington, Robert Lincoln, former American minister to the Court of St. James and son of the man whom Victoria had admired above all other United States presidents, called Victoria "one of the wisest women—probably *the* wisest woman—who ever lived." He added: "I do not mean to say that she is a genius, but her great gift of common-sense, reinforced by her vast store of knowledge, has enabled her to counsel men and women of all classes and conditions with a wisdom which could not be excelled." It was a sentiment many Americans shared.

❖  7  ❖

After each of the most important members of the Queen's family arrived and had the chance to compose themselves, Reid took them individually to see the sleeping monarch. First the Prince of Wales was escorted into Victoria's bedroom by the physician; it was the first time the Heir had seen his mother since the onset of her serious illness. Next came the Kaiser, followed by the Duke of Connaught, and finally the Duke of York. They could do little more than look at their matriarch from the foot of the bed, the doctor having advised each that he thought it best if no attempt was made to arouse her or speak to her. Reid was, however, little concerned about his patient becoming over-excited even should she awaken and see visitors: her eyesight was by now so bad that she probably wouldn't have been able to detect anyone in the room unless they spoke.

Later in the afternoon, the physician took a break from his vigil at the Queen's side to have a brief tête-à-tête with the German Emperor. William expressed great concern as to his grandmother's real condition. Reid promised to get him in to the Queen's bedside alone when she awakened, so the two monarchs might have a last talk together. After the Kaiser promised not to do or say anything that might excite her, the doctor again assured him he would do his best to make arrangements. As much as the princesses wanted William kept away from the sickroom—now a fairly cruel preoccupation, seeing that the Kaiser was actually at Osborne—some of the family was softening in its opposition to the man they considered a bull in their midst. The German monarch's behavior had so far been most acceptable—thoughtful, quiet, and uncharacteristically humble—a fact that was quickly picked up on by many of his relatives.

Though the housekeeping staff at Osborne was accustomed to large numbers of visitors at any of the sovereign's residences, it was rare indeed that such a high proportion of the visitors were so august in rank. No royal person, whether emperor or empress, king or queen, prince or princess, could get along on anything like his or her own devices. All were accompanied by retinues, squads of servants and attendants who did virtually all their masters' work for them: equerries who served as secretaries, aides-de-camp functioning as what in modern terms might be called "gofers," ladies-in-waiting who got their mistresses sorted out with the extraordinarily complex clothing requirements (but who themselves were prohibited from appearing in anything "too smart"), as well as the more menial maids and valets (who quite literally removed and put on their employers' clothing for them) and military guards, the latter charged with watching over Queen Victoria's vulnerable family. All of these persons had to be housed, all according to strict protocol requirements, with attention paid to the minor nuances of rank and station, especially in relation to their employers' rank and station.

The great majority of the family and their retinues were put up, together with the Queen's higher Household, in the Main-Household block adjacent to the Pavilion. Three floors of bedrooms equaled the facilities of a good-sized hotel, with dozens of rabbit-warren rooms for menials tucked in the cellars, kitchens and the odd space between the real bedrooms. Princess Beatrice's suite on the top floor of the Durbar Wing off the other side of the Pavilion had for the duration to be converted into rooms for the higher-ranking guests.

Thus the whole of Osborne—the Pavilion, the combined Main and Household block, and the Durbar Wing—now housed one of the most closely packed collections of European royalty in history. Bertie and Alexandra with their children and grandchildren; the Connaughts and offspring; the Petticoats Lenchen, Louise and Beatrice and their families; the Duchess of Edinburgh and Saxe-Coburg-Gotha, Affie's new widow; the Duchess of Albany, Leo's widow; various German *Hoheiten*; all kinds of necessary companions like Charlotte Knollys (who kept the Princess of Wales amused) and Herr von Pfyffer (who did much the same for the Kaiser).

And, of course, the most exalted of them all—the Kaiser. Fortunately for the space planners, William was without his Dona, the Kaiserin remaining in Germany to take care of her mother-in-law. Bigge made sure William got the best room of all—a lovely suite on the seaview side of the ground floor of the Main Wing, its French doors opening onto the broad terraces that skirted the lawns. The Kaiser must have been aware, with at least some measure of pensiveness, that the suite had once been his mother's rooms before she married his father.

Strewn about the remainder of the estate were quarters for family and courtiers and their suites who were either junior or whose egos didn't need to be stroked quite so much as those magnificences housed in the center of the beehive. Bishop Davidson got to share Kent House with Princess Helena Victoria of Schleswig-Holstein, Lenchen's grown daughter. East Cowes Castle took in Beatrice's boys, the Battenbergs having been turned out of their rooms in the Durbar Wing; with them were a clutch of high aides and functionaries. Osborne Cottage sheltered the Queen's phlegmatic cousin, the Duke of Cambridge, who had until recent years been commander-in-chief of the British army. The duke shared his quarters with the little Schleswig-Holstein princes as well as the Teck princelets, the latter the Duchess of York's uninhibited brothers. Albert Cottage had Princess Elisabeth of Hesse, May Cottage put up General von Scholl of the Kaiser's staff under the same roof with Lady Reid, Dr. Reid's wife. Barton Manor was equally full-up with various officials. Not to waste any space, even the royal yachts lying at anchorage in the Solent were turned into floating hotels: His Serene Highness Prince Louis of Battenberg was quite comfortable in a spacious stateroom on the *Victoria and Albert.*

Anxious to visit his mother for what he knew very well might be the last time, Bertie asked Reid if he would take him into the Queen's bedroom when she awakened. The doctor did so, there leaving them alone. Whether the sovereign and her Heir were able to remove any of the shadows that had for so long clouded their relationship isn't known, but when Reid and Mrs. Tuck later went into the room and stood by the bed, the semi-conscious Victoria took her doctor's hand and kissed it over and over. Reid recorded in his diary that he felt the Queen believed she was kissing her son's hand, Bertie having just left the room. Mrs. Tuck came to the same conclusion, and asked her mistress if she would like to have her son return. Victoria said yes, and the Prince of Wales was notified, and he immediately came back to his mother's bedside. Her only words to the man who was about to inherit the world's largest empire were, "Kiss my face." A little later, Reid took Alexandra in to see her mother-in-law, the last visitor of the day. He finally left her alone, turning off all the lights in the Queen's chamber except the little *veilleuse*, the nightlight she had always wished to be left burning until the dawn arrived.

Bishop Davidson had spent the day visiting with various members of the royal flock. While at Kent House, he and Princess Helena Victoria of Schleswig-Holstein exchanged anecdotes and little bits of intelligence about the Queen. The princess told the bishop about the small signs of her grandmother's failing health she had been noticing for the past several weeks. The principal problem was the Queen's sleepiness, she judged, particularly at times when always before she had been alert. The granddaughter added that the family had especially dreaded Lord Roberts's visit the prior week, which had led them to attempt the subterfuge designed to get the general in and out of the royal presence as quickly as possible. Ironically, her grandmother's anger at this impertinence did much to give the family hope that her present indisposition might be a fleeting one.

Queen Victoria's equivocal attitude toward religion was made evident in the stories her namesake granddaughter shared with the bishop. The princess told Davidson that she and her grandmother had spent many hours in the past weeks talking about illness and death. The Queen was still badly shaken by the death of the princess's brother, Christl. When Thora, as Helena Victoria was called in the family, told the Queen about her brother's last day in the hospital in Pretoria and how he had asked for the ministrations of a priest and expressed a wish to take Communion, the monarch mused, "I wonder whether he really *wanted* to receive the Holy Communion, or whether they 'got' him to have the service!" When she tried to assure her grandmother that her brother was in earnest, the Queen retorted, "Well, I don't feel at all sure that I should wish for it just then, but I should certainly like to have prayers." To Davidson, this came as further evidence of the sovereign's dislike of "over-churchiness."

After dinner in the Household Dining Room, the bishop went to see the three physicians, the trio taking a brief break from their duties with the Queen. He found the men in the Stockmar Room, the chamber that once belonged to the man who had guided Prince Albert through the rocky and largely uncharted shoals of marriage to a sovereign queen. Reid, Powell and Barlow had just issued the latest bulletin, which stated that "the slight improvement of this morning is maintained." Davidson wanted to know if the note of hope was really justified. The medical men confided that it was the Prince of Wales who asked for the optimistic tone, and, furthermore, that it went against their own wishes. Though not calling the words "untrue," they did tell the bishop such a bulletin was bound to raise hopes where none existed.

Clearly fascinated by the company, the prelate asked the doctors to tell him what the prognosis would be if the patient were not Queen Victoria but "Mrs. Smith in Sloane Street." Embarrassed glances shot between them. Finally Powell spoke. "I should expect her perhaps to live for four or five days." Barlow agreed. But all said the end could come at any moment—or that she could hold her own, and enter into some kind of lasting "vegetable life." Davidson asked if it was prudent for him to return to Kent House, or should he stay at Osborne itself in case he might be needed suddenly in the night. The doctors told him he could leave—that there would be time "in any case" for him to rush up to the Pavilion when needed.

Davidson ended his day with an intimate chat with the Kaiser and the Duke of Connaught. What the pair wanted to discuss with the bishop was the meaning of the Queen's life if she were to go on with only a "bare modicum of life." The distinguished-looking duke wasn't prepared to think of his mother as a vegetable, but neither he did he want her to die; Davidson thought the fifty-year-old soldier's comments made him come off a "simple schoolboy."

Not so the Kaiser. The Queen's grandson made it clear that there was no choice between dying and living on as less than she had always been; he told his uncle and the bishop that there must not be a "mean or unfitting close" to his grandmother's life. Though Davidson thought he sounded rather like he was pontificating "ex cathedra," nonetheless William spoke with no small eloquence, remembering the "splendid life" the Queen had lived, how "early her greatness had begun," and "how undimmed it was even now." Perhaps the supreme compliment from the Kaiser's perspective was when he compared Victoria with his paternal grandfather, affirming "Grandpapa and the Queen have both been lives of iron, and when it is broken it does not waste away but goes crack!" His logic as well as his syntax may have been a bit off, but the idea nevertheless came through. Prince Arthur diplomatically drew his nephew's ruminations to a gentle close by telling Davidson how good it was for the family to have the Queen's old spiritual adviser on hand.

———

One more bulletin was issued this Monday night. Again, if the words were noncommittal, the tone was still a good deal more optimistic than the true circumstances warranted.

Midnight

> There is no material change in the Queen's condition. The slight improvement of the morning has been maintained throughout the day.
> Food has been taken fairly well and some tranquil sleep secured.

The beautiful estate, filled with royalty and the high and mighty from all over the Queen's great empire, settled down to sleep under what was still a clear sky sheltering the island. Osborne had just ended its last full day as the home of a British monarch.

# *Tuesday,*
# *January 22*

❖ 1 ❖

Two days of clear, cold sunshine turned this morning to far more familiar January weather. Harsh winds gathered on the Solent and scoured the island, keeping inside all but the heartiest of those gathered for the royal deathwatch. Upstairs, Victoria in her bed was aware neither of the weather nor of her assembled kin. Again the trio of physicians had spent much of the night with the Queen, Reid in her room without once leaving, Powell and Barlow often called in for consultation by their intrepid but now exhausted colleague.

Victoria lay only half-conscious as the weak winter light began to penetrate the tall windows. Reid noted that his patient was now almost totally unable to swallow; he had tried to get a little liquid food down her, but the monarch could barely tolerate it. Most ominous, signs of a final death struggle had begun during the long night. Victoria now clearly emitted the sound of tracheal rales, the dry, crackling sound from the windpipe made in the death throes of the mortally ill. This harbinger of death meant that fluids were slowly filling and congesting the Queen's lungs; where before her cough had been bringing up the congestion in her throat, now even that defense mechanism was unmistakably breaking down.

At eight o'clock, the three doctors issued the first bulletin of the day. It was short, and held out no false hope. "The Queen this morning shows signs of diminishing strength, and her Majesty's condition again assumes a more serious aspect."

At around nine-thirty, leaving Powell in charge, Reid went back to his room in the Household Wing to clean up and get into some fresh clothes. Within moments of returning there, he heard a knock on his door. It was Powell, who urged his colleague to come back immediately to the monarch's bedroom: he was certain the Queen was going to die at any moment.

Davidson had just awakened at his lodging in Kent House, when he too was frantically summoned to get up to the Pavilion. A royal carriage waited for him in the gloomy driveway, then sped the bishop to the big house. Rushing up to the Queen's suite on the second floor, he found the apprehensive family beginning to gather, the doctors having summoned all the Queen's children and grandchildren who were on the island. He saw the Prince of Wales standing on the Queen's right, the Kaiser on her left, and about a dozen other royalties grouped behind and around the two men. Characteristically, the Princess of Wales hadn't yet arrived, her habitual lateness for anything—even her mother-in-law's death-watch—a trademark to which the entire family had long since grown accustomed.

The bishop could clearly see that the Queen was having a great deal of difficulty in her breathing, her movements jerky and betraying obvious discomfort. A nurse was standing at the head of the bed holding Victoria's head so the monarch might more readily cough up some of the phlegm congesting her throat. Powell and Barlow had just been re-joined by Reid, the latter now administering oxygen from a bulky iron tank. Davidson, who as chaplain of the Order of the Garter lent a historical note to the scene, immediately began to murmur prayers for the dying; he judged, with more hope than certainty, Victoria alert enough to be aware of his words. When she weakly asked her grandson George who it was speaking, he answered "the Bishop of Winchester." The Queen said she understood and asked, "Is Mr. Smith here too?" Canon Clement Smith, vicar of Whippingham Church, was a favorite of Victoria, and even in her weakened state she realized the cleric would be grieved if he thought his services weren't now needed at her bedside. An aide was sent immediately to the small church on the estate, where Smith was invited to come to the monarch's room.

The Queen's three daughters made an effort to let their nearly blind mother know who was in the room, but—still unrelenting —wouldn't say that William was standing next to her. Reid thought the omission was cruel, taking the Kaiser's exemplary behavior since he had arrived as evidence that he would do nothing to upset his grandmother. Turning to Victoria's heir, the doctor whispered, "Wouldn't it be well to tell her that her grandson is here too?" But apparently Bertie thought the excitement might be too much, still believing that if Victoria knew William had come from Germany she would realize that her condition was held to be hopeless.

Victoria's physical agitation soon calmed a bit, and she looked like she wanted to sleep. All the emotional tumult in the small room made it difficult for the medical staff to properly treat their patient—the more so since Victoria's oversize mahogany bed still stood, empty, next to the fireplace. The doctors quietly asked if everyone would leave to give the Queen a chance to rest alone for a while.

Timing their second bulletin of the day for a noon release, Reid, Powell and Barlow wrote out the bare facts of the Queen's condition. Even though they made an obvious effort to reduce its bitterness, no truthful words could now hope to disguise the facts.

> There is no change for the worse in the Queen's condition since this morning's bulletin.
> Her Majesty has recognized the several members of the Royal Family who are here.
> The Queen is now asleep.

❖ 2 ❖

Though much of the Queen's work was merely *pro forma*, that work nonetheless continued to play an indispensable part in the functioning of the British government. Her ministers realized that the logjam awaiting the sovereign's attention would have to be broken soon. The law courts were among the first to feel the Queen's incapacity, as judges were beginning to be held back from fully dispensing justice without the necessary warrants that were signed by the sovereign. Furthermore, appointments all through the kingdom's administrative layers could simply not be brought to completion without the personal sanction of Queen Victoria. There was no question of fudging the procedures—a thousand years of constitutional niceties may have brought the government to such a constitutional impasse, but it was an impasse still perfectly real.

Under normal circumstances, it would have been the Prime Minister at the center of this crisis in the nation's life. But as a peer and thus ineligible to sit in the Commons, Lord Salisbury was represented by his nephew as the leader of the House that truly governed the nation.

In fact, Balfour was in many ways the Queen's principal minister, not only because of his uncle's increasing ill health and absence from much of the day-to-day governmental affairs, but because of his own leadership qualities. Adding to Balfour's authority was the fact that the Prince of Wales had quietly informed Lord Salisbury that he didn't expect his mother's Prime Minister to come down to the island. Understanding the premier's dangerously weakened health, Bertie didn't want Salisbury further undermined by a journey from London in wintry weather. Though Salisbury had in fact just arrived in the capital from Hatfield, the Cecil country seat in Hertfordshire, it was made clear by Marlborough House that Balfour could represent the government leadership at what all now realized was a deathwatch. Aware of the checks on government the Queen's incapacity was causing, Balfour knew the time was approaching when he would have to summon a Privy Council to act in Victoria's name—no matter what happened at Osborne. But for the time being, the Leader would go down to the island and appraise the situation firsthand.

Balfour's secretary made arrangements for him to catch an ordinary train out of Charing Cross at mid-afternoon, but an urgent command from the Prince of Wales summoned the minister to change to the special government train that had been held under steam all night. Balfour set out from Downing Street at one-thirty in the afternoon, and arrived at Charing Cross a quarter of an hour later. At the station, he was notified that the Duchess of York and the Duke and Duchess of Connaught's three children would be journeying down with him, delaying the departure until the royal party arrived a few minutes later. At Portsmouth, the party boarded the *Fire Queen*, the private yacht of Sir Charles Hotham, commander-in-chief of the naval station. If they glanced in either direction along the port city's quays, they would have noticed hundreds of onlookers straining to see across to the island.

The scene that greeted Balfour on his arrival at Osborne late in the afternoon astounded him. Since the onset a week ago of Victoria's inability to do any desk work, the pileup of her "boxes" meant that a small mountain of accumulated state and government documents was awaiting attention. Balfour seemed stunned at this "mass of routine work" the Queen had to do, and he and Frederick Ponsonby wondered "how the machine could go on without her." On hearing from the Queen's assistant private secretary that Victoria was failing rapidly, Balfour quickly surmised the need for a Privy Council to complete state business would within hours be obviated by the accession of a new monarch.

❖ 3 ❖

Reid wholly intended to redeem the promise he had made to the Kaiser to somehow get him in privately to see his grandmother. A little before noon, the doctor went to the Prince of Wales's room to report on the Queen's condition. Imposing on the preoccupied about-to-be monarch, Reid seized the chance to ask if he might be allowed to take the Kaiser in to see the sovereign, explaining diplomatically that he had told the Prince's nephew he would do everything in his power to give him the opportunity to be alone with Queen Victoria one last time. Bertie, whose humanity could exceed that of almost any other member of his family, understood. He swiftly gave his permission to Reid, and said to tell anyone who objected "that the Prince of Wales wishes it."

At last, the physician was free to take the Kaiser for what he knew would be a historic final meeting between the sovereign rulers of two empires. He also knew, that unless the Queen could by some medical magic be brought to a state of at least semi-alertness, the visit would serve little purpose.

Armed with the Prince's leave, Reid went to the Kaiser's suite in the Main Wing. Though the rooms were the best the estate had to offer, and had housed William's own mother as a girl, they were a far cry from the opulence of the royal palaces in Berlin or Potsdam. Reid found the Kaiser busy reading cables and urgent messages from Berlin, dictating official responses to the most pressing of them. When the doctor told William he wanted to take him to the Queen's room now that no other member of the family was present, the Kaiser smiled appreciatively—both for the chance to see his beloved Grandmama *and* to get away from the ubiquitous but boring routines of kingship. But he had clearly been hurt by the coldness some of his relatives were showing him in spite of the efforts he had made to keep a low profile and to let his uncle stand out as the imminent head of the family; William wasn't used to taking second place to anyone, and the effort had taken its toll. "Did you notice this morning that everybody's name in the room was mentioned to her except mine?" the Kaiser asked Reid, obviously stung by the incident. Reid said he had, and that the omission was the chief reason he now wanted to make sure the two monarchs should have a few moments together.

Leaving the Main Wing, the Kaiser and the physician walked down the long corridor leading to the junction with the Pavilion. At the entrance to his patient's bedroom, Reid stood aside to let the German Emperor enter the room ahead of him. He asked the nurse and the dressers to leave. Taking the Queen's grandson to the edge of the low bed, the doctor murmured to Victoria, "Your Majesty, your grandson the Emperor is here; he has come to see you as you are so ill." Miraculously, she was alert enough to smile her appreciation, and Reid left the two alone in the room.

Some sources speculate that Dr. Reid was only able to bring the monarch to a state of semi-alertness for the visit with her grandson by giving her generous amounts of champagne and brandy, a few hinting that even stronger stimulants were used. (*The New York Times* headlined the disclosure that the Queen had been "drugged" so she could visit with the Kaiser.) In those of his diary entries that were published, Reid makes no mention of any such medications given his patient, though at this point in her illness it wouldn't be difficult to conjecture that he might have done so without recording it for posterity. He clearly understood the importance of the Kaiser having a last moment alone with Queen Victoria, knowing that whatever could be done to cement close ties between the royal houses of Britain and Germany would be useful.

When Reid later saw the Queen after her five minutes alone with her grandson, all she said to Reid was, "The Emperor is very kind." The Kaiser left no hint in his own memoirs what final words passed between himself and his grandmother.

❖ 4 ❖

A t Windsor, Reginald Brett, the second Viscount Esher, was in a quandary. As Secretary of the Office of Works, the dexterous and astute courtier held formal charge of the royal palaces, a position that had often brought him into close contact with the Queen. Over the half-dozen years of his service, Victoria had come to regard this Old Etonian and arch-establishmentarian with no small measure of admiration, the patrician Esher fully returning the sentiments. Although he accepted that the Queen's death was a matter of time now, he was still deeply grieved at the message from Osborne that Victoria was in fact dying.

When Albert died, the design and building of his mausoleum had been one of the few activities that gave his distraught widow some relief from her anguish. Victoria commanded that her kingdom would never let the memory of Albert pass out of the public consciousness, and committed herself to establishing far-flung monuments dedicated to her husband's labor on behalf of his adopted country. The greatest of these memorials would be the mausoleum she would build for his remains and, eventually, where her own would join for eternity those of her husband. Four days after Albert died, Victoria chose the Windsor gardens near Frogmore House as the place in which to erect this temple. The finished structure would resemble a good-sized basilica, and the Queen would, out of her private purse, spend £200,000 on it. It was "enough," as one socially minded biographer put it, "to rebuild the slums of Windsor."

Directly under the mausoleum's Victorian Florentine dome lay the sepulcher, the heart of this royal temple. The sorrowing monarch commissioned an Italian sculptor, Baron Carlo Marochetti, to carve not only an over-sized recumbent figure of Albert to lie atop his sarcophagus, but at the same time to fashion one of herself against the day it would be placed alongside. The two magnificently detailed effigies were brilliantly lifelike, and still rested on their blocks in Marochetti's studio when the sculptor died. After Albert's white marble figure was hoisted atop his new tomb on the Frogmore Mausoleum's completion in 1868, that of his widow was stored away in a recess in the walls of Windsor Castle. Workmen eventually bricked the recess up, their motives or instructions now obscure. This second effigy was forgotten by virtually everyone.

This was the state of affairs over which Lord Esher's quandary arose. For some days, since it was considered proper and reasonable for the courtier to surmise that the monarch's illness might be fatal, Esher had begun to prepare the Frogmore Mausoleum for her burial. But amazingly, no one had the least idea where, three and a half decades earlier, workmen now presumed long-dead had sequestered the huge object that was now needed. Inquiries throughout the royal establishment were hastily made as to its whereabouts.

While at Osborne the Queen's family was gathered, Esher received a note from Mr. A. Y. Nutt, the obscure official to whom he had given responsibility for finding the missing monument. Nutt had, to Esher's immense relief, tracked down one of the workmen involved with the disposition of Marochetti's monument. The venerable retainer told him exactly where, in a secluded recess of the castle, bricks and plaster had more than three decades earlier concealed the effigy of a grieving and still young Queen Victoria.

✧ 5 ✧

London's uneasy reaction to the news of the Queen's condition had since yesterday moderated to a degree. In the West End, knots of well-dressed people in the streets still talked of little else, and emotions continued to run high, but it seemed to many that the Queen's subjects had accepted the inevitability of the news they knew must soon come. The flood of anguish had, as *The Daily News* put it, "exhausted itself in the rush upon the rock cliffs of despair." Awaiting the end, the people of the metropolis held themselves in a vise of patience that one observer found "positively painful to watch."

Elsewhere in the world, press preoccupation with the events on the Isle of Wight was still all but driving other news from the front pages. Page one of this morning's *New York Times* had over four of its seven columns filled with the latest details from Osborne. News services from every major world capital carried stories of the Queen's condition, reporting that courts and governments around the globe were soberly preparing for their own eventual proclamations to mark Victoria's passing.

At Buckingham Palace, Lord Roberts, still ruddy brown from the African sun he had so recently left behind, arrived to sign his name in the visitors' book. While entering this sign of condolence, he asked the official in attendance for news of the Queen; intense sadness marked the field marshal's face, his eyes set fixedly. He uttered not a single word to the military officer who accompanied him up St. James's Street to the palace, nor did he seem to notice in the least the brash but well-intentioned crowds that followed behind. Roberts's presence betokened to many that Victoria's travail had completely overshadowed the war in South Africa. But among those gathered outside the palace, some of whom had spent the night on the bone-chilling pavement, one was heard to ask a bobby if the whole thing hadn't been a ruse simply gotten up to stimulate volunteering for South Africa. The policeman shot back a look that expressed his contempt for even imagining such lese majesty.

The earliest of the evening papers were on the streets an hour after noon. The display bills of two rival journals told totally different stories as to Victoria's condition. "QUEEN UNCONSCIOUS, SINKING FAST," said one, while another took a contrary lead: "QUEEN RALLYING, HAS EATEN & SLEPT. OFFICIAL." The boys crying out the headlines were both smiling, apparently only too glad to have the increased business on this historic day.

Marlborough House remained the center of court activity in London. On the side of the Prince's house facing St. James's Palace a huge crowd milled, often bulging into the middle of Marlborough Road. The object of everyone's concern was a small bulletin board on which was periodically placed a sheet of cream-colored notepaper, headed in green lettering "Board of Green Cloth, Buckingham Palace." (This ancient judicial institution of the royal household was responsible for the work and finances of the Lord Steward's department of the royal palaces.) It was there that the Master of the Household—Lord Edward Pelham-Clinton—communicated to the public the news of the sovereign's condition. As each successive notice of the Queen's state was posted, the crowd pushed harder to see if the ultimate had yet occurred.

At Cowes, the throng of journalists was growing massive. Nearly all climbed the mile of steep streets up to the little stone Lodge Gate at Osborne, hoping to get some new tidbit of information that just might have eluded their colleagues. This afternoon a number of reporters spotted the Kaiser and the Prince of Wales strolling on the estate's lawns, a fact soon wired around the world. A sprinkling of artists worked the crowd, drawing vignettes for their employers' front pages. Both German and British detectives mingled unobtrusively, the former to watch for threats to the All-Highest, the latter to guard against potential hazards to *any* of the gathered dignities.

Passing the reporters in a carriage, one untypical party especially attracted their attention. A trio of brilliantly turbaned Indians from Madras drove right through the gates, which had parted for what the gatekeepers assumed to be some sort of an official delegation. Because of their bejeweled costumes, they were thought to be princes, an assumption not, however, shared by the police overseeing the scene. When stopped and asked their business, the three men said they were going to Osborne Cottage, Princess Beatrice's

*The Queen.*

*The Queen at 81.*

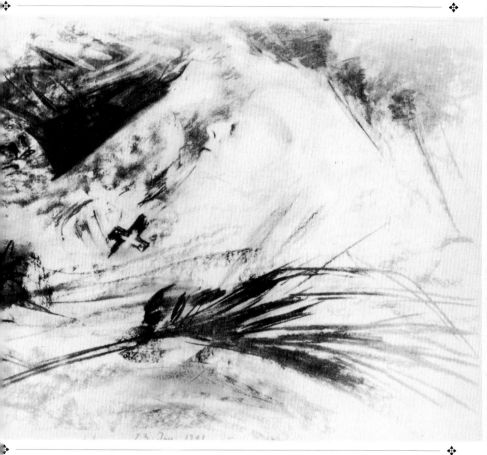

*Deathbed sketch by Emil Fuchs.*

*The Queen lying in state, Osborne House.*

*Start of procession from Osborne House.*

*Procession to the pier at the Isle of Wight.*

*Royal Train waiting for the Queen.*

*The catafalque in the train.*

*Kaiser Wilhelm II, King Edward VII, and the Duke of Connaught
at Paddington Station.*

5512.

*Farewell in Splendor, London.*

 *Farewell in Splendor, London.*

*Farewell in Splendor, Windsor.*

H.M. The Queen.

# Osborne House

### DURBAR WING

1. Durbar Room
2. Durbar Corridor

### PAVILION BEDROOM FLOOR

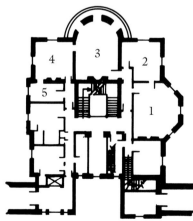

1. Queen's Bedroom
2. Queen's Dressing Room
3. Queen's Sitting Room
4. Prince Consort's Dressing Room
5. Prince Consort's Bathroom

*Plan of Osborne House (by Merl Grossmeyer, 1994)*

# PAVILION GROUND FLOOR

1. Drawing Room
2. Billiard Room
3. Horn Room
4. Dining Room (Chapelle Ardente)
5. Queen's Lift
6. Queen's Entrance

# MAIN/HOUSEHOLD WING

1. Council Room
2. Audience Room
3. Privy Purse Room
4. Grand Corridor
5. Kaiser's Suite
6. Household Dining Room
7. Library

# PAVILION NURSERY FLOOR

1. Nursery Bedroom
2. Nursery Sitting Room

*Osborne House.*

residence now occupied by the Duke and Duchess of Connaught. The police courteously objected. On further questioning, the distinguished-looking interlopers, all of whom improbably claimed to be converts to Christianity, explained they had been lecturing in the north of England and decided to journey to the island to offer, through the Queen's famous Indian servant, the Munshi, expressions of their own sympathy, and, furthermore, to have a "glimpse" of their great sovereign before she died. "We have come to pay our tribute to our Empress, but these conventionalists stand in the way," they unhappily explained later to reporters with the lilting inflections of Tamil-accented English. Thwarted in their demands, they had to be satisfied with an assurance from the police to send a message to the Queen's chief Indian secretary. Jeweled headdresses glinting dully in the misty light, the three turned around and headed back for the Cowes Hotel, where they promised to "await a reply."

❖  6  ❖

Epidemic influenza had hit Washington especially hard this January, with many of the victims quickly advancing to the dreaded sequel of pneumonia. President William McKinley had been sick in bed for days, his first serious illness since coming to the White House four years earlier. Fortunately, the chief executive seemed to have eluded pneumonia, and today, for the first time, he left his bedroom in the Executive Mansion for a meeting with his cabinet in his office overlooking the Ellipse.

The major item of business on the President's agenda required him to select a new attorney general to replace John Griggs, the only cabinet officer since McKinley's reelection the prior November who had decided to return to private employment. The man the President had in mind for the spot was his old friend Philander Knox, of Pittsburgh. As Griggs started to give his counsel on the selection of his successor, the President's secretary brought in an urgent telegram from the embassy in London. The Queen was "sinking rapidly." The gathered men agreed that humankind was about to lose a constant in an inconstant and increasingly contentious world. The President asked if anyone believed there would be objections to lowering the flags to half-mast on the White House and on all the executive departments on the day of Victoria's death and again on the day of her funeral. No one thought this would raise any questions or objections.

❖ 7 ❖

At Mansion House, hundreds of businessmen had over the morning inquired of the Queen's condition. When the noon bulletin from Osborne was posted, a whiff of hope for her recovery inexplicably arose. There were even a few muted cheers. Only at the posting of the 4:00 P.M. message, one addressed directly to the lord mayor, were hopes quietly dashed by reality.

> My painful duty obliges me to inform you that the life of the beloved Queen is in the greatest danger.
> [signed] Albert Edward

❖ 8 ❖

All day the little dress shops and couturier salons hedging in both sides of Mayfair's Bond Street had been unaccustomedly crowded with clients both old and new. They knew that once the sovereign's death was announced, the appearance of the entire city—especially its westerly districts with their legions of well-off women—would change drastically.

Mourning involved some of the strictest and most bizarre customs of nineteenth-century England, and following its rules often placed substantial financial strains on families whose station in life required their compliance. But for those unwilling to risk losing the status of "respectability" that anchored Victorian culture, to ignore the demands of mourning was unthinkable. While mourning requirements usually applied only to deaths within one's own family, the passing of a sovereign imposed this distinctive deportment on anyone even remotely connected with officialdom or "society." By the beginning of the twentieth century, men's clothing had already reached a stage of somberness approaching perpetual mourning, but for women of middle to high status, mourning involved an extravagant, expensive, and total change in their appearance.

For those in the social heights of British womanhood, mourning the Queen would mean putting aside virtually every item of their ordinary clothing, and in its place adopting black for everything—excepting only the diamonds that would, to a limited degree, still be permissible. Not only did all of one's clothing have to be black—outerwear, underwear, everything—it further had to be made of the dullest, most lusterless materials available. Shiny fabrics, like satins or velvets, were taboo. Instead, to obtain the requisite lifelessness, the mourning industry used twilled and ribbed weaving techniques to break up the cloth's surface, thus eliminating any shine. Bombazine, the near-habitual dress of the Queen, was one of the most popular of these fabrics (although by the turn of the century it was considered somewhat old-fashioned); woven from a silk warp with a worsted weft, the technique gave bombazine its characteristic matte surface, one that absorbed light rather than reflected it. A cheaper version of bombazine, made of cotton, was used for servants' clothing.

The sine qua non of mourning was crepe, endless yards and bolts and cases of it. It was used in every conceivable way to mark one's official sorrow, not only made into clothing, but covering furniture, doorways, carriages and everything else on which it could be flounced or draped or pinned to show proper respect for the dead. The black silk gauze-like fabric was further treated by a heat process to make it stiff and duller than was its normal wont, attributes it would quickly lose in even the mildest drizzle. Courtauld's was the nation's leading crepe manufacturer, the firm's owners having grown enormously wealthy by cashing in on the national obsession.

The tiara of death was the white widow's cap, the mark that Victoria took unto herself in 1861 and to which she clung tightly until the day she died; most women wore these caps precisely for a year and a day after their husbands' deaths, but of course Victoria wasn't most women. The white muslin cap with its long streamers was often rigged up with a so-called Marie Stuart peak in front, the particular style that had been adopted by Victoria's daughter, Vicky.

Nearly every imaginable artifact fashionable women used had to be changed or adapted for mourning. Perfume bottles and mirrors, sunshades, umbrellas and cardcases, wristwatches, blotting book and bookmarks all had to be suitably darkened, edged or marked in funereal tones to acknowledge the debt of the living to the dead. Widows' notepaper and envelopes were invariably bordered in black for a year. Predictably, the personal stationery of the super-observant Queen had been edged in black, double-wide for forty years.

❖ 9 ❖

At mid-afternoon Reid judged it was time to again call the members of Victoria's family to her bedroom. The physician had earlier jotted a note to his wife, saying that "she doesn't look like dying just now: and I can't help admiring her determination not to give up the struggle while she can." He added that "she often smiles when she hears my voice, and says she will do 'anything I like.' " A quarter hour after sending these optimistic tidings to Susan, he knew—now unequivocally—the Queen's last hours were at hand, and he began to notify those closest to the Queen of this now-unalterable fact.

By three o'clock, each member of Victoria's family had quietly entered the room, all treading lightly as if the Queen were merely asleep and shouldn't be disturbed. Looking at the woman lying on the bed, they saw the right side of her face was still slightly flattened from the stroke, a sight that shook many. Alexandra went and held up her mother-in-law's head and shoulders as William helped the trio of doctors and the nurse with the "cumbrous" process of administering oxygen to Victoria. The Queen lay deathly quiet, looking white and thin. She obviously didn't know what was going on around her.

Davidson and Canon Smith, who had been in the Drawing Room all morning and early afternoon, had just been finishing luncheon, when at about a quarter after two the pair was summoned by Ponsonby to go "at once" to the Queen's bedroom. As soon as they entered the room, both men began almost automatically to recite prayers. The bishop could tell that the monarch was unresponsive to their words, but he still thought he detected a flicker of recognition on the Queen's face as he murmured the last verse of "Lead, Kindly Light." They were deep in their prayers as the family members began to be ushered into the Queen's presence.

After an hour or so—at about four o'clock—Dr. Reid yet again asked that the room be cleared so he could let his patient be made as comfortable as possible in her bed. For the next five minutes, the Queen was attended only by her women. She came to, enough so that she again murmured for Turi to be brought to her. The little Pomeranian was carried into the room, this time only for a very few minutes, since Reid feared the rambunctious animal might agitate the sovereign. Reid and his colleagues went next door to the sitting room to write out what would be the last medical bulletin of Victoria's life.

4:00 O'CLOCK, OSBORNE HOUSE.
THE QUEEN IS SLOWLY SINKING.

Reid heard muffled sounds from the corridor as a few more members of the family arrived at the house and were brought up to the second floor. Victoria's cousin, the Duke of Cambridge, got to the island just this afternoon, having crossed the Channel from Calais. The *Osborne* brought Prince and Princess Louis of Battenberg—Princess Louis was Princess Alice's eldest daughter, her husband Beatrice's brother-in-law. The prince joined Bertie and the other men of the family in the Prince Consort's sitting room, where amidst swelling tension they talked quietly amongst themselves.

Vicar Smith went back to the Queen's bedroom to continue his prayers. But Reid, fearful that the prayers might be painful to the Queen if she knew what was happening, left to ask the Prince of Wales if it mightn't be better to have them discontinued until the actual moments of death. "Certainly, tell him [Davidson or

Smith] not to come into the room until I send for him," Bertie told the doctor. Reid explained the situation to Davidson, who agreed with its appropriateness.

Davidson, who had temporarily left the death chamber to Vicar Smith's ministrations, began to chat with the Kaiser in the sitting room. The bishop found him "full of touching loyalty" to his grandmother—William referring to her, as always, as "Grandmama." "She has been a very great woman," the Kaiser told Davidson and whoever else was within earshot. "Just think of it: she remembers George III [the Kaiser may have meant George IV] and now we are in the twentieth century. And all that time what a life she has led." Warming up to his tribute to the only woman in the world he both loved and respected, he added, "I have never been with her without feeling that she was in every sense my Grandmama and made me love her as such. And yet the minute we began to talk about political things she made me feel we were equals and could speak as Sovereigns. Nobody had such power as she!"

Being taken seriously was serious business for William, and that his Grandmama did so was probably the most fundamental grounds for his attachment to her. When Davidson said the Kaiser's coming to England would unquestionably be a great good, William instantly agreed, responding that "my proper place is here; I could not possibly be away!" For good measure, the Kaiser repeated his declaration several times, lest anyone miss the sentiments.

William's musings were suddenly broken off a little after four, when Reid and the other physicians asked him and the rest of the family to come back into the Queen's bedroom. Though Victoria had long ago made her wish known that she didn't want a crowd to witness her last moments, she was now beyond caring—or ordering; the unique historicalness of the occasion meant this could safely be one time when the Queen's command might be ignored. Every adult at Osborne was profoundly aware that what was transpiring in their presence represented a watershed in history, one of the dividing lines between epochs and a definable edge in the nation's existence. As mournful and trying as the scene was, not one of those gathered around Victoria's bed would have chosen to be anywhere else at this moment.

William assumed the symbolic mastery of the occasion. Quietly kneeling down on the right side of the bed—at Queen Victoria's left—he gently put his strong right arm under his grandmother's pillow, his left arm hooked in his jacket pocket, the small limb all but useless. He gently raised the monarch's upper torso off the pillow, evidently in the hope that his action would make her breathing a bit less labored, that his presence might somehow reassure the dying woman. Victoria's face was white and already waxen, and her long gray hair cascaded thinly across William's arm and down onto the pillow; the hair was startling to the assemblage, none having seen it arranged in any way other than the severe coiffure that she had worn since the outset of her reign. A tiny flutter of the high-arched nostrils and an almost imperceptible lifting and sinking of her frame were all the signs that remained of life.

Opposite William, on Victoria's right, Reid helped the Kaiser hold the Queen in a semi-sitting position. Both men kneeled as though made of marble, Reid unable to switch arms because of the Emperor's affliction, and William unwilling to allow anyone to usurp this last duty to his beloved grandmother. To the physician's right, Alexandra kneeled and stroked her mother-in-law's still hand, a hand now without any of the might which it had for so many years wielded over her vast domains. Her ordained successor knelt at the end of the bed, thinking God knows what thoughts as his long-awaited destiny was almost upon his brow. He was already an old man, worn down by tobacco, alcohol, uselessness, debauchery, too much food, not enough to do. Whatever his thoughts, surely they included more than a bit of resentment at the nephew he had always abhorred once again in the limelight at this the most poignant scene that can transpire between sovereign and heir.

Packed tightly around the highest-ranking mourners was the remainder of the family: the Petticoats—Lenchen, Louise and Beatrice—all red-eyed and wet-cheeked as they watched the sole reason for their uniqueness dying; Arthur, always his mother's favorite son, perhaps wondering how much she knew about his long-time relationship with Leonie Jerome, the sister of Lady Randolph Churchill; George, about to become Heir Apparent, and his wife May, who relished the prospect of taking over as Princess of Wales in her mother-in-law's stead; one of the Queen's sons-in-law, the Duke of Argyll, forever an interloper in this the most closed of families; the Duchess of Saxe-Coburg, having such a short time ago lost her duke; the slew of grandchildren and great-grandchildren: little Yorks, a pair of whom were destined to be kings and one of whom would one day nearly bring down the whole structure of British monarchy; pretty Connaught girls and rambunctious Battenberg children and little Schleswig-Holsteins, and Alice's daughter Victoria, whose sister Alexandra remained in Russia distracted by her inability to give her husband an heir as the future Tsar of their troubled empire.

A few in the room weren't royal, but filled vital roles in the life of the kingdom. Her Prime Minister's representative, Arthur Balfour; the chief courtier, the Lord Chamberlain, the Earl of Clarendon; the physicians and dressers and chaplains whose lives were dedicated to making the Queen's life healthier or more comfortable or more holy. Downstairs, in the Drawing Room, the youngest members of the family—mainly great-grandchildren—bided the hours; lords- and ladies-in-waiting sat with them. Most of the principal corridors were lined with servants, given permission by the Prince of Wales to be there in light of the history that was being made in the large corner bedroom. The working quarters of the estate remained fully manned, primarily by the cooks and kitchen workers even now attending to the preparation of one of the gargantuan meals normal to the Queen's residence. The fact that the mistress of the mansion was dying had no effect on the requirement that hundreds of people, both mighty and modest, would soon have to sit down to their dinners.

A few times in the last hours of the long afternoon, Victoria had feebly looked at Reid and implored, "Sir James, I'm very ill," as if beseeching that the opposite should be the truth. Each time, the doctor responded, "Your Majesty will soon be better." All around the room, the members of her family began to call out their names, apparently hoping that this ruler of a quarter of the world's people would know they were there—or even that she might remember them when she got to heaven. Young Prince Maurice of Battenberg, Beatrice's boy, started crying so loudly that he had to be taken from the room for fear his commotion might hasten the end.

The only sound other than the infrequent murmurings of the physicians was the alternating prayers from Davidson and the overwhelmed little vicar of Whippingham Church, now again fully engaged in their incantations, with the Prince of Wales's permission. Occasionally a sob could be heard, from Alexandra, or from one of the Queen's daughters. Even Bertie and William's cheeks were wet with tears, the two men assured enough in their positions to be able to cry openly before this assemblage. Darkness had already settled onto the island, and the only light in the room came from flickering gas lamps, the Queen herself having long ago banned the new electrical contraptions because she didn't care for the sharp glare they produced. Bertie quietly passed the word to an aide to make sure the ring of policemen around the estate was absolutely unbreachable—the first word of the Queen's death must not be leaked to a journalist by an excited servant, but rather be officially dispatched by the new monarch himself.

By six o'clock, Reid and the Emperor had been holding Victoria up for nearly two hours. Though the doctor had been able to shift a bit to relieve the strain, William hadn't the luxury. The latter now ignored the numbness in his big arm, so intent was he on holding on to his Grandmama and so unwilling to show his relatives the slightest weakness or hesitation in fulfilling his "duty." Princess Louise had left the little knot of her sisters and come next to the bed, kneeling on the carpet on the physician's right. Mrs. Tuck stood at the top of the bed.

With the chimes of the clock striking six times, Davidson's voice was the clearest sound in the room as he recited the Prayer for the Dying. "O Almighty God, with whom do live the spirits of men just made perfect, after they are delivered from their earthly prisons: We humbly commend the soul of this thy servant, Her Gracious Majesty the Queen, into thy hands, as into the hands of a faithful Creator and most merciful Saviour; most humbly beseeching thee that it may be precious in thy sight."

Long minutes then passed without any sound at all. Suddenly, Alexandra took a sharp intake of breath that all around her noticed. The Queen's hand had moved in hers, and Victoria's eyes were opening as though she were awakening from a long sleep. She seemed able to see everyone and everything clearly, as do many on the precipice of eternity catching their last glimpse of the world and its life. Davidson, just ending the Aaronic blessing, stopped his praying.

Victoria's now-aware eyes appeared to turn slightly to the right, gazing over the fireplace, at the picture of the *Entombment of Christ*. She was now "sinking into death," in the words of a son-in-law, like a "great three-decker ship." In her last seconds of life, her eyes lingered on the Prince who was about to become King. Victoria murmured her last word: "Bertie." She smiled and her head turned a fraction, as though she knew Albert was awaiting just across the next blink. Queen Victoria then, at last, closed her eyes for all eternity. It was exactly 6:30 P.M.

Reid laid down her hand, and kissed it. He then raised his arm, the signal by which the family knew that all was over. Unsteadily, he rose to his feet, his knees frozen from more than two hours of kneeling. Victoria's eyes still slightly open even in death, Reid asked the Prince of Wales—*the King*—to close them. The first real rustle of activity was the children of Victoria murmuring quiet thanks to the physician for all he had done for their mother. The Kaiser, painfully raising himself on now-sore legs, came over to Reid and squeezed his hand without a word passing between them. The tension in the room was palpable: the woman who was the raison d'être for these people was gone. That someone else had in the flicker of a heartbeat ascended to her eminence couldn't yet be comprehended. Least of all by the man who had been so elevated.

In the British system of monarchy, the legal principle governing the throne is that it is never—not for so much as an instant—vacant. When the monarch dies, there is no interregnum, no period of time before the successor ascends completely and entirely to his or her predecessor's eminence. There is no question of succession for any Parliament or deliberative body to ponder or decide or parley over; the order of succession is as ironclad as the laws of mathematics. As the breath left Victoria's body, the mystical quality of sovereignty just as surely entered Bertie. He was now fully, without reservation or pause, possessor of all the powers that had been his mother's. He was fifty-nine years, two months, and thirteen days old.

❖ 10 ❖

Queen Victoria's death was caused by cerebral failure, but, in the simplest terms, she died of old age. The wonder was that this almost entirely sedentary woman lived as long as she did.

*The Lancet*, the official journal of the British Medical Association, reported that the secondary cause of Victoria's demise (after cerebral failure) were the "private griefs" and "public anxieties" she suffered, especially those that marked and plagued the last eighteen months of her life. Many British newspapers of the period gave out that "overwork" was the reason the Queen died. Insofar as people don't die of "overwork" itself, especially when such exertions consist of reading, writing and holding audiences, such reports can be understood as well-intended but not entirely accurate.

For a year, Victoria's health had been rapidly deteriorating. Her lack of appetite had led to a dramatic weight loss, and eventually to a kind of starvation. Her chronic insomnia of the last few months further weakened her body's capacity to restore itself, with the small strokes she had suffered disabling her health generally. The move to Osborne in late December had been a physical trial for the debilitated Queen, and in its wake she never regained the strength that had for so long sustained her. Only through the discipline ingrained through decades of self-control was she able to beguile her ministers, family and visitors into the belief that she remained the same woman with whom they had dealt for so long.

In light of the many infirmities and weaknesses that beset her at the end, Victoria's heart itself remained amazingly strong throughout her ordeal. Furthermore, her arterial system was, in Reid's view, relatively little impaired for a woman of her age, and the thoracic and abdominal organs remained in good functioning order. In the last hours, a respiratory insufficiency of the Queen's lungs set in; although, again, her heart continued strong. Most notable in light of Victoria's unique position and the fact that she remained in full nominal charge of her constitutional powers until she died, the monarch suffered little from any kind of senile confusion, the Queen's most important organ—her brain—remaining in good working order up until only the final few days of her reign. As *The Lancet* summarized her fatal illness, "the end came as a

peaceful and natural conclusion to a long, full and beautiful life."
Few could wish for more for themselves.

❖ 11 ❖

A fter their shock at the Queen's actual death abated to some
degree, everyone except the members of the family left the
bedroom. For a final few minutes on this dramatic scene, her kin
would have their matriarch to themselves. No one recorded what
happened in those moments. Though it can reasonably be assumed
that the realization of Victoria's death still held most of the adults
in shock, every member of this family was trained since earliest
childhood to respect the relative rank and station of even their own
parents, spouses, siblings, cousins, nieces and nephews. And thus
it was that in the wake of the sovereign's passing, the old ranks
changed as instantly as did the person of the monarch. Those who
had been children of a regnant queen now became siblings of the
new king, a position that dropped their relative rank a material
notch; the precedence of Bertie's own children now stood above
that of their aunts and uncle.

It is likely that during these private minutes Bertie's family
made their obeisances to the new monarch—a kiss of his hand, a
bow, a curtsy as appropriate. The new King quickly let it be known
that he and his new Queen Consort would for a while in the privacy of the family remain as Prince and Princess of Wales. Nonetheless, he knew that the moment he stepped from the death room
into the corridor, he *was* King regardless of any private hesitation
or compunction to the contrary.

The new sovereign's most urgent order of business remained
the official notification of his mother's death to the nation's highest
officials. The first telegram went to the Lord Mayor of the City of
London; fifteen minutes after Victoria died, the King wired: "The
Prince of Wales to the Lord Mayor—My beloved mother, the
Queen, has just passed away, surrounded by her children and
grandchildren. Albert Edward." Similar wires followed to the
Prime Minister and the Archbishop of Canterbury.

With those telegrams safely dispatched, the waiting journalists at the Gate Lodge could be informed. Police Superintendent Fraser was sent down to the gate to give the word to the assembled reporters; Fraser had been Victoria's chief personal bodyguard at Osborne, and was grief-stricken at the task he had been assigned. His only words to the gathering, spoken in a voice shaking with emotion, were achingly brief and to the point. "Gentlemen, the Queen passed away at half past six o'clock."

After a quick raising of hats, the mass of newspapermen stampeded toward town, many shouting at their comrades "Queen dead! Queen dead!," all having already composed their flash stories for transmission to their newsrooms. A few rushed toward carriages they had hired, others jumped on bicycles for the downhill sprint to the now-besieged telegraph office in East Cowes. One man started off at a full gallop on horseback. Just as they were rushing off to report the news to every corner of the world, one last member of the family—Prince Christian of Schleswig-Holstein, Lenchen's husband—was arriving at the Lodge Gate. The prince had left for Osborne too late to see his mother-in-law die. By this time, he had probably forgotten all about today being his seventieth birthday.

## ❖ 12 ❖

As much as London expected the worst, the news of Victoria's death still struck with the force of an earthquake. From Whitechapel to Mayfair, streets that had been filled with the usual throngs of the capital in nighttime suddenly turned deserted and desolate. Blinds on the huge West End mansions came down so that not a glimmer of light shone through them, and usually bright Pall Mall looked Stygian as the gentlemen's clubs turned down nearly every lamp. The metropolis almost literally stopped when the first bulletins from Osborne were received, the news carried to every corner of the city by thousands of bellowing newsboys and confirmed by suddenly tolling bells from a hundred churches both mighty and modest. The sound carrying above all others was the mournful pealing from the belltower of St. Paul's, a booming that rattled the timeworn City to its foundations. Every minute tolled another clap, eighty-one times all together, one for each year of the dead Queen's life.

Sir Spencer Ponsonby-Fane, Comptroller in the Lord Chamberlain's office in St. James's Palace, immediately dispatched the following notice to every metropolitan theater, all of which came under the Lord Chamberlain's licensing authority:

> I am directed by the Lord Chamberlain to desire that, in consequence of the death of the Queen, the theatres licensed by his lordship shall be closed this day.
>
> A further communication will be addressed to you as to any future occasion when it may be proper to do so.
>
> Whilst sending this formal communication, the Lord Chamberlain feels sure that such an order on his part is superfluous, and that the loyalty and good feelings of the managers would have led to the same result. —I am, Sir, your obedient servant
>
> S. Ponsonby-Fane

In fact, nearly every place of entertainment had closed on first hearing the news, not waiting for the Lord Chamberlain's telegram. Because of the late hour involved, a few had already begun their plays. At Drury Lane, where the evening's show had just started, the curtain was immediately lowered and the audience told the news; everyone rose and silently left the hall, either their money being refunded as they left the door or their tickets exchanged for a future performance. At the Gaiety and the Lyceum and the Empire, and at dozens of others, arriving playgoers found black-bordered notices on the theater doors, announcing that "owing to national mourning this resort of entertainment will be closed until further notice." Not a single incidence of an indignant patron was recorded.

So, too, at the Crystal Palace, probably the city's most popular amusement center—and the Prince Consort's most durable monument—the management instantly stopped the entertainments on hearing of Victoria's death. The visitors congregated in the great Central Transept of this mammoth glass concoction, where the organist Walter Hedgcock broke into a solemn and inspiring version of Handel's "Dead March" from *Saul.* Not a licensed entertainment resort of any kind remained open. The Royal Aquarium and the London Hippodrome and the Egyptian Hall all went dark, all for "the duration"—meaning until after the Queen's funeral.

But inevitably, Londoners wanted to be with other Londoners on this historic evening. So the Strand, part of the great thoroughfare connecting the City and East End with the affluent west, had by 8:00 P.M. become the center of the whirlwind. Masses of the poor and the just-getting-by from the east flowed westward to mix with the sophisticated, those living in the west wanting to be close to the heart of their dead Queen's great metropolis. In this ancient highway these two vast waves met in a surging tide, uniting all ajumble with the theater crowds and late office workers. Sprinkled like sequins through the scene were the members of the theater companies who poured into the streets, stage paint and costumes still on many of the actors, the musicians loaded down with their instruments, carpenters and scene-shifters dressed in their overalls. No one could remember such a sight before, but neither could anyone remember a night so pregnant with historical transition.

Above the crowds, the throaty notes produced by the sixteen tons of hollow metal that made up St. Paul's Big Tom continued to clang joylessly, the reverberations clashing with equally despondent notes from the belfries of Wren's smaller masterpieces. From further down the Strand, where it became Fleet Street, newsboys rushed toward waiting customers, knowing the people would buy any paper to get more details. The bicycle delivery boys picked their way through what few gaps remained in the throng, with their just-printed sheets. Every paper sold out within moments, and the bicyclists wasted no time in turning around to fetch fresh loads.

Trafalgar Square was ringed with full-to-overflowing omnibuses. The platforms on top of the horse-drawn conveyances made perfect viewing platforms for the spectators who wanted to witness and remember the great tumult: with every place in the metropolis closed, there was, after all, very little else to do. When a cold drizzle began to fall, the bus-tops emptied; by midnight, even the Strand was deserted.

❖  13  ❖

The two dinners at Osborne—one for the royals, another, larger, for the Household—were subdued. Nonetheless, the squadrons of chefs and sous-chefs and pastry cooks who formed one of the most powerful battalions in Osborne's army of servants had done their best to placate whatever appetite the assembled mourners had worked up over the long and trying afternoon and evening. Junior chef Gabriel Tschumi, busy over his entremets and spitted Welsh lamb, heard of the Queen's death from his cousin, one of the Queen's dressers. She told him the Queen had promised to leave her a few of her black bombazine dresses, a great thrill both for the token of esteem it conferred and because both women wore the same size. Tschumi hoped something had been definitely arranged in the sovereign's will so his cousin wouldn't be disappointed.

Back in the Pavilion, the new King asked Bishop Davidson to hold a small service in the dead Queen's bedroom. While waiting for the family to gather, the prelate was buttonholed by Arthur Balfour. Evidently wanting to make the most of every minute of his valuable time, the House Leader sought Davidson's thoughts on who might be an appropriate replacement in the recently vacated bishopric of London. Davidson had just been reading the Queen's journal entry from her own accession day almost sixty-four years earlier. When Balfour noticed the book, he asked if he might borrow it. An eternity had passed since Britain's sovereign had last changed, and the politician wanted to know what rubrics were involved.

In the death chamber, Dr. Reid was helping move the Queen from the temporary bed into her own larger bed. Assisted by carpenters, the small bed was taken out of the room, and the regular one then returned to its normal position. The dressers covered the Queen's body with lace and strewed a few flowers over the covers, finally placing in the corpse's folded hands the little cross that had hung over the headboard. Reid noticed while undressing the body that Victoria had sustained a ventral hernia and a prolapse of the uterus, not unusual for a woman of her age and one who had undergone nine childbirths. It was remarkable, he thought, that this was the first time he should know these intimate facts about the woman who had been his patient for two decades.

Around a quarter past ten, Davidson's rites got under way. He later described the little ceremony as "calm and bright," and wrote of Victoria looking "pale and quite calm and almost youthful." He apparently was pleased with his performance, since he concluded his journal entry with the observation that "all, I think, liked our little service."

Exhausted, Reid still had a few more details to attend to before he could leave the Pavilion for his own bedroom in the Household Wing. The first of his priorities was to make arrangements for the coffin. With the new King ultimately responsible for Victoria's funeral, Reid sought him out, and finally found him in Keeper of the Privy Purse Sir Fleetwood Edwards's room, gathered with a few members of his family. The preoccupied little group was reading the late monarch's written instructions as to what she wanted for her funeral, intricate and sometimes unorthodox instructions which her eldest son would feel obliged to carry out down to the smallest details.

Victoria had long harbored an unambiguous image of what her own coffin should look like. Members of the Royal Family had been interred in the vaults at Windsor Castle's St. George's Chapel for centuries, and this sovereign wanted a container much like the others in St. George's. Reid told his new sovereign that the Lord Chamberlain's department would be responsible for obtaining her coffin—or what would actually amount to a series of coffins within coffins. Bertie asked the physician to get to Lord Clarendon—who was on the island, at East Cowes Castle—on the double. Reid left immediately for the castle, and when he arrived told the man who was head of the Queen's working household that Victoria's body was to be placed in her innermost coffin (the so-called shell) on Thursday morning. This left Clarendon just one full day to order the coffin, have it made, and get it delivered to Osborne.

With this bit of business completed, Reid could finally return to his own quarters for a few hours of sleep before facing what he knew would be a hectic day tomorrow. That night, Susan Reid wrote to her mother-in-law about the events of the past hours.

Filled with pride in her husband's competence and the fact of his place at the center of such a historic occasion, the physician's wife ended her letter: "When it was all over, the family came, one after another, to Jamie to thank him for all he had done for the Queen. . . . He was very exhausted and worn out with the emotions of the day, but not harassed by thinking anything more could have been done. He has all the Queen's last wishes written down by her, so of course there is still much to do."

❖ **14** ❖

On reaching Berlin, word of the English Queen's death spread like a firestorm. Special editions of the city's newspapers almost instantly appeared on the street, their editors, having expected the tidings, only waiting to get the long-prepared obituaries into print. The press reported that virtually every department of the government was ordered into official mourning, with later instructions to be issued regarding the more complex particulars of the court, the army and navy, and every ministry. The news that the Empress had left earlier to be with the Dowager Empress was sympathetically received, notwithstanding widespread antipathy among many Germans toward Victoria's eldest daughter.

"Semiofficial reports," referring to off-the-record statements from government officials, assured Germans that the new British King would not pursue policies hostile to the Reich. In the event, most Germans didn't understand the constitutional differences between the two nations, believing that the English monarch wielded the same sorts of prerogatives as did their own sovereign. Still, those of the Kaiser's subjects attuned to the growing rift between London and Berlin felt distinctly uneasy about the loss of Victoria and her strong German ties.

In Washington, the President's cabinet meeting had stretched on into the evening, when it was interrupted by one of the telegraph office clerks handing the chief executive a flash from London. Reading it, McKinley immediately ordered that the flag atop the mansion be lowered to half-staff. The more historic-minded of the capital's residents noted that this was the first time in the history of the United States that such a token of mourning had been authorized for a foreign monarch. It was a telling marker for the maturing country, a nation that had gained its independence during the reign of Victoria's grandfather.

Ready for the news, McKinley had earlier given his secretaries instructions to have the formal messages of condolences ready to be sent. Dispatched that afternoon from Washington via the Atlantic cable was the official expression of sympathy from the American people to their British cousins:

> Washington, January 22, 1901
> His Majesty the King, Osborne House, Isle of Wight:
> I have received with profound sorrow the lamentable tidings of the death of her Majesty the Queen. Allow me, Sir, to offer my sincere sympathy and that of the American people in your personal bereavement and in the loss Great Britain has suffered in the death of its venerable and illustrious sovereign, whose noble life and beneficent influence have promoted the peace and won the affection of the world.
> WILLIAM MCKINLEY

Following the President's message within minutes, the State Department wired its own official cable of condolences via the embassy in London's Victoria Street:

> [Joseph Hodges] Choate, Ambassador, London:
> You will express to Lord Lansdowne the profound sorrow of the Government and people of the United States at the death of the Queen and the deep sympathy we feel with the people the British Empire in their great affliction.
> JOHN HAY

The Senate had gathered for an executive session when the news of Victoria's death reached the chamber, doorkeepers passing it around to the milling senators. Senators William Boyd Allison and John Tyler Morgan took the lead in composing the body's message of sympathy to its British parliamentary counterparts. Senator Henry Cabot Lodge, the Massachusetts patrician, spoke for many of his colleagues when he met the press: "The Queen has always been a steadfast friend to the United States. . . . Americans can never forget that England was withheld from active interference in our own civil war largely, if not wholly, by the influence of the Queen and the wise counsels of Prince Albert." Speaker David Bremner Henderson would speak for the House in much the same tones. Both chambers of the government adjourned early in token of the Queen's passing, an act, like the White House's lowering of its flag, that was unprecedented.

In every one of the United States, a sense of loss and shock greeted the news of Victoria's death. Chicago immediately set to planning for elaborate memorial services in the Queen's honor; legislators in Boston's State House prayed for the "proper guidance of the English nation"; Charlestonians were reminded of the message of condolence they received from the Queen when an earthquake severely damaged the South Carolina city in 1886; legislators from Little Rock to Sacramento to Olympia adjourned their bodies out of respect to Britain's loss. Former President Benjamin Harrison worried in Indianapolis that "a mighty influence on the side of peace" had been lost in Europe but assured his countrymen that the new sovereign "will be loyally supported by all men everywhere."

Not every American met the news with the same sense of decorum. In Chicago, British subject Robert Dawson filed a notice with the city clerk of his intention to renounce his allegiance to the new British King. In New York, an imbroglio of a farcical nature upset the plans of Henry Zimmer, British subject, who was this day to become an American citizen. While in the act of forswearing his allegiance to the Queen of England before the Naturalization Court, a clerk rushed into the chamber to announce the death of the very sovereign whose name was being invoked. But the precise words which when spoken would officially make Mr. Zimmer an American hadn't yet quite been reached. A hasty consultation ensued among the court's officials, the upshot of which was that the chief clerk refused to naturalize any more British subjects until the word of Queen Victoria's death was *officially* confirmed. Mr. Zimmer expressed his regret at the turn of events, but promised to be back "as soon as the throne of England had been filled."

The tolling bells of Trinity Church—the first time that church had offered this mark of its respect since President Garfield's assassination two decades earlier—were the first indication many New Yorkers had of Victoria's passing. William Broughton, the church's sexton, received a private cable from a personal source in London as soon as the news was received in the British capital. At 1:00 P.M. Broughton began tolling the famous bells, a signal few of those within earshot missed for their intended meaning. Elsewhere in Manhattan, newspaper extra editions were on the streets within a half hour of Broughton's signal, with news vendors doing their best business in memory.

In Wall Street, the news broke at a quarter past one. Every bank and brokerage firm immediately displayed flags at half-mast, until the financial heart of the country looked like a continual line of bunting straight down to the East River; the only effect the news had on stock prices was a slight halt in the tide of trading, the market recovering within minutes. All over the commercial centers of Manhattan, the biggest department stores and specialty shops immediately hung their premises with black drapery and Union Jacks, Tiffany's, Steinway's and Arnold Constable's especially prominent for their lavish displays of respect and mourning.

A frisson even ran through the insurance community. It was widely taken for granted that large amounts of American insurance coverage were outstanding on the life of the British monarch. But according to the three largest insurers in New York, that assumption was false. Mutual Life, New York Life and the Equitable reported in *The New York Times* that no one, or no one they knew, carried any policies dependent on the life of the Queen. Likewise, reports that Victoria personally held large real estate interests in New York were refuted by city officials. One explained that "reasons, such as fears of revolutions . . . which might prompt other monarchs to invest part of their money outside of their own country[,] would not hold good in the case of England . . ."

In its wall-to-wall coverage of the Queen's death, even *The New York Times* ran an article speculating on the nature and breadth of Victoria's fiscal estate. After admitting that only officials of London's Coutts and Company, a private bank with longtime court associations, knew the true extent of the royal fortune, the newspaper went on to report that "sources" nonetheless placed the amount as high as £6 million (in 1901 about $30 million, with late-twentieth-century purchasing power immeasurably higher). The writer explained that the royal fortune had grown steeply since the death of the Prince Consort, when her expenses plummeted but her income continued to grow from a wide variety of sources.

Though Victoria had inherited nothing from her bankrupt father, and only about £600,000 from Albert, she had in fact gained another half million pounds in an entirely novel manner. A Mr. John Cameron Nield, a goldsmith's son, lived his entire life as a miser so he might leave his money to his sovereign. Fortunately for his sovereign, Mr. Nield had done very well, financially speaking, and Victoria duly inherited every penny of it. The fact that he left nothing to his relatives bothered Victoria to the degree that she arranged they should have some annuity, the amount never being disclosed. The interest on the principal grew in her private account at Coutts until by her death the total had doubled to about a million pounds. What with the annual £385,000 from Parliament in the form of a Civil List and another £70,000 in her Privy Purse payment, not to mention the £100,000 she took in every year from her inherited position as Duke (*not* Duchess) of Lancaster, the whole thing meant that Victoria had just about all she could have possibly needed or used. The *Times* article speculated that the new King would most likely have a special parliamentary grant to pay off those debts that he had incurred as Prince of Wales, at least of those that were of a nature as to "embarrass" him.

Across America, though news of Victoria's demise was the chief topic of interest, life nonetheless went on with its own peculiar American-style gusto. Carry Nation, saloon-buster extraordinaire, had been up to the well-known antics of imparting her own moral code with the working end of a hatchet. Having been arraigned for smashing a Wichita saloon on the very day Queen Victoria breathed her last at Osborne, the bonnet-topped little zealot informed the judge that she fully intended to carry on with her "program" the moment she got out of the courtroom. Which she did. Saloon men in her part of Kansas were said to be "very uneasy" anticipating Mrs. Nation's "program," and hired "lookouts" to warn them of the approach of this enemy. The wife of one saloon-keeper placed herself on the front steps of her husband's establishment to keep the hatchet-wielding fanatic at bay.

Elsewhere in the world, the Queen's death created ripples shaped by local conditions. In the Netherlands, it was decided not to postpone the wedding of Queen Wilhelmina planned for early February; instead, in light of the requirements of royal etiquette, the celebrations would be "curtailed as far as may be practicable." "Usually well-informed" court sources in Berlin were said to have no idea whether the Kaiser planned to stay in England through his grandmother's funeral, worrying Germans whether their All-Highest's birthday five days hence—William's forty-second— would still be marked in the usual fashion as a national holiday. In Dublin, traffic stopped dead in the main thoroughfares on the city receiving the news from Osborne, reporters noting that the transformation of the streets from their normal commerce to utter stillness was a sight Irishmen would never forget. In Canada, where a dirge from church bells rang unbroken from Labrador to Vancouver Island, the immediate reaction was to "set aside Victoria's birthday for all time as a memorial to the Victorian era." A native chief in South Africa when told of the Queen's death said that "tonight I shall see another star in the sky."

Throughout South Africa, religious leaders, both English and Boer, eulogized Queen Victoria, characterizing her loss as a blow to peace prospects on the still-bloody veld. In fact, the Boer leaders were pressing on relentlessly in their effort to drive the British out of their hard-pressed republics. Commandant-General Louis Botha and Christian de Wet spent the day of Victoria's death deep in conference in Standerton, struggling with whether to keep up the offensive in the Natal. The hawks carried the day in light of the still-fully prepared Boer armies. A Boer attack on the Brakpan electric light works on the outskirts of Johannesburg left most of the greatest of the Boer cities in British hands in darkness, a chilling reminder to the occupying forces of the continuing capacity of Kruger's followers to inflict damage.

One of the more memorable eulogies marking Queen Victoria's death expressed with great simplicity the extraordinary scope of the reign that had just ended. It tallied those whom this sovereign outlived or outserved:

> . . . all the members of the Privy Council who were alive in 1837; all the Peers who held their titles in 1837, except Earl Nelson, who was 14 in that year; and all the members who sat in the House of Commons on her accession to the throne. She saw five Dukes of Norfolk succeed each other as Earl Marshal, and outlived every Duke and Duchess, and every Marquis and Marchioness who bore that rank in 1837. Her Majesty saw eleven Lord Chancellors, ten Prime Ministers, six Speakers of the House of Commons, at least three bishops of every See, and five or six of many Sees, five Archbishops of Canterbury and six Archbishops of York, and six Commanders-in-Chief. She saw eighteen presidents of the United States, eleven Viceroys of Canada, sixteen Viceroys of India, and France successively ruled by one King, one Emperor, and seven Presidents of a Republic.

One might note that Victoria also outlived all nine of her bridesmaids.

# Wednesday, January 23

❖   1   ❖

Under a murky sun that this morning seemed to rise only grudgingly, Osborne languished in obvious pain from yesterday's trauma. The sounds of a sporadic carriage or of a servant scuttling across the courtyard were all that disrupted the stillness. Profound events had altered this corner of the kingdom, and Osborne was now different. For the first time in its existence, it awoke to a world without the woman who lent this place its very being.

Exhausted though he was, the new King knew he couldn't take time to mourn privately. Having risen early and dressed in the deepest black of mourning, Bertie came down before breakfast to see Mr. Balfour, his chief minister present. The men discussed the consuming ceremonies the aging sovereign would have to get through today. The royal yacht was waiting at the Cowes pier to take him and an official party to London, there to meet with his Privy Council and swear a solemn oath on his accession as sovereign.

Davidson too had risen early, and soon went up to the main house. Before the King and Balfour would leave for the mainland, the bishop wanted his new sovereign's instructions as to the first memorial arrangements for the dead Queen, still in her bedroom one floor above. Bertie had obviously given the matter of his mother's lying in state his consideration during the night. He first told Davidson he wanted the Dining Room in the Pavilion turned into a chapel for the Queen until her body would be taken to Windsor. The Dining Room was the house's largest appropriate chamber (the more spacious but garish Durbar Room was apparently never considered), and would for several days be transformed into what was called a *chapelle ardente*, or "glowing chapel" in which monarchs lie in state, so-named from the candles that are placed around the catafalque. Commanded to have the room ready to receive the Queen's body by the next day, Davidson set off to his task.

The bishop's assignment proved to be thornier than either he or the King had anticipated. Lenchen, Louise and Beatrice—the latter letting others know that she considered herself chief mourner—all had fixed ideas about how their mother's remains should be arranged for the coming ceremonials. For starters, they told Davidson they wanted the portraits on the Dining Room walls unchanged throughout the lying in state, suspecting something more somber might be hung instead. Reasoning that these huge family canvases represented happy times for both their parents and for the family as a whole, they informed the bishop it would be "nice" for their mother to have these looking down on her as she lay in her coffin. To the conservative prelate, the idea was preposterous. That such colorful and indisputably temporal images should intrude on his *chapelle ardente* couldn't be countenanced.

Since the new King had already left for London, Davidson took up the matter with the Kaiser. William agreed that nothing out of keeping with the solemnity of the occasion should intrude on Grandmama's dignity, and after the princesses heard of their nephew's views, they decided it best not to risk riling the incendiary Emperor. Davidson now wired London for the crimson hangings and other funereal artifacts he would need. They were promised for the next train.

Victoria's loyal dressers were this morning busy preparing their mistress's body as well as her bedroom for a private showing for the estate's servants and tenants. Overseen by Dr. Reid, who took Powell and Barlow in to see the corpse while the preparations were in hand, the women turned the little corner chamber into what the press would melodramatically call "one of the most solemn and beautiful spectacles ever presented to mortal eyes."

With the women's work done, Victoria lay clothed in a white sleeping gown in the center of her bed (contrary, by the way, to her habitual sleeping position at one side, in memory to the missing Albert). Her hands were folded over her breast, on which was also positioned a large silver cross. Her head inclined slightly to the right. Over the bed coverlet the dressers had strewn fresh flowers—snowdrops and lilies of the valley, with a few green leaves setting off the paleness of the flowers. A veil of almost impossibly sheer white net covered Victoria's face, so fine that it allowed her features to remain clearly visible. Every trace of suffering seemed to have evaporated from those features. When Davidson peeked in on the scene, he noted that her appearance had "changed somewhat" since the previous night, but that "she still looked gentle, peaceful and dignified."

In the company of his son George and brother Arthur, Bertie reluctantly left his grief-stricken wife and the privacy of Osborne for what he knew would be a very public ordeal in London. Departing the estate through its principal gate, the royal party took a trio of open pair-horse carriages to East Cowes's Trinity Pier, and from there via boat to Portsmouth and the train to the capital. In addition to the King and his son and brother, the group included Lenchen's and Louise's husbands and Arthur Balfour, together with a number of courtiers. Though Bertie acknowledged the quietly respectful crowd at Trinity Pier with a raise of his black silk top hat, he quickly passed through the throng to the waiting yacht. At 9:45, the *Alberta* steamed off across the glassy Solent, the Royal Standard running up as he stepped on deck. No salute was fired, and the yacht carried the sovereign standard at half-mast, which the passengers could see was reciprocated on the Clock Tower at Osborne. At Portsmouth, after Bertie received the mayor to thank him for his message of condolences, the special Portsmouth–London royal train sped across the southern English countryside, reaching the metropolis at 12:55. It was the first time an English King had entered the capital of the kingdom in almost sixty-three years.

For the monarch's arrival at Victoria Station, orders had been passed along to the officials in charge that the ceremonies should be kept to the barest minimum in keeping with protocol. Thus only a few members of the station management together with a sprinkling of courtiers were in place on the platform when the King's train arrived. Bertie stepped out of the carriage onto the platform first and, hat in hand, strode the few steps to his waiting carriage, with only a fleeting salute to the reception committee. His son and an aide rode with him, a mounted policeman escorting the closed brougham up Buckingham Palace Road. On the streets, the silent crowd strained for a first look at the noticeably pale King. The silence was almost eerie throughout the short ride to Marlborough House, only the clattering of the horses' hooves breaking the stillness.

The route from Victoria to Bertie's London town house grew increasingly dense with spectators as the carriage approached its destination. At the point where St. James's Palace looks across to Marlborough House, they were especially thick, and Bertie leaned forward to nod his head slightly to his silent subjects. Every man paid the King the compliment of a bare head, but even as the brougham glided through the throngs in front of the palace that had been the home of the Prince and Princess of Wales for forty years, the scene continued to remain almost bereft of human voices.

The cause of Bertie's coming to London—his Accession Council—faced him within the hour. First, however, he hurried up to his bedroom to change into appropriate garb, for this unique ceremony the uniform of a field marshal. Just before two o'clock, the magnificently re-garbed King was driven in a state carriage, down Marlborough Yard and by way of the Mall to the garden entrance of St. James's Palace, the scene where this ceremony had been traditionally enacted. On his left breast he wore a Garter star, its facets barely glinting in the weak afternoon light. Accompanied by an escort of scarlet-coated cavalry, the procession entered the ancient palace through its garden entrance, where the highest officers of state waited to greet their sovereign.

In the palace's gilded Banqueting Hall, the Duke of Devonshire as Lord President of the Council spoke to the glittering assemblage of Privy Councillors, many arrayed in ancient and colorful robes of office that had been little seen over the past four decades. This council had assisted the monarchs of England long before the Houses of Parliament had even existed. Representing the greatest of the nation's institutions, it was a virtual who's who of the United Kingdom: members of the Cabinet and leaders of the Opposition, the highest ecclesiastical dignitaries of the Church of England, the greatest and richest and most powerful peers of the realm, judges and lawyers who had risen to high position from the courts, others who had achieved power in the civil and diplomatic services and from the empire's commercial life. The statement the duke delivered was an official notification of the death of Queen Victoria and the consequent accession of her son and heir, the Prince of Wales. He recited a summons whose antique text reads "whereas God had been pleased to take to Himself the late Sovereign Queen Victoria, his Majesty the King has called the members of the Privy Council together to take the oath of allegiance." The duke concluded by ordering that the new King should so be informed of the Council's summons.

Bertie, waiting in a separate room, was brought in by the royal dukes (all of whom were his near relations, of course) and by the lords of the Council to hear officially what had just been announced. He found his gold and crimson chair at the far end of the hall, a table facing it, and four smaller chairs to its right for the princes; everyone would remain standing except for the King and the quartet of kinsmen who accompanied him. First, the Archbishop of Canterbury administered the customary oaths to the assembled Councillors. Next it was the turn of the new King to make his first declaration as sovereign. Bertie knew his speech would be crucial, that he would be widely judged by what he was about to say.

He acquitted himself with such eloquence that those who heard it would never forget. His speaking without notes, however, meant that the King's words went unrecorded. But Lord Rosebery, the former Prime Minister and a man with an exquisite sense of the history being made, immediately thereafter wrote out a version that came to be thought of as near-verbatim. (Afterward, the King expressed surprise that shorthand notes hadn't been taken.) Bertie began by stating that "this is the most painful occasion on which I shall ever be called upon to address you." What followed bore a dignity that astonished many who were expecting less.

> My first and melancholy duty is to announce to you the death of my beloved mother, the Queen, and I know how deeply you, the whole nation, and I think I may say the whole world, sympathize with me in the irreparable loss we have all sustained.
>
> I need hardly say that my constant endeavor will be always to walk in her footsteps. In undertaking the heavy load which now devolves upon me, I am fully determined to be a constitutional sovereign in the strictest sense of the word, and, as long as there is breath in my body, to work for the good and amelioration of my people.

Then came the surprise that caused a palpable rising in the room.

> I have been resolved to be known by the name of Edward, which has been borne by six of my ancestors. In doing so I do not undervalue the name of Albert, which I inherit from my ever lamented great and wise father, who by universal consent is I think deservedly known by the name of Albert the Good, and I desire that his name should stand alone.
>
> In conclusion, I trust to Parliament and the nation to support me in the arduous duties which now devolve upon me by inheritance, and to which I am determined to devote my whole strength during the remainder of my life.

These spontaneous first public words of King Edward VII, the general composition of which he had determined on the morning's train ride up to London, and the new King's poise in delivering these words, dazzled many. But what caught almost all unawares was the name under which Bertie determined to reign. Generally expected to be King Albert Edward—the first male sovereign bearing a new name since King George I nearly two hundred years earlier—instead he would reign as Edward VII. He later explained his actions by saying that he wanted to leave the "memory of his father's name as the exclusive treasure" of his mother. In fact, he wanted nothing to do with a double name, which he knew sounded "foreign," and he wanted even less a name of which he had throughout his entire life been told he wasn't worthy.

The remainder of the ceremony involved Bertie taking the oath of allegiance to the kingdom, which he did seated in the throne at the head of the council chamber. Lifting his right hand, King Edward swore fealty to his own kingdom, and to the maintenance and security of the Church of Scotland. He then signed the parchment, his signature countersigned by his son, the Heir Apparent. This finished, the members passed before their sovereign, each pausing and kissing his hand before leaving the Throne Room. When George came to make his obeisance to his father, Bertie extended his hands over his son's head in a silent act of blessing.

❖   2   ❖

The dressers' handiwork was a breathtaking success. The hundreds of inhabitants of the Queen's estate who had been invited to file past their dead mistress were overwhelmed at the beauty and drama of the scene. The occasion would remain with most as a treasured memory to the end of their lives.

The idea had been her eldest son's, to give the hundreds of servants and tenants of the estate a last look at the monarch. Lined up in a neat queue through the halls of the Pavilion, they would in fact be the only of her hundreds of millions of subjects who would see Victoria in death, as her coffin would be closed just before her body was taken from this room. This represented the first time in the royal residence's history when so many ordinary men and women were given leave to see the Queen's most private rooms up close.

Guarding the end of Victoria's bed throughout the showing were two of her Indian servants, their Hindu silks and paisleys contrasting sharply with the somber black that otherwise filled the chamber. In a corner, bishops praying in rota mouthed their invocations near-silently. Among those in the line of viewers walked scullery maids from the kitchens, young women who spent their lives in what might have been the other side of the moon in comparison to the splendor of the royal living quarters. With them trod farmers and their families, secretaries who formed the wide base of the steep Household pyramid, even a few soldiers of the 2nd Battalion of the Rifle Brigades Reserve who guarded the estate. The highest ranking were the officers from the *Osborne*, the *Victoria and Albert*, and the *Alberta*, the royal yachts lying in the waters at the foot of the royal estate. One man described the scene as "the solemnest moment of my life," and remembered "feeling nervous, and hanging my head, and treading very softly." Those expecting a palatial apartment ablaze with gilding and scarlet were visibly amazed at the homely intimacy of Victoria's bedroom.

What most captured the eye of all who shared this unparalleled scene was the body at the center. Under a painting of Christ, Victoria lay looking little different than if she had been asleep. Her golden ring—the wedding band Albert had given her sixty years earlier—was still buried on a fleshy finger. The white hair, parted in the center and combed severely back, was clearly visible under the wisp of fabric that lay on the rises of her features. From outside, booming minute guns from Portsmouth gave a martial tone to the scene, oddly accentuating the stillness that was otherwise only broken by the gently shuffling feet on the soft carpets. Susan Reid, who was among the three hundred or so who visited the room, later wrote of her husband's patient: "Her face [was] like a lovely marble statue, no sign of illness or age, and she looked *"the Queen"* . . . all so simple and grand. I shall never forget it!"

By late in the afternoon, almost everyone from the estate had passed through the bedroom, and the family told Davidson it wished to have another private service at the Queen's bedside. Shortly after teatime, the bishop joined most of the family members around the bed and led them in a ceremony only slightly more elaborate than the spur-of-the-moment bedside prayers he had conducted the prior evening. As he had been throughout, Davidson was struck by the Kaiser's dignified demeanor. So often had William played a chaffing, pompous bore during his visits to his English relations that such churlish behavior was expected again; such had been, of course, the principal reason the Queen's daughters had tried so hard to keep him from coming to his grandmother's sickbed in the first place. But this evening his manners remained, as they had since his arrival, exquisite. Though few knew it, the Emperor's chief advisers in Berlin were feverishly entreating him to return to Berlin at the soonest moment, his absence causing serious complications in the dynasty's bicentenary celebrations. Many in Berlin secretly feared their master would embarrass himself or his government in the bonhomie atmosphere of his English family gathering, another reason they wanted him home. But William reveled, wholly in his element, enjoying the gentle Englishness of the occasion. He knew it couldn't be replicated in Germany, and he didn't want it to end any sooner than it had to.

Where royal requests are concerned, they tend to be taken as commands, and Davidson's phone requests to London for the *chapelle ardente* fittings were very much taken as a command. Thus early in the evening and right on schedule, a team of men arrived with the furniture and the hangings and crucifixes that would turn the Dining Room into a temporary but proper repository to receive the Queen's body.

Once the bishop and the workmen got started, it didn't take long to transform the gilded setting for countless royal dinners into a splendid if somewhat busy stage set for the Queen's catafalque. Crimson hangings from ceiling to floor now completely covered the cream and gold walls. An altar borrowed from the mansion's own chapel was set up at one end of the room, with the gold furniture of the church lavishly spread about. A painting by Verrocchio, taken from Albert's bedroom, hung over the altar, facing the Queen's de Ferrara *Madonna and Child* at the opposite end of the room. Over the crimson draperies were tacked tapestries from the Household Wing's Council Room. The indispensable embellishment to any Victorian setting—massive potted plants and palms—were set about in their huge and valuable containers. Fussy but impressive floral arrangements—wreaths, crosses, whatever— added to the feeling that the dining room had been turned into a hothouse. A platform was centered in the room, where the huge mahogany table normally stood, and was covered with expensive Indian carpets, a Royal Ensign where the coffin would rest.

Missing the right sort of ceremonial illumination, Davidson telegraphed St. Paul's Cathedral to ask that its set of magnificent candelabra be sent down to the island; he had seen them at the Bishop of London's recent funeral and thought they would be perfect for the present situation. Thanks to the power of the royal request, the gorgeous objects arrived later in the evening. But the bishop was disappointed when he saw them here. What had been exactly right under St. Paul's soaring dome managed in the squat dining room of Osborne to dwarf everything else. In the end, half a dozen of the Queen's own tall candle sticks were used to surround the plinth, which now awaited only Victoria's body.

After the six o'clock family service, Reid went up to the Queen's room to make sure everything was in order. With him was Emile Fuchs, a Viennese painter and sculptor who worked in Berlin. The Kaiser had asked the artist to make a deathmask, then a common memento of the dead, and Fuchs needed to take a casting of the dead Queen's features; he was about to start the sketches he would need for the final work. The Petticoats somehow got wind of the plan, and the trio immediately set out to cancel what they considered a desecration of their august mother's body.

Agreeing with them that such an undertaking would represent a vandalization of the monarch's corpse, Reid knew the quickest way to scotch the plan would be to get the King on his side. To this end he asked the new Queen to telephone her husband in London to get William's orders rescinded. Not wanting his mother's face smeared with sculptor's plaster any more than did his sisters, Bertie instantly agreed. As Fuchs was still working on his drawing, the Kaiser's secretary now looking on, Reid quietly instructed the dressers not to leave the body alone for a moment.

❖  3  ❖

Earlier that afternoon, the now-declared King left St. James's Palace. The crowd that had been silently respectful when Bertie entered the palace this time raised heartfelt cheers as the royal carriage passed. Many shouted "God save the King"—the first time in the new reign this cry was heard in the streets of London. Though the carriage was a closed one, and the drivers sped it at a smart clip the short distance back to Marlborough House, those who had been waiting for hours in the bite of the January air agreed that they had gotten their reward.

A mile to the east, yet another great concourse of Bertie's new subjects had just gathered for a mourning service at the metropolitan cathedral. St. Paul's now presented a very different aspect than it had at Victoria's Diamond Jubilee triumph four years earlier. Five thousand worshipers came together for the four o'clock service, filling every seat in the vast nave as well as those under the dome, in the choir, and in the transepts. The forty-five-minute rite, celebrated on an altar table heavily draped in black, concluded with the majestic strains of Bach.

At the Palace of Westminster, where members of both houses of Parliament remained until late in the afternoon to pledge their allegiance to the new sovereign, the issue of the legal effects of the demise of the Crown were being carefully studied. Many aspects of the official life of the nation were affected by Victoria's death, in some cases substantially, in others only because the sex of the monarch had changed. In Parliament, the central and most vital organ of the state, the change of sovereign was governed under statutes adopted in 1867. The latest act made clear that both houses would continue in their same makeup, without any interruption caused by the sovereign's death. (It had before Queen Anne's reign been the custom to dissolve Parliament on the demise of the Crown.) As to the kingdom's courts, statutes specified that Victoria's death would not affect any "pending writ, plea or process, or any other proceeding" in criminal or civil law, though "Queen's Counsel"—the most eminent barristers—would now, of course, become "King's Counsel."

❖ 4 ❖

Late Wednesday night, after all had viewed Victoria's body, and after the family had been led in bedside prayers by the Bishop of Winchester, one final task remained to be completed in the royal bedroom. The Queen's body, now dead nearly thirty hours, was to be embalmed. In stuffy Victorian interiors, decay would set in quickly. In the Queen's case, some persons present had already noticed the flattening of her features under the gauze shroud. Though it was expected that Victoria would be sealed in her coffin the following morning, more than a week still remained before she would be consigned to her final resting place.

The technique of embalming was fairly straightforward. An artery was pierced—most likely in the fold of the groin—with a large syringe connected to a supply of embalming fluid, usually pure formaldehyde. At the same time, a vein would be punctured with another syringe connected to a drainage catheter. While the formaldehyde was being forced through the first syringe into the body's blood vessels, the body's several quarts of blood drained through the second syringe. Since clots would most likely have formed in the hours since death, the process was generally imperfect, the formaldehyde being blocked in many of the vessels in spite of the vigorous pressure applied to push the fluid through the clots. Even so, the result was a body that would last far longer without decomposing and giving off the disagreeable odors that accompany such decomposition.

## CHAPTER XI

# *Thursday, January 24*

❖  1  ❖

LORD CHAMBERLAIN'S OFFICE,
ST. JAMES'S PALACE, S.W.,

*24th January, 1901.*

ORDERS for the COURT to go into Mourning for HER LATE MOST GRACIOUS MAJESTY QUEEN VICTORIA, of Blessed Memory, viz.:—

THE LADIES to wear black Dresses, trimmed with Crape, and black Shoes and Gloves, black Fans, Feathers, and Ornaments.

THE GENTLEMEN to wear black Court Dress, with black Swords and Buckles.

The Mourning to commence from the date of this order.

The COURT to change the Mourning on *Wednesday, the 24th July next, viz.:—*

THE LADIES to wear black Dresses with coloured Ribbons, Flowers, Feathers, and Ornaments, or grey or white Dresses with black Ribbons, Flowers, Feathers, and Ornaments.

THE GENTLEMEN to continue the same Mourning.

And on Friday, *the 24th January next*, the COURT to go out of Mourning.

❖ 2 ❖

"I wish I were dead, too." When the German Dowager Empress was told about her mother's death, such were the despairing words she was reported to have uttered. It was a wish that would come true in a tragically short time. Lying miserably in bed in her Hessian *Schloss*, Vicky had, to all appearances, taken the news as stoically as possible, although the Empress's servants were deathly afraid to break the tidings from Osborne, so sure were they the knowledge would kill their mistress.

Vicky wrote of her loss in her diary: "Oh, how can my pen write it, my sweet darling beloved Mama; the best of mothers and the greatest of Queens, our centre and help and support—all seems a blank, a terrible awful dream. Realise it one cannot." She had always been able to relieve her feelings by setting down on paper her innermost thoughts, usually in long, heartfelt letters to her widely dispersed family. To her daughter Sophie in Greece, the Empress poured out emotions that were full of anguish. "Is she *really* gone?" she wrote. "Gone from us to whom she was such a comfort and support. . . . What a Queen she was and what a woman!" The pain of not being at her mother's bedside was in some ways worse than that of the cancer eating away at her spine.

❖ 3 ❖

After all that had happened in the last few days, the all but spent Dr. Reid still managed to get up to the Pavilion this morning at an early hour. First visiting the Queen's bedroom, the physician found the problematic Fuchs again busy charcoal-sketching the corpse at the center of the room. But now a new character had joined Fuchs. Professor Hubert von Herkomer, the Bavarian-born portraitist who had made a name for himself since moving to England, was in the middle of his own deathbed portrait of the Queen. Reid wasn't sure who had commissioned Herkomer, but he noticed that the artist was creating what seemed to him an ethereal and altogether flattering portrait of the Queen.

Looking over the arrangements in the Dining Room in the

company of Lenchen and Beatrice, Bishop Davidson reveled in his own creation. His pleasure, though, was brief. Shortly after entering, he was handed a message that the undertaker had arrived. Expecting that the coffin was being delivered, Davidson was surprised to instead find a "rough, ordinary" man waiting at the Queen's bedroom door, cap in hand, and clearly coffinless. Davidson knew that Reid had written Bantings, the London undertaker, on the night of the Queen's death—any sooner would have been unseemly—specifying that the coffin shell had to be at Osborne by Thursday. Reid had given the letter to the Lord Chamberlain to take with him to London. But the Lord Chamberlain, not used to attending personally to what he considered a "minor" detail, gave Reid's letter to a subordinate to deliver to Bantings. No one knew what had gone wrong, but this was Thursday, there was no coffin, and the man from Bantings told Davidson there wasn't a hope that one could be gotten down to the island until the next day—at the soonest. Meanwhile, the man wanted to take the "preliminary measurements" to be sent to London, computations without which Bantings couldn't finish the shell and get it down by tomorrow. Davidson and the princesses informed the undertaker's assistant that this scenario was "out of the question," at which the man shrugged and said such were his instructions, and they could take them, or, in effect, leave them.

With a corpse that needed prompt enclosing, Davidson took little time in deciding to go to the one person whose word could put a chill up almost anyone's back. Going to fetch the Kaiser from the suite overlooking Osborne's sloping lawns, the bishop knew the Queen's grandson could demand—command—what was needed, and that it would be gotten. Describing to the Emperor the undertaker's demands to take the Queen's measurements, the two men decided only to allow the Bantings man to get the figures he needed, and then take them to the leading undertaker in Cowes, here on the island, where the liner could be quickly run up. When informed of the decision, the frightened little undertaker's assistant mumbled that this wasn't satisfactory at all, what with his *own* employer getting short-changed. But when the name of the German Kaiser was invoked, the man from London was quickly humbled into acquiescence.

When the bishop brought the Emperor up to the Queen's

room, William was shocked by the appearance of the undertaker's assistant. Both Kaiser and bishop judged the Bantings man so "unsuitable" for the princely task of measuring Victoria's body that together they decided against allowing him to actually touch the corpse, lying so majestically under its white gauze pall. As it turned out, Davidson and William, now joined by Reid, demanded the undertaker tell them precisely what measurements he required, and they then set out to take the necessary calibrations themselves. Watching the trio running their tape measure along Victoria's body and calling out the figures, the man from Bantings clearly wanted nothing more than to get done and get out. The Queen's dressers had to take a few more discreet measurements alone when the doctor, bishop, and Emperor finished, and gave these last figures to the little interloper.

The whole affair came to what Davidson referred to in his memoirs—in dry understatement—as a "curious scene." For his part, Reid recorded in *his* remembrances of the day's events that Davidson had made "rather too much" of his own importance at the body measuring, archly noting that the prelate "[made] himself," in the doctor's words, "prominent in giving directions." As for William, who seemed in the first place to get involved because he shared Davidson's doubts about the undertaker, he oddly agreed with Reid about the bishop's unbecoming sense of self-importance. To the doctor, the Kaiser remarked that "if I were dead and my pastor came in the room like that, he would be hauled out by the neck and shot in the Courtyard!" Clearly, tempers and turf sensibilities were rising in Osborne's increasingly overheated atmosphere.

❖ 4 ❖

As the coffin episode was getting under way at Osborne, a second grand ceremony in as many days was just beginning in London. The public proclamation of the new sovereign had in prior reigns taken place on the same day as the Accession Council, but this time court officials decided to delay it a day. Newspaper reports said the ritual would start at 8:00 A.M., and crowds had begun to gather an hour earlier in the St. James's Palace courtyard where the King-of-Arms would deliver his ritual proclamation. Another damp and cheerless morning frowned on London, the choking coal smoke spewing from a million chimneys and mixing poisonously with the thin mist. The nasty air was accompanied by a feeling of gloom. One perceptive observer, Lady Battersea, born into the Rothschild family, described the capital's atmosphere in words that many would have understood: "The emptiness of the great city without the feeling of the Queen's living presence in her Empire, and the sensation of universal change, haunted me more than any other sensations." Lytton Strachey remarked that "it appeared as if some monstrous reversal of the course of nature was about to take place."

The bone-numbing weather combined with the early hour of proclamation should have been enough to discourage casual sightseers. But the proclamation of a British sovereign had always been a colorful and popular spectacle, and already untidy knots of stalwart souls obstructed the confined streets around the gritty brown palace. Yellow gaslight still flickered from the ornate poles in a half-vain attempt to brighten the morning's demi-light. Most onlookers roused considerably when the leading squadrons of Life Guards came trotting stolidly by, the troopers muffled in long crimson cloaks and glossy black boots, looking promethean high atop their black mounts. Though by tradition the new King himself didn't attend the ceremony, virtually every other great officer of state would be present, nearly all clad in the antique and stately raiment of their offices.

Officials had reserved the parapet of the balcony overlooking the palace's Friary Court for the most privileged of the spectators, including members of the new monarch's Household and the elite of the diplomatic corps. Every window overlooking the small courtyard was filled, with a few cumbersome cameras peeping from cracked windows to provide an historic record of the pageantry. Shortly before nine, police closed the gates between the palace and Marlborough House to prevent any more spectators from pushing into the confined area. A few minutes later, with a sense of great moment a group of mounted officers rode into Friary Court, causing cheers to rise from the crowd when it recognized the now-familiar face of the new commander-in-chief, Field Marshal Lord Roberts, who was leading the formation; Roberts's tunic was distinguished by the cornflower-blue sash of the Garter, the order he had so recently received from the Queen's own hands.

With all the dignitaries drawn up in their positions, at precisely nine o'clock the middle window of the balcony opened. From it emerged officials in scarlet and gold and black, this knot of fairy-tale characters led by the Duke of Norfolk, the kingdom's chief peer and Earl Marshal. Wiggling in behind the head of the venerable Fitzalan-Howard clan were the various kings-of-arms and heralds and pursuivants, each dressed in some variation of the crimson tabards wrought with the new golden coats of arms of Edward VII. Overloading the balcony to the point it looked about to shear off were state trumpeters, backed by four of the King's serjeants-at-arms bearing the gilded sovereign's maces. In the words of the *Times* reporter on the scene, the dowdy courtyard was transformed as though it were "a flowerbed that had in a matter of moments gone from bud to blossom."

Finally, the leading king-of-arms drew himself up to his full height and raised to his eyes the parchment bearing the words that represented the reason this cross-section of Britain's high and mighty had gathered this morning. The state trumpeters blew a long, exultant flourish that seemed to hang in the chill, and in a voice pregnant with nobility, the official read the following text:

> Whereas it has pleased Almighty God to call to His Mercy Our late Sovereign Lady Queen Victoria, of Blessed and Glorious Memory, by whose Decease the Imperial Crown of the United Kingdom of Great Britain and Ireland is solely and rightfully come to the High and Mighty Prince Albert: We, therefore, the Lords Spiritual and Temporal of this Realm, being here assisted with three of Her late Majesty's Privy Council, with Numbers of other Principal Gentlemen of Quality, with the Lord Mayor, Alderman, and Citizens of London, do now hereby, with one Voice and Consent of Tongue and Heart, publish and proclaim, That the High and Mighty Prince Albert Edward, is now, by the Death of our late Sovereign of Happy Memory, become our only lawful and rightful Liege Lord Edward the Seventh, by the Grace

of God, King of the United Kingdom of Great Britain and Ireland, Defender of the Faith, Emperor of India: To whom we do acknowledge all Faith and constant Obedience, with all hearty and humble Affection; beseeching God, by whom Kings and Queens do reign, to bless the Royal Prince Edward the Seventh, with long and happy Years to reign over us.

*God Save the King*

As the King-of-Arms finished the last four words, the whole assemblage uttered spontaneously and in unison the same stirring final phrase. The trumpeters blasted out a flourish, the troops stood to the salute, the King's Color was lowered, and the band struck up the majestic and peculiarly Germanic chords of the national anthem.

Though the St. James's ceremony was the paramount rite of the day, the ceremonial declaiming of sovereignty hadn't yet concluded. The entire company of officers of state got themselves back up on their horses or into their carriages and processed, by way of Pall Mall and Duncannon Street, into the Strand and toward Temple Bar. Here was the site of an ancient archway that had been demolished early in Victoria's reign but whose memory continued to mark the boundary between the cities of London and Westminster. In a space less confined than that around St. James's Palace, the crowds had come in far greater numbers, the throng made up mostly of office workers set on glimpsing the royal pageantry. The Lord Mayor of the City came to Temple Bar in his own considerable state to grant entrance to the King's officers-of-arms, the latter about to proclaim the new King sovereign within the ancient kernel of the metropolis. Since a gate no longer existed to be ceremonially opened, a red silk rope had been stretched across the thoroughfare, a squad of burly constables having been charged with the duty of ensuring no one disturbed this barrier prior to its ritual cutting.

When this second proclamation finally got under way, the Lord Mayor read out the Order in Council requiring him to proclaim His Majesty. With the silk rope severed and Temple Bar opened, the whole procession moved off yet again, this time to Chancery Lane, where the proclamation was repeated. For a final time, all progressed still further eastward, down toward the heart of the City and the Royal Exchange, where the last act in this day of London's proclaiming its sovereign would take place. From her privileged perch on the balcony of the facing Mansion House, the Lady Mayoress watched the scene over which her husband presided, while on the roof of the Bank of England the directors claimed their prerogative to view the ceremonies from the best seats of all. The perfection of the ritual was momentarily broken when one of the busby-topped troopers of the Horse Guards was suddenly thrown from his mount, which apparently was startled by a threatening movement from the crowd pressing into the great commercial crossroads; the rider speedily regained his saddle, evidently none the worse for his tumble. Soon the Common Crier, a highly nervous lieutenant colonel named Burnaby, demanded silence. Filled with pride, the Lady Mayoress watched her husband read the order for the proclamation. The Somerset Herald thundered out with the ancient words, like his predecessors concluding with "God save the King," by which formula all present knew their monarch had been well and truly proclaimed the lawful sovereign in this land.

Having presided over a second Privy Council, this one at Marlborough House, King Edward left London shortly before noon to return to his mother's lying in state at Osborne. An interloper at Victoria Station sent the royal bodyguards into a momentary scare when the man approached the King on the platform, apparently only to hand him a petition. Quickly hustled away by the railway police, the paper he was pressing on the monarch vaguely demanded that he "be permitted to see my beloved Queen"—presumably Bertie's mother, not the new Queen. After being searched, nothing suspicious was found, and following a few quick inquiries, he was released.

When Bertie arrived at Portsmouth to cross the Solent, he found that the navy had dressed the fleet in colorful flags arranged like rainbows. As the King boarded the *Alberta*, the sleek little steam-yacht his mother had ridden so often between the mainland and her island home, its captain ran the Royal Standard smartly to the top of its mast as the massed ships fired a second salute, their guns joined by those in the batteries ringing the Spithead forts.

Waiting for the sovereign at Osborne, Davidson received a special request, notifying the bishop that the King wished to have a Communion service conducted at his mother's bedside as soon as he returned to the island. The prelate thought the King—or the messenger—had made a mistake, assuming that what would be required would merely be a simple bedside service, with Communion given in the newly rigged-out *chapelle ardente* the following morning. However, on Davidson's checking His Majesty's orders, an imperious reply back came that no mistake had been made.

An hour and a half after Bertie's two-thirty arrival, the rite got under way. Davidson didn't think it "right" to move the furniture from the Queen's room, and since there was a great deal of it in the cluttered fashion of the era, the gathering was uncomfortably cramped. Since the entire family wanted to attend, a fair amount of jostling went on around Victoria's corpse, especially when protocol required that an "appropriate" space be reserved for Bertie and Alexandra in their new dignity. Davidson managed the whole thing without too much discomfort, and even the late Queen's dressers and her page, Waite, squeezed into the overly warm room. A new crop of flowers lay around Victoria's body, a small imperial crown at her side. Davidson thought her face was losing a little of the "fine look" of the previous day, but nonetheless judged that she still appeared "most calm and peaceful."

Later that afternoon, Dr. Reid saw to the final preparations of the Queen's body before it was to be placed in its coffin. Before the sovereign's body could be placed in the coffin, the doctor and the dresser first removed its white nightgown, replacing the garment with a white satin dressing gown; Victoria had unequivocally commanded that she wanted to meet Albert dressed not in her black of forty years but in the traditional color of matrimony. The Queen had always been extremely proud of her role as head of Britain's orders of knighthood, and of no order was she prouder than that of the Garter. Specifying that she be buried in the order's insignia, the pair arranged the blue sash, draping it from her left shoulder to the right side of the waist, and then attached the diamond-studded star to the left breast of the dressing gown. Finally, Mrs. Tuck cut off her mistress's hair, how much or for what reason Reid didn't comment upon in his diary. After a last adjustment of the fresh flowers scattered artfully around the corpse and a rearranging of the veil over the Queen's face, Reid and Mrs. Tuck could turn to the matter the coffin itself.

The man from Bantings had promised to have the shell ready this evening and, faithful to his pledge, finally arrived with the vital artifact at about seven-thirty. When the new Queen—Alexandra had been tiresomely pretending all day that she wasn't yet Queen, still insisting everyone treat her as the Princess of Wales—saw the little man lugging the artifact in the front door, she appealed to Reid to allow the body to remain on its bed for one last night, assuring the physician that there was "no smell" yet. The reason she wanted the delay was to give her son George, ill and in bed with a fever (which was about to develop into German measles), a last chance to see his grandmother. Reid quickly acceded to the wishes of the new mistress of the house.

After dinner, the King announced that he would receive his mother's Household to thank them formally for all they had done these last trying days. Reid had to leave his work with Mrs. Tuck to attend. At ten o'clock, in the ornate Council Room in the Main Wing, all the Queen's principal servants who could be corralled were individually presented to Bertie, each formally brushing his hand with their lips. Davidson, ever mindful of the minutiae of social relationships in the service of royalty, noted the proceedings were considered "strange" by the men who had been in the Queen's most private service to find themselves "introduced by a new Equerry into the Sovereign's presence."

When he was finally able to get away from the Council Room, Reid hurried back to the dead Queen's bedroom to take care of the last requirements of the day. The exhausted doctor, who had left the house for hardly more than a few minutes at a time since the past weekend (Powell and Barlow had returned to London earlier this afternoon), headed a little group of servants who carried the shell into the bedroom, which they gingerly laid on the floor by the bed, on the fireplace side of the room. There it would wait until morning to receive the body, as Alexandra had requested.

Expecting to carry a loaded coffin down to the Dining Room, a contingent of sailors from the *Victoria and Albert* had been standing around all evening. Reid allowed them to file past the bed—a signal privilege for all who had been accorded this honor over the past three days—and were finally sent back to their ship with orders to return to Osborne by ten o'clock the next morning.

An affecting piece of news was received in London from the Cape Colony. Wishing to pay a tribute to their enemy's dead sovereign, the Boer inmates at the great Greenpoint prisoner-of-war camp in Cape Colony decided to suspend all amusements until after the Queen's funeral. In no way, though, was this a concession to British arms. Outside the prison, the fighting continued, and wouldn't stop until the war was ended by an armistice a year later.

# *Friday,*
# *January 25*

❖    1    ❖

One of the few European sovereigns not related to Victoria,
Emperor Francis Joseph nonetheless sent to Osborne a remembrance that would have much pleased his British counterpart.
From the incomparable Schönbrunn conservatories, the seventy-
one-year-old Austrian monarch ordered for Victoria a wreath made
up of flowers native only to Great Britain or its colonies. When it
arrived this morning, the tribute was placed conspicuously next to
the Queen's deathbed.

❖    2    ❖

Victoria's closest retainers woke this morning to what each
knew would be one of the most sensitive and emotional tasks
they would ever face. The dead Queen was to be placed in her
coffin today. The minutely detailed instructions the sovereign herself devised had been completed in December 1897. Victoria
sealed them in an envelope, and marked on it "For my Dressers
to be opened directly after my death and to be always taken about
and kept by the one who may be travelling with me." She had
clearly given the matter a great deal of thought. Reid was chosen

by Victoria to be responsible for her body until the actual moment it would be sealed in its coffin. The physician, who regarded his mission with the utmost gravity, determined to see that the precise wishes of the late sovereign were carried through without a single omission.

On Wednesday evening, Mrs. Tuck had privately read to Reid the memo Victoria had left, listing those things she wanted buried in the coffin with her. The mandate made it clear that some of the items weren't to be seen by any member of her family, Victoria evidently not wanting to be embarrassed or challenged—even posthumously—for what even she must have known were unconventional choices. Yesterday, the physician and the dresser began to assemble the artifacts from the Queen's trove of a lifetime of souvenirs, Mrs. Tuck having in fact started to put the collection together only hours after the Queen's death.

Having just examined the Duke of York—the prince's increasingly dangerous fever was beginning to worry the family—Reid headed for the familiar corner bedroom. There in company with Mrs. Tuck and one of the junior dressers, the physician undertook what many would come to regard as one of the most remarkable elements in the saga of Queen Victoria's dying and death.

No members of the family were present to eavesdrop on what the small group of retainers were about to do. Before getting to Victoria's instructions, Reid and the women first had to prepare the coffin shell, which was lying on the floor next to the Queen's bed. They spread it with a layer of charcoal, neatly pushing the little nuggets around to an even depth of about an inch and a half, the charcoal meant to absorb whatever fluids might still remain in the body. Following this task, they finally began the careful arranging of the treasures Victoria chose to remain with her forever.

Victoria wanted her last passage to be made in the comforting company of a cornucopia of mementos from her long life, the bounty of oddments and heirlooms she selected symbolizing a lifetime as diverse and interesting as few people in history have known. Some of the items she specified were priceless, others mere bibelots whose value derived from their associations with happier times. Favored jewels, some of which held little intrinsic value, were joined with more modest gifts that had simply pleased her—favorite shawls and hand-embroidered handkerchiefs. Reid put in scores of carefully specified photographs, images not only of her family but of old friends and loyal servants. Some of the famous collection of carved limbs of the Queen's family members were tucked in, most notably Albert's alabaster hand. Folded in neatly was the Prince Consort's dressing gown, a robe that had been lovingly embroidered by Princess Alice, the first of the Queen's children to die.

With the layer of mementos thus arranged, Reid and the women went on to the next task. Bantings had provided a quilted cushion to precisely fit the interior of the leaden shell, and it was now fitted and laid. It perfectly covered the relics, the effect of which was to conceal the contents from the eyes of the family. Reid now turned to the carpenters who were standing by ready to assist. He asked them to move the coffin around to the side of the bed nearest the door. There they propped it up on a frame so that it rested at the same level as the top of the mattress. It was now flush with and only a few inches away from Victoria's body. The physician then ordered the men to withdraw into the adjoining dressing room.

Now the physician was ready to let a few close members of the family see the Queen's mortal remains while they still rested on her bed. King Edward and Queen Alexandra came into the room first, and spent a few minutes alone with the woman who had dominated both their lives for so many years. Alexandra—still insisting that she wasn't yet Queen—tenderly arranged a few flowers on her mother-in-law's body, and withdrew.

Bertie remained while Reid brought William in to see the body. The Kaiser's attitude was one of reverence, his volcanic mouth still subdued by the aura of the dead sovereign. Arthur then entered, with his son behind him. Finally, led by Mrs. Tuck, the dressers—Miss Stewart and Miss Ticking—came in, together with the small crew from the carpentry shop who had been helping earlier. It was then up to the family members, the dressers and the physician to lift the corpse into the waiting container, using straps that had been laid under the body. William spontaneously stepped forward as if he meant to pick up the body alone. The Kaiser's impulsive gesture was too much for the new King. Bertie instantly caught his brother's eye, and the two men quickly interposed themselves between their mother and their nephew, claiming what they instinctively held as their prerogative to initiate this last familial duty regarding the body of Queen Victoria. William made way for his uncles.

Reid then gave the signal. With himself and Mrs. Tuck holding Victoria's head, two dressers the feet, Bertie and Arthur holding one strap each on the left and William and young Prince Arthur of Connaught holding a strap each on the right, all either straddling the coffin or kneeling on the bed to keep their balance, the group hoisted the little bundle down into the coffin shell. Her weight down to a fraction of what had once reached 162 pounds (at a bit less than five feet tall), it is doubtful that Victoria gave much trouble in this final chore.

Reid now asked the Queen's relatives and the workmen to leave the room, allowing only Mrs. Tuck and the two junior dressers to help him with another chore that the Queen had wanted to remain unknown to her relations. Neatly rearranging the dressing gown, the quartet first put Victoria's wedding veil over her face and upper torso. Then bags of charcoal wrapped in muslin were tucked along the body's flanks, the charcoal's purpose, like the purpose of that under the quilted cushion, to absorb moisture. Finally the moment arrived to keep the pledge that Victoria commanded most earnestly: Reid placed in the Queen's left hand a photograph of John Brown, the man she loved but her family despised. The physician enclosed a lock of Brown's hair, wrapped in tissue paper and hidden by the flowers Queen Alexandra had placed in the coffin a short while earlier. After a last glimpse to make sure his work was done, Reid left to go downstairs to the Drawing Room, where he told the female members of the family who had gathered there that they might now go up for their own last look.

The women greatly outnumbered the men. Leading off was the new Queen, the only woman who had so far today seen the body on the bed. With Alexandra was her daughter-in-law, the Duchess of York; May was having to get through this trying ordeal alone, her ailing husband now, on Reid's orders, bedridden. A large group of princesses followed: Affie's widow joined the queue with her daughter. Arthur's wife came with Leopold's widow, the

Duchess of Albany, who had her daughter Alice in tow. The Queen's daughters walked in with Princess Thora and Princess Victoria Eugenia of Battenberg, the latter destined one day to be Queen of Spain. Reid asked the King if the ladies of the Household might also see the corpse, and Bertie graciously permitted Harriet Phipps and Charlotte Knollys to go up. The King then asked that the male members of the Household be invited to look in on the scene, and, in a typically thoughtful gesture, Bertie even sent for the Munshi, his mother's overbearing Indian servant who was frowned upon by most of the family. The male members of the family then squeezed back into the room. Reid held the coffin lid for a moment, and looked at the King. For a few seconds, Bertie stood speechless, clearly stricken with his own memories. Then he said quickly, "Close it finally. It must not be opened again."

Carpenters quickly sidled quietly past the royal mourners, knelt down with their tools and carefully screwed the lid onto the coffin, lastly covering it with a gleaming white pall. The party of waiting sailors from the Queen's yacht then marched down the hall and into the room. The bluejackets gingerly raised the small but heavy box that was, unknown to most in the room, now filled with the objects betokening one of the most indelible lives ever lived. They carried it out of the room and back down the hall and grand stairs, turning in to what had been a dining room but was now a sanctuary glittering with crimson and gold and tall, white, flaming tapers. Tightly sealed against any more of the prying eyes Victoria had tried so long to avoid, the coffin was settled onto the bier, which stood where the table had been. Bertie set his mother's beautiful little diamond crown atop the coffin, and with it the insignia and ribbon of the Garter. The velvet and ermine furls of Victoria's scarlet parliamentary robe was spread out around the base of the plinth. With everything in order, the King departed for London, leaving Beatrice and William in charge at Osborne.

❖  3  ❖

At Windsor, harried courtiers were trying to figure out how to bury a monarch. The only thing they knew for certain was that in accordance with Victoria's express wishes, there would be neither services nor a lying in state in the capital. Only a regal but relatively short procession through London would give the inhabitants of the empire's key metropolis the opportunity to pay their final respects. What was more, the Queen had commanded for herself not a state funeral, but specifically a *military* funeral, a privilege fitting for a monarch who had been immensely proud of her standing as head of the nation's armed forces.

There could be no question that St. George's Chapel, the ecclesiastical home of the British monarchy, would serve, as it had so many times already, as the site of the funeral. Many of the grandest celebrations of Victoria's reign had been carried out in this exquisite cathedral-like chapel, one of the oldest churches in the kingdom. St. George's connected directly with another, much older, structure. The latter building had been known for centuries as the Wolsey Chapel until Victoria changed its name to honor her husband. Running underneath the two was a crypt, reaching roughly from the altar of St. George's to the nave of the Albert Chapel. There beneath worn stones were entombed the bodies of the preeminent members of the British Royal Family, including King George III, his sons and successors George IV and William IV and many members of their families; at least one sovereign from every dynasty since the time of Edward III was entombed in his or her own crypt on the main floor of St. George's. In recent years, foreign royalty had been memorialized near the tombs of the British sovereigns: in 1879, Victoria ordered that Alamayu, who was the son of the Abyssinian Emperor Theodore and who as a young Etonian had been taken under Victoria's protective wing, be remembered with a brass marker near the west end of the chapel.

By the end of Victoria's reign, Windsor Castle had been the home of English sovereigns for eight centuries. Named for the village of Windesores, or "Windlass Shore" (referring to a mechanism used to haul boats out of the river), its commanding chalk heights overlooking the Thames had centuries before led King Edward I to found a royal manor on the site. A few years later, William I—"the Conqueror"—replaced it with a military post meant to safeguard the river-highway that served as the principal commercial artery from London to the interior of his English possessions. William erected his castle in what was then the revolutionary "motte and bailey" fashion, its bulk overwhelming the still-near-savage natives. The fortress's central feature, the "motte," was a large flat-topped earthen mound topped by a wooden fortress, the whole thing encircled by a protective ditch, this in turn surrounded by the "bailey," a larger walled area where locals and their animals sought refuge from the wrath of William's enemies.

Over the centuries, the crude fortress was transformed into, first, a relatively comfortable castle, and, gradually, into a luxurious palace. Nearly every English sovereign lived in it, and nearly every one who did altered it. Edward III founded the Garter, England's premier order of chivalry, at Windsor. Edward IV began the building of the chapel that would serve as the order's headquarters, naming it after the England's patron saint, leaving it to Henry VIII to complete it. The chapel stood as England's most renowned example of the Gothic perpendicular style and one of the world's sublime ecclesiastical structures.

Charles II, a king perhaps best remembered for his collecting of acquisitive mistresses and siring of troublesome bastards, turned the so-called Upper Ward of the castle complex into the general outlines of the modern palace. His State Apartments on the ward's north side were until the reign of George IV the site of the royal family's own quarters. It was George IV, perhaps the most practiced plunderer of the nation's treasury in its history—albeit the possessor of an unparalleled vision of the proper setting for an English sovereign—who was responsible for building the setting in which Queen Victoria spent the greatest part of her life.

In the closing days of January 1901, courtiers busy in the magnificent rooms that lined the palatial corridors of the Upper Ward found themselves confronted by an endless list of questions about the impending ceremonies. Though no funeral of a sovereign had been held in sixty-four years, the officials in the Lord Chamberlain's department could only hope that the answers to those questions were arrived at soon.

❖ 4 ❖

At Osborne, nearly all of the senior courtiers were passing the day dealing with details that were surging over the Household officials like an unstoppable landslide. But aside from the matters related to the funeral, many in the now combined Households were absorbed with the preservation of their own status. So determined was everyone who had served the late Queen to maintain cordial relations with their new opposite numbers belonging to the King that both camps were letting telegrams go unanswered for fear the others might take exception. Bertie's people were, of course, *official* now, those of Victoria technically having ceased to hold their appointments. The King sensed the problem, and told Fritz Ponsonby that he wanted everyone to continue "just as usual," and to await further orders. The old Household, understandably at sea, found itself lending unaccustomed assistance to the late Queen's daughters—especially to Louise, who was struggling with several hundred telegrams to which neither experience nor inclination had enabled her to cope.

One of the issues giving difficulty involved the ceremonial guarding of the Queen's coffin in the Dining Room. Senior Household members had formed a temporary guard, but it was apparent to the family that something more splendid than mere courtiers was required. What was needed, in fact, was a military guard. Unhappily, the only available soldiers were the 60th Rifles, stationed at the nearby Parkhurst Barracks—the Rifles were unquestionably military but carried little of the status or panache of the aristocratic units of the Household regiment in London. When their officer in charge found out what his men were expected to do, the hapless colonel admitted that he didn't have the least idea how to mount a royal guard, his soldiers totally ignorant of such maneuvers as reversing arms, an esoteric but necessary maneuver his drill book didn't discuss. Nor was he even sure how to set up a smooth rota of watches; in light of the nauseating smell of tuberoses and gardenias pervading the dining room, he knew the men would have to be relieved at short intervals, and that it would have to be done smartly and precisely. Only with trepidation did the Riflemen manage to post guard at each of the coffin's four corners, hoping that the colonel would prove a quick study and come up with the appropriate choreography.

In spite of their makeshift air, these arrangements seemed to satisfy everyone for the time being, and for nearly a whole day the Queen was watched over by some of the humblest of her warriors. But later in the afternoon the Duke of Connaught looked in on the scene. This punctilious soldier abruptly asserted that the privilege of mounting guard over the defunct sovereign belonged to the Queen's Company of the Grenadier Guards, the smartest, most socially prominent unit in the kingdom. Since Uncle Arthur was taken to be an authority on such matters, a wire was sent to the Grenadiers' London headquarters immediately. Within hours, a contingent of the red-jacketed troopers arrived at Osborne. Unluckily, its two officers in charge, St. John Coventry and Miles Ponsonby, didn't have any more idea of what to do than had the 60th Rifles. A decision was made for the Grenadiers to simply copy the drill the Rifles had been carrying on with for the last several hours.

Not long after the advance Grenadier contingent arrived, their commander arrived on the scene, clearly intent on making sure that the regiment's performance not dishonor the unit. Working out an intricate routine in which the new guard would do all its changing in slow time and with weapons reversed, the new arrangements were put into effect and quickly assumed an impressive martiality. The Grenadiers—the four tallest men taking the first detail—stood at the corners of Victoria's bier as though marble statues, their gloved hands crossed over rifle butts, the weapons' muzzles on the toe of each man's left boot. To honor the faithful Household members, a lone courtier remained in the coffin-head position; on Fritz Ponsonby's shift, the overpowering smell of the massed flowers in the overheated room almost did the Private Secretary in. With lighted candles flickering on eight massive candlesticks, masses of wreaths that included Louise's white lilies and Beatrice's Wedgwood-blue hyacinths, red velvet hangings covering the walls and the sparkle of the Imperial and Garter jewels twinkling from atop her coffin, the gloomy old Dining Room took on an otherworldliness Victoria would doubtlessly have pronounced most successful.

Matters of status and its preservation danced around the heads of the Royal Family as much as they did those of the court. To few persons were such concerns more important than they were to the wife of the new Heir Apparent. The Duchess of York never possessed the easy and ethereal security of Queen Alexandra. But in May's case, insecurity was understandable—the relative penury and the humiliating deference the Tecks had been obliged to pay the more senior members of the family had long rankled all the Tecks. On marrying the heir to the second heir to the throne, May's position took the ultimate leap, yet she remained obsessed by rank and station, a fixation dovetailing with her passionate desire for valuable possessions.

The prize May most coveted was the title her mother-in-law had borne for almost forty years. The direct male heir to the British throne has for centuries been created Prince of Wales, his wife automatically becoming Princess of Wales. The title is the second highest in the kingdom, subordinate only to that of the sovereign. It is not, however, a perquisite of birth, but rather the "gift" of the monarch, the only automatic title to which the heir is due by birth being that of Duke of Cornwall.

Though the Queen had been dead for only three days, May already surmised her father-in-law was not going to advance her and George to the titles she believed should have been theirs on Victoria's death. She evidently reached this conclusion because the King hadn't yet even raised the subject. Suspecting that her mother-in-law was opposing another woman using a title that had been her own for four decades, May put two and two together, and the arithmetic was annoying her badly. To her old governess, Mme. Helene Bricka, May registered her grievance: "We are to be called D. & Dss. of Cornwall & York and I don't think the King intends to create G. [George] Pce of Wales. . . ."

May enlisted the help of someone who shared her feelings about this sort of thing. Sir Arthur Bigge, an ardent traditionalist and her husband's new Private Secretary, spoke to the King about the problem, making clear his disagreement with the monarch's apparent delay in passing on his and Alexandra's longtime titles. He even told the sovereign that the action might even imply that George was in disfavor, or that the King lacked confidence in his heir. Meanwhile, May again took to her pen, setting down her concerns in a letter to her aunt Augusta, the elderly Grand Duchess of Mecklenburg-Strelitz and a granddaughter of King George III. The thrust of her complaint was that she "dislike[d] departing from traditions." It was a position in which Aunt Augusta minced no words in agreeing. From Strelitz a letter came to Osborne saying ". . . my *ire* was up & hot that the legitimate historical Title is not to be continued nor borne by you & George! Oh! what a terrible mistake so to upset old traditions! and *why?* because *he* will not be superseded? what can it be else? . . . The "Dauphin" can't be suppressed nor the Pce of Assturias [sic] in France & Spain. What reason can the King give?"

Both May's concerns and the grand duchess's response seem fatuous in retrospect. As it happened, the King did indeed quite purposely refrain from the immediate conferring of the title on his son, doing so for what he held to be good—and, certainly, unmalicious—reasons. For sixty years, he himself had been Prince of Wales, his wife the Princess of Wales for the nearly forty years that she had been married to him. Bertie felt that to transfer the name to another couple too abruptly would only create confusion in the public mind. If Alexandra in fact influenced her husband in his decision, it, too, was understandable that she wouldn't especially fancy the immediate transference to another woman of a name that had for so long been her own.

Eventually—ten months later, as it turned out—King Edward created his son Prince of Wales; May, of course, became Princess of Wales at the same time. But the younger woman never quite forgave her mother-in-law for what she imagined to be a deliberate slight, a notion abetted by the fact that Alexandra would never address May by the new title. In justice to Bertie's concern (which itself seems trivial today), many letters mailed by the public to the "Princess of Wales" were meant for Queen Alexandra, long after the old title ceased to be hers.

With Victoria now lying in semi-state on her bier, the first group of those invited to view the scene came down the Pavilion's Grand Corridor this afternoon. In the lead were some forty journalists and artists, specially invited to describe or draw the scene for the national audience. Behind them filed in many from the countryside surrounding Osborne, the Queen's neighbors whom the new King wished to accord this privilege. Each arrival was carefully identified in the courtyard to prevent those without legitimate claim from entering, the Royal Family well aware that if the lying in state were opened to all comers, the event would quickly become unmanageable. Still, the family was solicitous in seeing to it none who had been important to the Queen were forgotten: the local veterinary surgeon who had treated the Queen's dogs took great pride in being invited to see Victoria resting in the beauty of her island home for the last time.

Late in the afternoon, Fritz Ponsonby was summoned by the King. With only a week remaining before the funeral, Bertie told the courtier he wanted him to assume overall supervision of the arrangements at Windsor. The monarch explained to the trusted aide that the actual service at St. George's would by tradition fall under the aegis of the Lord Chamberlain, but that Ponsonby should oversee all the other arrangements at the castle. The courtier—*and* the King—were shortly to discover that the Earl Marshal, the hereditary organizer of Britain's great ceremonies of state, would have his own notions as to who was going to be in charge.

## CHAPTER XIII

# Saturday, January 26, through Thursday, January 31

## SATURDAY

### ❖ 1 ❖

Henry Fitzalan-Howard, Knight of the Garter, Privy Councillor, member of the Noble Pontifical Order of Christ, fifteenth Duke of Norfolk, and—by virtue of his holding the oldest dukedom in the kingdom—hereditary Earl Marshal of England, was looking forward to the upcoming pageant. He had held his title for all but the first twelve of his fifty-three years. The education of the fledgling duke, possessor of the greatest Catholic peerage in the kingdom, had been carried out under the personal supervision of Cardinal Newman, a charge meant to ensure that the young nobleman receive a grounding with which to lead the Catholic laity of England. The irony of Norfolk's inheritance was that for the rest of his life he would manage the Protestant rites that lie at the heart of this kingdom's ceremonial life.

Though one titled lady had described him as looking like "the most insignificant of mechanics," the diminutive duke possessed a strength of character that would serve well in the arduous task of burying the most famous person in the world. Having directed Victoria's two jubilees to their glorious conclusions, Norfolk had already displayed incontestable competence with arranging royal ceremonial. When he arrived at Osborne this morning at the King's bidding, he found assembled there some of the main actors in the upcoming rites: the King; the Lord Chamberlain—Lord Clarendon—who would take charge of many of the funeral ceremonies; Sir Spencer Ponsonby-Fane, comptroller of Clarendon's office and his principal assistant; and the ever-useful and seemingly omniscient Lord Esher, who as secretary of the Office of Works would control much of the ritual at Windsor Castle, the site of both the funeral and the entombment.

Very quickly, the distinguished gathering got down to the main outlines of the complex formalities. Norfolk and Clarendon quickly locked horns over a turf-based conflict, both men claiming the ultimate authority over the entire funeral. Clarendon took the view that the role should be his since he clearly possessed the greater experience in handling funerals, having already been in charge of a number of so-called royal funerals, a species one step below the top category that was reserved for dead sovereigns. Norfolk shot back that as Earl Marshal he possessed an absolute right to take charge of Victoria's last rites, a position in which he was backed by both precedence and tradition. Bertie, the ultimate arbiter, declared that his premier peer would indeed assume overall charge, while assuaging Clarendon and others with important segments for which they would be directly responsible to the King himself. When he confirmed Fritz in general charge at Windsor, he added the proviso that the courtier was to take orders from the Dean of Windsor regarding anything touching on the rites at St. George's Chapel.

The funeral date was fixed firmly for the following Saturday—one week from today. Victoria would be taken to Windsor Castle in a complex two-day, two-stage journey. Both of the military services would be involved, with tens of thousands of soldiers and sailors detailed to accompany the Queen along every foot of the route from Osborne to Windsor.

For the tricky crossing of the Solent, the Queen's body would travel from Cowes to Portsmouth within the embrace of a cordon of some thirty of the Royal Navy's capital warships—eighteen battleships and twelve cruisers; the Admiralty had already directed a number of the ships home from the Mediterranean Fleet to participate in this floating honor guard. To space the ships along the eight-mile crossing, a mere two and a half cable lengths—about 1,500 feet—would separate one vessel from the next. Four German warships, ordered by the Queen's grandson from what he considered his personal navy, would be anchored in pairs at either end of the British armada. It wasn't yet agreed where to place ships that other navies were sure to send.

After having crossed the Solent, on Friday evening the body was to remain under guard in Portsmouth's Clarence Victualling Yard, while the royal mourners accompanying the Queen across the strait were to spend the night on their yachts—the *Alberta*, the *Osborne*, the *Victoria and Albert* and the *Hohenzollern*—moored in the harbor of this traditional home of the Channel Fleet. The following morning, the royal train would set off for London's Victoria Station, from which a gun carriage would then transport the coffin, followed by the royal party, through the streets of the capital to Paddington Station, there to once again entrain, this time for Windsor and the afternoon's funeral service. Two days later, on Monday, the last ritual would be performed when the Queen's body was to be taken from St. George's Chapel to the mausoleum at Frogmore, where it would, finally, join that of Albert.

To carry out this dauntingly complex program, Norfolk and Clarendon faced endless details that had yet to be resolved. Among the most overwhelming of logistical problems concerned the stationing of troops along the lines of march in London and Windsor. Every regiment in the country wanted to be represented, nearly all considering it a matter of honor that they should be so. The principal decision makers as to the specifics of military planning would be the commanding general of the Home District and army commander-in-chief Lord Roberts, with the Earl Marshal the arbiter of last resort in all questions pertaining to any of the ceremonial.

Particular attention was being given to the gun carriage that would serve as the hearse, the symbol that more than any other would turn the funeral into the military affair Victoria wanted. Built in the Royal Carriage Department at the Woolwich Arsenal, by early this morning the rig had already been dispatched to London. Plans called for the muzzle of a fifteen-pounder field gun to project from the front of the vehicle, its breech and trunnion covered by the gun carriage platform the same size and shape as the coffin. The entire affair would weigh in at about two and a half tons.

❖  2  ❖

While these matters were being thrashed out in Osborne's Council Room, yet another family member was arriving on English shores, this time via the German imperial yacht *Hohenzollern*. The yacht had deposited the German Crown Prince William this morning at Port Victoria, from which he had taken a train to London and on to Southampton. The same time the impetuous young Prince was stepping ashore, the Kaiser was setting out on the *Alberta* from Cowes. Father and son would meet in Southampton, and return to the island together on the *Alberta*.

A few hours later, the Emperor and his heir slipped into Cowes's Trinity Pier, a considerable crowd having gathered in the town's center to get a look at the lavishly uniformed German royals. Later in the afternoon, the officers and men of the Kaiser's yacht—the *Hohenzollern*, which had sailed into Cowes in the wake of the *Alberta*—trooped up the hill to the royal residence. There, at the invitation of the British King, their first duty was to make their pilgrimage to the *chapelle ardente* to pay respects at Victoria's bier.

The *Alberta* remained busy with round trips between the island and the mainland. It returned yet again to Cowes toward the end of the afternoon, bearing another family group—Princess Victoria and her sister and brother-in-law, Prince and Princess Charles of Denmark—to pack even tighter Osborne's already overflowing rooms. A bit later, the old Duke of Cambridge arrived with the Secretary of State for War, the Marquess of Lansdowne and the commander-in-chief of the army, Lord Roberts.

Bishop Davidson, away for most of the day yesterday on diocesan business, returned to the estate earlier this morning, crossing by the early boat from Southampton. Pleased to see that during his absence the coffin had been brought safely downstairs, he now busily organized a little bier-side service, which most of the Royal Family would attend. Since by this time Victoria's relatives in the house had turned into a sizable throng, the service was closed to all but the family, but the congregation was still uncomfortably crowded. Hymns were dispensed with in light of the makeshift nature of the rite, but scriptural readings lent the occasion the requisite solemnity.

This duty accomplished, Davidson filled the rest of his day with social chores. The most important bits involved meeting with the King to iron out some details for the funeral. Oddly, at least to Davidson's way of thinking, the monarch again brought up the business about the recently vacated London bishopric, a detail that Davidson seemed to think preoccupied him. Between smoothing logistical upsets for a number of the royals and officials packed together, the bishop tried to do a little sermon writing for tomorrow's big service at Whippingham Chapel. Davidson's wife arrived on the island late in the afternoon, giving him an excuse to break away from the wearing protocol permeating the royal residence and everyone in it. It wasn't until an hour before midnight that he finally got an hour to himself to gather his notes into a coherent sermon.

Victoria's death naturally filled the obituarial world this week, but hers wasn't the only passing of overriding international fame. Giuseppe Verdi, the son of a poverty-stricken tavern keeper and grocer who had risen to be one of the nineteenth century's musical giants, died this morning. Six years older than Victoria, he learned his first lessons in music from a traveling fiddler. The operas for which he became so famous were said to have had their last acts written first, a technique to ensure that the finale would show no "signs of fatigue." The critics sniped that such was the reason his third acts were invariably inferior to what followed them.

# SUNDAY

❖ 1 ❖

This morning's sun rose on the first Sabbath since the Queen's death, and churches all over England, indeed in virtually every outpost and oasis of empire, were full from pulpit to front door. Dr. Frederick Temple, Archbishop of Canterbury and England's preeminent cleric, preached to a standing-room-only crowd at St. Paul's, whose doors had to pushed shut against a massive crowd struggling to enter the largest temple in the kingdom. At Westminster Abbey, the text was taken from Acts 13. The venerable octogenarian dean George Glanville Bradley, his long white hair partially crowned by a skullcap, spoke of the Queen's coronation in this building, a ritual he himself had witnessed over six decades earlier.

But this Sabbath morning's premier service was celebrated at Osborne's own little flint and plaster parish sanctuary, Whippingham Church. The cozy chapel that Albert had altered to suit his and his wife's taste was now filled with an unprecedented sweep of royalty. Hardly a glint of color showed from the mourners, the women especially, looking like apparitions under the black hangings that shielded them from head to toe. The special sermon that Bishop Davidson had toiled over only a few hours ago used 1 Corinthians 15 and its promise of resurrection as its foundation. He displayed a diplomatic sensitivity by including amongst his rather overlong remarks a warm tribute to the Kaiser. Commenting on the "two great kindred branches of our race," Davidson noted how impressed "all England" was that William was "simply taking his quiet place as the grandson of our Queen, and thereby cementing by the force of a sentiment which is keener and further reaching than any force on earth the undying friendship" of these two nations. The Reverend Sir Walter Parratt, Victoria's private organist, followed up with Mendelssohn and Schumann, as well as a little Hebrew lament for the dead, and ended the service on the resolute notes of Beethoven's "Funeral March."

After what for him had been a taxing service, Davidson spent what he hoped would be a quiet afternoon in the company of the

Duke of Norfolk. But the bishop found himself put out that the placid little duke didn't seem quite up to his responsibilities for the next week of high ceremonial. In fact, Davidson's conversation left him convinced the duke was "curiously ignorant" of even the basics of what had to be done—things that everyone else seemed to be both aware of and worried about. The prelate thought the Earl Marshal might at least have studied the topography of Windsor: the fact that Norfolk didn't know how far it was from Great Western Station in the town to St. George's Chapel in the castle seriously alarmed him. In discussing this particular element of the logistics (for which Davidson had no real responsibility), the bishop interpreted that the procession as Norfolk envisioned it would have the head of the marching unit far past the chapel by the time the coffin was just being taken off the train. Davidson suggested Norfolk alter the route by "going along Park Street and up the hill," a route which would solve this particular problem. He confessed to his diary to be "nonplused" at such denseness.

For his part, Norfolk, the kingdom's most prominent Roman Catholic peer, expressed his own puzzlement at seeing a crucifix atop the late Queen's coffin. Davidson savored confiding to his diary the intelligence that this seemed "new" to the duke, who evidently didn't realize that Lutherans—"and therefore the Prince Consort"—had no "objections" to this symbol of piety and, furthermore, that the Queen "never shared the antipathy of English Protestants to that figure."

Throughout the drama at Osborne, the biggest surprise remained the Kaiser. Today, William would receive his reward from a family that a few days ago unanimously wished he wouldn't even have come to the island. This was William's forty-second birthday, an occasion treated in Germany as a national holiday but here in the bosom of his English family would be more simply marked as a relatively cozy private fete. Having left the Main Wing to spend the remainder of the week aboard the *Hohenzollern*, the yacht anchored in the Cowes road, the Emperor's happiness would be magnified by being able to celebrate with his family on what amounted to a small piece of sovereign, and highly luxurious, German fatherland.

At the late-afternoon party, Bertie gave his nephew what was by far the Kaiser's most prestigious birthday present. Well aware of William's fascination with the minutiae of military rank and the uniforms that went with them, the King conferred on the Kaiser one of the greatest gifts at his command—the baton of a British field marshal. The trophy overwhelmed the speechless William, who already held the equivalent rank in the Royal Navy, thanks to his grandmother's generosity. Some in the family suspected Bertie's generosity was based on ulterior motives, namely the desire not to be outshone in the funeral procession by a nephew outfitted in the unmatchably ostentatious uniform of the Prussian Garde du Corps.

One additional token remained this afternoon for the King to bestow on his nephew. Queen Victoria had herself planned to send her grandson this gift she knew would appeal to William's sense of theater; instead, Uncle Bertie would now do the honors. Having just handed the German caesar the baton of a field marshal, the King reached behind to an aide who passed him a blue leather box. As Bertie opened it, the lights from the crystal chandeliers of the *Hohenzollern* reflected off the facets of a constellation of diamonds set in a specially made Star of the Garter.

## *MONDAY*

❖ 1 ❖

A s ships carrying foreign royalties and dignitaries poured into England's ports for the coming funeral, those huddled at Osborne were watching the weather turn increasingly raw, with pelting rains driven by blasts of frigid wind. Still, between the cloudbursts, a weak sun would come out and glint coppery rays for grateful spells. Workers from all over the island returned to farms and shops and workbenches after a Sabbath marked by church attendance at levels few could remember. On the royal estate, the cast of the national drama dutifully prepared for rites whose ancient grandeur would have been relished by the one person who would be so conspicuously missing.

In place of what was proving to be an intense boredom among

relatives many of whom he barely knew, eighteen-year-old Crown Prince William, Queen Victoria's still very callow great-grandson, was to be inducted this morning into the Order of the Garter. Already worrying his family over the dissoluteness that would become the chief characteristic of a lifetime—few weren't aware that the barely pubescent Crown Prince spent his days chasing hobbleskirted beauties throughout his empire—Willie was about to be accorded the highest British honor the Crown could bestow, an honor due solely to Willie's position rather than to any intrinsic merit on his part. As Heir Apparent to the throne of the German empire, it was in the interest of the new British King and his government to strengthen ties with a Kaiser whose relationship with the United Kingdom had just lost one of its staunchest bonds, and the morning's rites would be aimed solely at these ends.

The ceremony, held in the Main Wing's ornate Council Room, was under the trying circumstances little more than a truncated version of the usually lavish rites by which new knights were normally inducted. There would be no ritualistic calling of the roll, no ceremonial robing of Willie in the mantle of his order. Still, the King insisted the ceremony be performed with as much dignity and pomp as could be mustered in the unavoidably muffled setting. Enough knights were within reach at Osborne to give the occasion the requisite profundity: on hand to bolster the knight-designate were not only the new King, of course, but the Duke of York, the Duke of Connaught and the Kaiser, Prince Christian, the Duke of Cambridge, the Duke of Norfolk and, finally, the most-recently knighted, Lord Roberts. Watching the ceremony was virtually the entire Royal Family and Household, as well as the German entourage that shadowed the fatherland's All-Highest: Generals von Kessel and von Scholl, Surgeon General von Leuthold, Commander von Krumme, embassy representatives Prince Lynar and Baron Eckardstein; even Captain Baudissin, commanding officer of the imperial yacht, received a special invitation from the King. Lining the periphery of the room were the remaining officers from the *Hohenzollern,* their studied informality lending an air of Prussian hauteur. Not wanting his own officers to be outshone by their Teutonic brethren, Bertie directed that every British officer at Osborne attend in full dress uniform. In the center of the assemblage, little Willie himself was outfitted in the splendid uniform of the Prussian Guards.

Arthur and Christian acted as their grandnephew's "supporter" during the ceremony. Davidson—the order's prelate—couldn't, unfortunately, get his official robes sent down to the island in time, so he instead officiated in evening dress, a solecism for the morning ceremony for which Bertie withheld his usual caustic observations at such lapses.

The proceedings got under way when Sir Fleetwood Edwards and Sir Arthur Bigge entered the room, each carrying a velvet cushion, one cradling the Garter, the Ribbon and the George, the other the Star and the Collar. All were expensive and beautifully crafted baubles that together signified the outward dignity of a Garter knight; theoretically, all were on loan, since the order's rules specified they be returned to the sovereign on the recipient's death. With Willie kneeling before the King, Bertie wrapped the Ribbon around the youth's shoulder and waist, after which the sovereign pinned the Star on his grandnephew's left breast. The rest of the raiment was simply handed to the new knight in its presentation cases.

The King followed with a religious homily appropriate to the occasion, one specifically meant to impress on Willie the blessings of friendly Anglo-German relations. Candid as to the provenance of the gift, the King pointed out to the new knight that "it was the wish of my beloved mother the Queen to bestow [the Garter] upon you as a mark of her favour, and I am only carrying out her wishes." Touching on the real objective of the morning's exercise, he added, "I desire to express a hope that my action . . . may yet further cement and strengthen the good feeling which exists between two great countries, and that we may go forward hand in hand with the high object of ensuring peace and promoting the advance of the civilization of the world." There was little doubt that the white man's burden was still something quite tangible to those who were gathered at Osborne.

Davidson, who thought the morning's ceremony was "very well done, and created evidently a marked impression upon the Germans," went on to what he described as a "rather worrying" day. Most worrying to him and the others was the fact that the Duke of York's flu was evidently beginning to acutely weaken the patient. Bertie's doctor, Sir Francis Laking, had taken charge of the thirty-six-year-old prince, and had let the family know that George's condition was showing signs of deteriorating into a more serious illness. No one yet thought a calamity might be in the making, but the situation increased the tension which was already beginning to overtake many.

Later in the afternoon, the senior members of Victoria's staff gathered in the Household Wing, their conversation centering on their futures. Few expected to retain their present positions in the new court, recognizing that the King had naturally grown close to his own people during his long years as Prince of Wales. Ponsonby admitted to his colleagues that he thought his own future uncertain. But Fritz's assistant, Sir Fleetwood Edwards, volunteered that the Duke of York had offered him the assistant comptrollership of his Household, though he turned it down because of his advancing years ("rightly," thought Davidson). Arthur Bigge revealed that he had accepted the secretaryship to the Duke of York, "a shift," Davidson noted that constituted "rather a drop" from his more visible dignity as private secretary to Queen Victoria.

# TUESDAY

## ❖ 1 ❖

The spell of winter sunshine was still blanketing southern England this morning, although freezing air subdued the splendor of the brilliant blue sky. From the Shetlands to the Scillies, the nation remained gloomy, the death of the Queen hitting the typical Briton ever harder with its compelling finality. In the capital, business had returned to something near its normal tumult, despite all resorts of entertainment remaining shuttered "for the duration." Only the anticipation of the great ritual which was scheduled for the week's end managed to buoy a nation's spirits that had plunged to unprecedented depths.

Bertie was feeling stuck at Osborne, his loathing for the place a fact which he did little to disguise. Not scheduled to leave the island until Friday, the King was burdened with the commodity he hated—time on his hands. There were few things he avoided with greater intensity than boredom, and he knew that he should spend this respite from official duties working out some of the many unsettled details of the funeral. Shortly after breakfast, he summoned Davidson to discuss a few hazy features in the printed program for Archbishop Temple's Privy Council service, one of the rituals that would figure in the funeral services. Davidson had to admit to his sovereign that he hadn't a clue as to what the Archbishop of Canterbury envisioned for the ceremony, so the King dispatched inquiries to Lambeth Palace to resolve his questions.

The monarch also told Davidson that he wanted no black bunting in St. George's Chapel on Saturday, Bertie obviously respecting his mother's injunction against it. Instead, he said only the floors would be black, covered with felt. Turning to the matter of the thousands of wreaths that were already pouring into the castle, the King ordered that all be kept as fresh as possible so they could be seen at their best advantage at Saturday's service.

He was pleased to be getting many of the details in hand, but the restless King could only stand so much busywork. Surprising his secretaries and contradicting the statements that had been released to the press, Bertie decided to leave these matters and go up to London this afternoon, his official excuse being to attend a Privy Council scheduled at Marlborough House. Taking along with him the Duke of Cambridge and his son-in-law, Prince Charles of Denmark, he quickly departed Osborne and crossed the Solent on the *Alberta*. When they got to Victoria Station, leaked news of the King's arrival meant that large crowds had already gathered along the route to Marlborough House, surprising the King with the public displays of affection that were attending his every move since the death of his mother.

❖   2   ❖

The titled, the celebrated, the rich and the powerful of the world were beginning to ornament London like a freshly laid tea at the Ritz. Each of the capital's official visitors—along with their lords- and ladies-in-waiting, their secretaries and aides-de-camp and equerries, and their multitudes of servants—had to be accommodated in hotels and palaces and town mansions that were rapidly overflowing with the unaccustomed onslaught. The responsibility for finding room for each of these official suites was split between the Royal Family and the foreign office—European royalty to be put up as family, the others to be treated as state visitors.

There was little problem with the immediate family. The closest of the King's English relatives stayed at their own London residences as they trickled away from Osborne for forays into the capital. George and May were at home at York House, a relatively modest wing of St. James's Palace where the cacophony of central London seeped into the royal couple's windows. Princess Maud and Prince Charles stayed at Marlborough House; without a London residence of their own, the King's daughter and her husband passed their time in the house in which Maud had grown up. Louise and her husband Fife were at their own ducal town palace in Portman Square. A suite of rooms at Buckingham Palace was organized for the Connaughts, their new quarters at Clarence House still housing its old occupant, the Duke of Edinburgh's widow. Of the Petticoats, Lenchen and Christian were at Cumberland Lodge and Louise and Argyll at Kensington Palace; Beatrice and her three Battenberg children had no need to leave Osborne. Leopold's widow and her daughter Alice were quartered at Buckingham Palace. The fusty old Duke of Cambridge was housed at his own town mansion, Gloucester House, in Park Lane. All these family members were accompanied by their own official suites, the Connaughts in the lead with six Household retainers (apart from near-numberless servants, of course) to help them get through the coming ceremonies.

Distant relations were quartered rather more creatively. The late Queen's Continental cousins, the Pawel-Rammingens, were put up in Chapel Street, just off Belgrave Square. Prince and Princess Louis of Battenberg were, appropriate to the prince's position in the navy, housed in the Admiralty. The Edwards of Saxe-Weimar were lent a mansion in Portland Place, the Tecks—the Duchess of York's family—one in Devonshire Place. Various spare rooms were found in St. James's Palace for the late Queen's other German cousins, the Gleichens.

Non-family guests were spread around according to their status. Generally, the royal ones were put in royal venues and the non-royal ones weren't. The little-used bedrooms in Buckingham Palace were aired out for Austria's Archduke Francis Ferdinand, Bavaria's Prince Arnulf, the sex-crazed King Leopold of the Belgians, Count Seckendorff (Vicky's personal representative), Hesse's Prince Frederick Charles, Italy's Duke of Aosta, Portugal's King Carlos, Schaumburg-Lippe's Prince and Princess Adolph, and Sweden's Crown Prince Gustav.

Sharing Marlborough House was a sizable group of Queen Alexandra's Continental relatives: Crown Prince Christian of Denmark, the Greek King George I (Alexandra's brother), the Hereditary Grand Duke Michael of Russia (who was, for the time being, Heir Presumptive to the Tsar). Other temporary royal lodgings included Clarence House, which besides Affie's widow housed the Prince of Hohenzollern and Prince Ferdinand of Rumania, Mecklenburg House with Duke Adolphus Frederick of Mecklenburg-Strelitz (May's cousin), and Cumberland Lodge with Prince Hohenlohe-Langenburg, Duke Ernest Gunther of Schleswig-Holstein and Prince Philip of Saxe-Coburg.

Spread around in less stately quarters were a growing army of minor-royals, not-quite-royals, and definitely-non-royals. Señor Don Florencis of Argentina was at a mansion in Kensington Palace Gardens. The Buckingham Palace Hotel rented out its best suite to Baden's hereditary grand duke. Representing the Prince of Bulgaria, Count de Bourbelon put up at the Carlton. Mr. Tchinn Pomm Yi, at the Cecil, was officially standing in for Korea's Japanese-puppet Emperor; just down the hall was Monsieur Homère Morla representing Ecuador's president. The Egyptian Prince Mohammed Ali Pasha, at the Berkeley, was deputing for his brother, the Khedive.

France checked its delegation into its embassy in Albert Gate; the contingent was headed by the startlingly low-ranking but influential Vice-Admiral Bienaimé, a man the King knew to be well-disposed toward amiable Anglo-French relations. A massive deputation from two German regiments—of which the late Queen had been and the present King was now honorary colonel—all stayed together at the Burlington, in Piccadilly. Colonel Baron von Klench, deputing for the Queen of Hanover and the Duke of

Cumberland, was at the Buckingham Palace Hotel. Baron Tadayu Hayashi, in London in the stead of the Japanese Emperor Meiji, registered at the Grosvenor Gardens; Count d'Assembourg of Luxembourg at Brown's; Count Bally d'Avricourt, representing the Prince of Monaco, at the Grosvenor; the Thakore Sahib of Morvi at Bailey's in South Kensington; and a substantial group from the Netherlands at Brown's Hotel. Room was found for His Serene Highness Prince Henry XXX of Reuss at Chesterfield House, along with the Hereditary Prince of Saxe-Meiningen and Prince John George of Saxony. The Siamese Crown Prince put in at the Buckingham Palace Hotel. Brook House, the residence of the new King's great and good friend and financial adviser, Sir Ernest Cassel, welcomed the Prince of Waldeck and Pyrmont and Duke Robert of Württemberg. President McKinley's representative, the American ambassador Joseph H. Choate, stayed at his own ambassadorial residence in Carlton House Terrace.

Keeping track of these widely dispersed VIPs, whose numbers were being augmented daily, was a job involving not only formidable logistical skills, but heroic social tact. Each thought of himself and his country fully as important as the next, and the Foreign Office's policy was to see to it that all were accorded every honor due rank and their nation, honors which were doled out in strict order of precedence. Every visitor had to be fetched by more or less high-ranking officials and greeters from wherever their ship happened to land, and each had to be met by an entirely new set of greeters when they reached their London rail terminus.

For those who were royal, the King had approved a special Order of Precedence for the duration of the funeral. William headed the list, unsurprisingly, his status as an Emperor *and* a King amplified by his additional status as the eldest grandchild of the deceased. Next, in order, were the three additional kings in attendance: Leopold from Brussels, George from Athens, and Carlos from Lisbon, each of whom was related in one degree or another to either Victoria, or Albert, or both. Following these monarchs came the assorted princes, their relative rank depending on a formula measuring the antiquity of the sovereign they represented, their nearness to the British Royal Family, and whether royal or merely serene.

———

According to the Reuters news agency, Berlin's *Militärwochenblatt* (*"Military Weekly"*) published the following dispatch from Osborne this morning: "The Emperor has appointed King Edward of England chief of the 1st Dragoon Regiment of the Guard, of which the late Queen Victoria was chief." It hadn't taken William long to show his uncle how much he appreciated the honors of the last few days.

# WEDNESDAY

❖ 1 ❖

By the KING

A PROCLAMATION

EDWARD R.

We, considering that it is desirable that Saturday, the second day of February next, should be observed as mentioned in the fourth section of the Statute passed in the thirty-fourth year of Her late Majesty Queen Victoria, chapter seventeen, and as a day of General Mourning throughout the United Kingdom, Do hereby, by and with the advice of our Privy Council, and in pursuance of the provisions of the Act aforesaid, appoint Saturday, the second day of February next, as a special day to be observed in manner provided by the said section, and as a day on which business shall be suspended in terms of the said section. And We do hereby appoint and direct that the said Saturday, the second day of February next, shall be observed as a day of General Mourning throughout the United Kingdom, and every part thereof. And We do by this Our Royal Proclamation command the said day be so observed, and all Our loving subjects to order themselves accordingly.

Given at Our Court at *St. James's*, this thirtieth day of *January*, and in the year of our Lord one thousand nine hundred and one.

GOD save the KING.

---

With most of the arrangements for the funeral in motion, the atmosphere at Osborne had jelled into a dull sameness. The King wouldn't return from London until late this evening. William was now on the *Hohenzollern*, so the stimulation of his undeniably provocative presence was missing from the Pavilion. Even many of the junior members of the family had departed for the mainland to prepare for their parts in the funeral. Davidson spent much of the afternoon walking in the grounds, particularly along the paths that skirted the bluffs above the Solent. The morning's weather remained beautiful into the afternoon, both here on the island and over much of southern England, raising expectations, or at least hopes, that it would continue through the momentous weekend. As the afternoon sun began to give way to dusk, everyone's attention turned to the shimmering lights that outlined the ships in the gathering naval armada, which, in Victoria's honor, was giving the Solent the appearance of a magic river from a book of fairy tales.

❖   2   ❖

In London, where the public just read in their morning papers that the coming Saturday had been proclaimed a national holiday, the excitement of anticipation took on a noticeable upsurge. With visiting delegations progressing through the city's tight streets, the entire metropolis seemed to sense the profundity of the unfolding events. The public's attention remained fixed on Marlborough House; though Buckingham Palace was now Bertie's to do with as he pleased, he still regarded as home the somber mansion that nearly two centuries earlier Sir Christopher Wren had been commissioned by Queen Anne to build for her intimate friend, the first Duchess of Marlborough.

Though Bertie would have grasped at almost any excuse to get away from the shadows at Osborne, the Privy Council remained the ostensible reason for his impulsive journey to London and one to which he was therefore obliged to lend his presence. The meeting was called to settle the rapidly escalating matters of state that

legally required the council's imprimatur. Today's g
the second such session of the Council in the new
several of the Councillors hadn't yet sworn their oath
sovereign, that formality became the first business of the
vows concluded, it took only a quarter of an hour for th
formally approve the matters before the Council, the most significant of which was the proclamation of general mourning that
would be shortly released to the public in the form of a supplement
to the official *London Gazette*.

Before wrapping up his official business, Bertie had one more
task to see to. Protocol demanded that his fellow monarch, Carlos
of Portugal, be welcomed by the King himself. Through their mutual descent from the House of Saxe-Coburg, King Carlos was
Bertie's cousin several times removed, and together with a sizable
party this reform-minded Iberian monarch—who in seven years,
almost to the day, would be murdered by an assassin—had been
invited to stay at Buckingham Palace for the duration.

Together with his brother-in-law Christian, Bertie received the
Portuguese sovereign in an elaborate ceremony at Victoria Station.
The trio rode from the station to the palace through a dense crowd
that lined the entire route and which good-naturedly cheered their
new sovereign and his guest. Probably only a few in the throng were
certain who their king's carriage companion was, but Dom Carlos,
lavishly clad in furs against the chilly air, happily doffed his hat to the
excited onlookers. Three carriages followed the pair of kings, with
the Marquis de Soveral—Lisbon's ambassador in London and one
of Bertie's closest friends—bringing up the rear. As the lead carriage
rumbled through Buckingham Palace's gates, the Royal Standard
glided up the tall flagpole over the great central entrance, the signal
that the sovereign was in residence. Remaining with his Iberian
cousin for only a few minutes to ensure Carlos's comfort, Bertie
quickly departed to begin the gloomy journey back to Osborne.

❖ 3 ❖

In obedience to his instruction from the King, Fritz Ponsonby
had arrived at Windsor this morning to begin his mission of
making sure that the funeral preparations were securely and cor-

.ctly in hand. This consummate courtier would have that consumacy tested in coordinating his authority with that of the Duke of Norfolk, the latter having already shown himself prickly where his prerogatives as Earl Marshal were concerned.

Meeting with Windsor's mayor and police chief, Fritz passed a few pleasantries before getting to the first decision that would have to be made. It concerned the funeral procession's route through Windsor. After weighing the options, the two men decided that instead of the line of march proceeding straight from the station to the Castle—a matter of only a couple of hundred yards—the elaborate procession would advance through the heart of the town, up the High Street and into Park Street, ultimately turning into the Castle via the Long Walk, the magnificent ceremonial riding path that led directly into the heart of the Upper Ward. Ponsonby reasoned that the greatest number of people would be able to see the procession using this route, a factor he knew would be important to the King. No final figures were yet available as to the numbers of people in the procession, so Fritz was, for the moment, forced to leave the final logistics to be decided later.

Ponsonby hurried back to Osborne after the meeting at Windsor. There he was told that the Earl Marshal was apparently preoccupied with the "London part" of the funeral to the exclusion of all else, meaning that important questions regarding the arrangements for the events at Windsor were being left dangling. Considering the significance of the events that would in seventy-two hours overtake the historical seat of the British monarchy, Ponsonby realized the urgency of getting the concluding part of the day's activities quickly nailed down. He decided to get up to London first thing in the morning and force as many decisions as possible from Norfolk.

Meanwhile, more members of Victoria's family were packing up to leave Osborne, all anxious to get back to the mainland to finish their own preparations for Saturday's rites. What had started out as a trickle of departures earlier in the week had by this afternoon become a flood. Yet one prince who couldn't leave the island was the Duke of York, George's German measles having taken a sufficiently serious turn to keep Dr. Laking almost constantly at the Prince's bedside. The horrifying notion was running through many minds that if the King's son were to succumb, the monarch's new heir would be a six-year-old boy. Though George was a central figure in the monarchy and would be missed at his grandmother's funeral, the decision was made to keep him at Osborne rather than risk aggravating his condition, as well as putting other members of the family and court at risk to a disease that represented a potentially lethal threat. George remained in his Pavilion bedroom, getting little sleep and less relief from his symptoms, his chief occupation watching the gathering fleet in the Solent, an armada that he knew would in two days' time salute his grandmother on her last journey across that familiar body of water.

Bertie finally arrived back at the estate in the late afternoon, and immediately asked Davidson to arrange a small service in the mansion's chapel. A group of choristers had earlier in the day arrived on the island from St. George's Chapel, providing for the family a musical accompaniment Davidson later described as "most beautiful."

The evening ended with the kind of minor contretemps that was beginning to unravel Osborne's tranquillity, one which Davidson had to invoke his not-inconsiderable moral authority to have his way about. The issue involved the late Queen's daughters and a Russian hymn. The princesses told the bishop that they wished this particular piece to be sung at Saturday's funeral because their mother had "liked it," and had, in fact, often requested it herself at family funerals. Immediately sensing a theological snag, Davidson discreetly explained to the sisters that allowing the performance of this particular hymn—"Give Rest, O Christ, to Thy Servants"—would "contravene" the wishes of the Established Church, a church of which Victoria had been and Edward was now "defender." The princesses remained unswayed. Taking the matter to the King for a decision, Davidson patiently explained to the monarch that the offending selection was, as "we bishops had more than once pointed out, unauthorized" for public services—as though it should be obvious to the sovereign. And, he reasoned, because the funeral at Windsor would be the greatest of public services, the use of a non-conforming hymn might put the brand-new monarch in the unwanted position of taking sides in a clerical controversy.

Though the sensible Bertie probably thought the matter an

absurd waste of his own energies, he still didn't wish to needlessly risk incurring the displeasure of the church he now headed. Angry sisters or no, the King felt he had to side with his bishop, diplomatically telling Davidson that "I see, what you want to protect is the Nonconformist conscience"—though how forgoing a non-conforming hymn would protect the non-conforming conscience isn't clear. At any event, the tactful prelate responded to his sovereign that "you might put it so without being far wrong." Davidson characterized the whole thing as, in his unique High Church mentality, a "near shave."

# THURSDAY

❖ 1 ❖

First thing on his arrival in London, Fritz Ponsonby caught a hansom cab directly for the Earl Marshal's office. Anxious to resolve the precise dimensions of his own responsibilities for the supervision of the funeral, the courtier decided to confront Norfolk and get every detail spelled out. Expecting to find some degree of efficiency at the duke's headquarters, instead and to his shock Ponsonby found "absolute chaos." The first officials Ponsonby encountered were the heralds, whom the courtier began to interrogate about the details that obviously hadn't been settled on and which he was determined to get nailed down. Ponsonby's quarry was apparently ready for him, though. Using the excuse that as there had been no funeral for a sovereign in almost sixty-four years, these experts in official ceremonial—the Earl Marshal's official assistants—claimed that the confusion they were doing their best to deal with couldn't be avoided. Furthermore, they reminded the plainly irritated Fritz that they were accustomed to working on the arcanities of genealogical tables and coats of arms, and that the crises caused by the Queen's death had "swept them off their feet."

When Ponsonby asked whether the official program for the Windsor service had been established, he was told Norfolk hadn't even gotten around to settling the Osborne and London segments yet. Inquiring with some barely concealed derision as to whether they were aware that "the funeral starts from Osborne tomorrow," the soft-spoken but resolute courtier met with little more than stony silence. Afraid that what he saw as an approaching disaster would be blamed on him—as far as the King was concerned, Ponsonby was expected to make sure Norfolk was doing his job—he demanded to see the duke himself.

The meeting with Norfolk at least convinced Ponsonby that the little peer's heart was in the right place, even if everything else seemed dangerously askew. In his encounter with Norfolk, whom Ponsonby generously judged "thoroughly businesslike and capable," he quickly saw the crux of the problem. Despite Norfolk's attempts at sensible orders, the subordinates who should have carried them out—the heralds and *their* assistants—hadn't done so. Norfolk went on to complain that the Lord Chamberlain had continuously and confusingly altered the roster of royal and official visitors, each of whose names had to be included in the programs, making it impossible to get a finished draft to the printers. Norfolk told Fritz that the one thing that the courtier should do immediately would be to see Lord Roberts, and in unison with the commander-in-chief (who bore ultimate responsibility for the funeral's military participants), make out a final ceremonial plan. That taken care of, the Earl Marshal ventured that everything else would likely fall into its proper place in short order.

Agreeing with the sense in Norfolk's suggestion, Fritz quickly left for the War Office, in Whitehall. To his chagrin, on reaching Roberts's rooms underlings responded that the field marshal could see no one at the moment, the subordinates giving the clear impression that the commander-in-chief was too busy to be disturbed—even by the King's envoy. Scratching out a message on a piece of notepaper that said, "Funeral arrangements—urgent" and signing his name, he managed to get the note sent into Roberts's office. It worked, and Ponsonby quickly found himself being ushered into Roberts's presence. The plainly harried field marshal listened to Fritz's description of the meeting with Norfolk, and then replied—perplexingly—that he had nothing to do with the funeral itself. But, he added, if Ponsonby wanted to give specific orders for the troops' participation on Saturday—now only two days off—he could invoke the commander-in-chief's express permission to do so, giving Roberts's precise words as authority to anyone who stood in the way.

With this newfound leverage in hand, Ponsonby hurried back to the Earl Marshal's office. There he got himself a shorthand stenographer—who, depressingly, told him this was the first time he had been employed at this occupation—and the two started to list the things that had to be done. Categorizing everything— "English Royal Family," "Foreign Sovereigns," "Representatives of Foreign Countries"—Fritz began to work out a detailed groundplan. But when he tried to resolve the specifics for the steps that had to be carried out, he encountered the same problem of which Norfolk had complained. Over the afternoon, the requirements pouring into Norfolk's office kept changing, in some cases by the hour: orders from Osborne, the military arrangements, requirements for the visiting suites. Working against snowballing chaos, Fritz still managed to get a number of matters settled, and late in the afternoon took his efforts to get the duke's approval.

First, however, Norfolk informed the courtier that his heralds had been quite put out with his "rudeness," considering Fritz's earlier hostility as a slur on their competence. The King's agent apologetically but firmly pointed out that had he not come to London to see what was going on, the upcoming rites might still be in a hopeless muddle, especially those matters dealing with the masses of soldiers and sailors whose presence was meant to honor the dead sovereign. Norfolk wanted to know from whom the military participants were to receive their orders. Ponsonby evenly replied that Roberts had given him *carte blanche* to handle such matters precisely as he saw fit. On that, Fritz took leave of Norfolk, ordered his shorthand assistant to get everything typed up, took the plans to the War Office and the Admiralty to make sure the orders were unmistakably understood, and, finally, left to return to Osborne. He got back to the estate at 2:00 A.M., dead tired but satisfied the journey had been a success.

❖ 2 ❖

Today's *Court Circular* contained two pieces of information whose release proved popular with a public that hungered for almost any scrap of information about what was going on at the late Queen's estate. First, and of most immediate interest, the royal doctors expressed their belief that the new King's heir had passed the crisis in his illness. The official announcement stated that "His Royal Highness the Duke of Cornwall and York . . . passed a very restless day yesterday, but after a refreshing sleep during the night his condition continued to improve." Much of the public did, however, remain saddened that Prince George wouldn't be participating in the funeral rites.

Of intense popular concern was the question of how much longer the Kaiser planned to remain in England. The press had made clear that the German government was most anxious that William return to Germany as soon as possible, his ministers in Berlin voicing increasing scorn that their master had come to his grandmother's deathbed in the first place. Happy with the English limelight in which he was basking, William allowed it to be officially announced that he intended to remain with his mother's family until after Monday's burial service at Frogmore. How, many Britons reasoned, could a man who would display such tender sentiment to the memory of the late Queen possibly pose a danger to their own kingdom?

❖ 3 ❖

At Windsor, with only one full day to go before the town would become the focus of the world's eyes, funeral planning had been going on all day at meteoric speed. Reggie Esher in particular felt as though he were in the middle of a tempest. One of the issues still causing the courtier confusion dealt with his own dress, specifically the touchy issue of decorations—touchy to the King, at least. Well aware of the monarch's attitudes on the correct wearing of orders and decorations, Esher sent a note to the Private Secretary asking whether he should wear the star of his order at the funeral. The forty-year-old viscount was relieved when a note came back saying "My dear Esher—The King says you may certainly wear your order—Yours ever—J. J. Edwards."

Aside from this sort of detail that saturated every level of official court life, there were plenty of serious things to worry about. Esher had ordered Mr. Nutt, the man who had so fortuitously uncovered the Queen's long-hidden sarcophagal statue, to take charge of getting temporary bleacher-style seating rigged up in front of St. George's. After he got the structure assembled, Nutt began to realize that if this hastily built erection were to keel over, it would take an appalling number of dignitaries along with it. Devising a little experiment to test his work, Nutt borrowed a sizable contingent of busby-topped Guardsmen, soldiers who happened to be practicing their drills in the castle courtyard, and had them march up and down on his temporary seating. The men were ordered to seat themselves, and then, on Nutt's order, to rise simultaneously and start jumping up and down with as much force as they could muster. The whole thing stood, without even a flutter, the risk to the King's soldiers adjudged a low price to pay for the peace of mind it brought.

Outside the castle walls, the town, too, was being transformed. All over Windsor, but particularly along the line of march, Victorian mourning preparations were changing the very look of the ancient streets. Purple hangings floated from every shop and every window, with even more of the bunting waving from newly erected flagpoles. Great banks of tulips and hyacinths and cyclamens, primulas and narcissuses from the flower market lent the sole patch of color to the otherwise somber streets.

In both Windsor and London, a high proportion of the windows that looked over the procession route had been rented to well-heeled spectators. In Windsor, though, the prices were cheap compared to what was being demanded for such vantage points in the capital. The big shops in London's Buckingham Palace Road had closed by Thursday so they could replace displays from their windows with that temporary seating that they knew they could rent for a premium, any kind of seating along the procession route in both cities being highly prized. In the quadrangle in front of St. James's Palace, two banks of grandstands had been reserved, one for court officials, the other for the diplomatic corps, and in Piccadilly the clubs were making special reservations for the accommodation of members, with some of the places going for upward of £150. One of the few "affordable" banks of temporary seating had been set up in Buckingham Palace Road, a seat with a fairly good view of the procession there fetching six or seven pounds, a sum that still represented in 1901 enough to provide a working-class family with food for six months.

Activities were in full swing at Portsmouth, too, where the royal yacht *Alberta* was being prepared for the unique role it would play tomorrow. This the smallest of the family yachts had been chosen to carry the Queen's body from the Isle of Wight to the mainland, and workmen were busy transforming it into a properly majestic conveyance for its short but august mission. The firm of Messrs. S. J. Waring and Sons was this afternoon putting the finishing touches to a deck pavilion for the yacht, one specially designed to shield the royal coffin from whatever elements it might meet on its crossing. Inside the pavilion a plinth had been built, over which hung a covering of red cloth. From the structure's ridge the workers draped a canopy of imperial-ruby velvet lined with white silk, with draperies of the same materials arranged at the four corners, the whole affair meant to echo, for an unfathomable reason, the look of the fifteenth century. At one end of the pavilion, pyramidal hangings framed a red-velvet cushion that would support a royal crown. The design had been approved by the King, who thought the "simple" effect seen in the artist's sketch preserved the essential dignity of the occasion.

Late in the evening, Davidson got into another of his ecclesiastical disputes. It had to do with singing again—or, more precisely, a *singer*. Following another of the interminable bier-side services in the Dining Room, the Reverend Sir Walter Parratt casually informed Davidson that, at the King's special invitation, the world-famous soprano Emma Albani was going to sing at the Sunday service in St. George's. Even though the selections that Parratt said Mme. Albani would perform were indisputably *hymns* and not something from Mr. Puccini, Davidson immediately concluded that such a program would be "most unfortunate." The bishop argued that it would not only be the first Sabbath on which an "outside, professional singer" would be performing in that hallowed place, but that the performer was a Roman Catholic.

After Davidson informed Parratt of the impossibility of such an exception to ecclesiastical propriety, even one at the behest of the King, the two men immediately set out to find their sovereign. When the pair of clerics were shown into the monarch's study, Davidson quickly began to set out the difficulties inherent in Mme. Albani's planned appearance. Bertie admitted he had indeed made the promise, Mme. Albani being, after all, his friend, and he wished to honor her with this invitation. The King said the whole thing amounted to little other than an unfortunate misunderstanding; nevertheless, the performance was being eagerly looked forward to by the soprano. Davidson diplomatically suggested that instead of allowing a lamentable precedent to be set, that the lady might instead be permitted to perform her hymns at a special, private *family* service later in the afternoon; he even thought Mme. Albani might consider this arrangement the greater honor—and St. George's would, happily, be spared the "innovation." After what the prelate confided to his diary as "some demur," Bertie agreed.

# *Friday,*
# *February 1*

The Solent looked this morning like a sheet of mercury glass. For the Queen's last crossing of this historic strait, Heaven had sent her the gentlest avenue in its power to bestow.

Bishop Davidson had arisen earlier than usual, knowing the day would be momentous and his part in its enterprise a central one. After getting his wife off on the morning mail packet for Portsmouth (from where she would go on directly to Windsor), the prelate left for the last time his rooms at Kent House, and walked up to the Pavilion. Following a rushed breakfast, he had a quick conference with the King, Bertie anxious to be sure that everything would be carried off with the punctilio for which his mother's reign had been distinguished. The monarch gave Davidson a few last instructions, queried him on an outstanding detail or two, and finally himself went upstairs to get ready to play his own role as chief mourner.

At half past noon—only an hour before the procession bearing the Queen's body from Osborne was to begin—Davidson entered the *chapelle ardente* to look over the arrangements for which he had in such large measure been responsible. He observed the crown and scepter and orbs all waiting to be solemnly carried along with the coffin, and he reflected on the quartet of soldiers at the bier's corners, knowing they were standing their last watch over the dead sovereign. Davidson took a few private moments to contemplate what the woman at the center of this drama had meant for so long, for so many peoples, for so great a part of the world. He would later remember these minutes as the "most solemn" time he had passed since being called to the sick Queen's side almost two weeks earlier.

The time inevitably came when Victoria was to be carried into the public light and the bosom of her subjects. The privacy for which she had fought, for which she had indeed risked her throne, would be given up for this last solemn and triumphal procession through her capital, on to Windsor, and to the claiming of her place beside her husband. At a little after one o'clock, a group of soldier-pallbearers marched into the Dining Room. There, on a softly spoken order, they lifted the coffin off its plinth, then smoothly lowered it to waist height by grasping its gilt handles, and carried it into the mansion's hallway, at the foot of the massive Queen's Staircase, opposite the majestic double-doors of the principal entrance. There, the waiting family tightly gathered around, and Davidson reading "*Nunc dimittis*"—"Prevent Us"—a lesson from the gospel of St. John.

With the prayers at Osborne concluded, the great doors slowly opened, and Victoria was borne out of her house by bluejackets from the royal yachts, with a party of Highlanders holding up the pall. From a second floor window, the new heir to the throne—still weakened from his measles—watched as his grandmother's coffin was carried out of her beloved Osborne and toward the path down to the estate's gates.

The day was described by the *Times* as though it "might have been out of Paradise." Under a blue and cloudless sky, with a gentle southeasterly barely rippling the Royal Standard that hung at half-mast from the Pavilion's flag tower, Victoria was placed on a gun carriage. Eight horses of the Royal Horse Artillery drew the burden slowly toward the gates. On the coffin rested the Imperial State Crown, replacing the smaller crown that had been used this past week in the *chapelle ardente.* Bands of island schoolchildren stood in privileged positions on the manicured drive, their numbers increased by warrant holders and local dignitaries whom the King had specially invited. Following the gun carriage on foot was the entire family, in the lead Bertie and William and Arthur and, slightly behind, the rest of the princes; all were dressed in military or naval uniform but bareheaded. Then followed the new Queen —walking with her well-known "Alexandra Glide"—together with the princesses, all of whom were draped from head to foot in flowing black crepe. Of all the family, it was William's face that seemed to stand out—tanned to an almost olive color, the weird mustache with its sharply upturned tips, his eyes hinting at a mental strain and betraying the sorrow he was feeling.

Lining the drive stood Grenadier Guards at attention, all in enormous black bearskin helmets, their numbers forming a sinuous avenue of scarlet. Facing inward, each man carried reversed arms, muzzles resting on their feet and their heads slightly bowed over the butts of the rifles. The pipers of the Black Watch skirled the ancient Highland dirge "The Flowers of the Forest." The procession passed first under the ilexes, trees the Queen herself had planted—their boughs almost joined above the winding avenue— and then under a giant holm oak that had been planted by Princess Alice fifty-three years earlier. This latter tree was thriving and in full vigor, a sad reminder to the family of a daughter and sister and mother now so long dead. At the gate, the pipers peeled away, and as Victoria passed through these portals, massed bands took their place, the melodies of the Highlands changing to the dirges of Chopin and Beethoven.

All the way down York Avenue—an ordinary, villa-lined street that led in a sharp descent from the Queen's Gate into the town —the raised and inwardly sloping sidewalks provided a perfect vantage for spectators, who congealed the entire route. In the more pretentious villas, at the top of the avenue, many little grandstands had been set up for the occupants and their guests, while outside the modest houses further down the hill the landscape was black with people standing shoulder to shoulder. With the passing of the gun carriage at the center of the procession, every hat was doffed, every feminine knee bent in a curtsy. Such was the stillness that when one ill-mannered sightseer called out loudly to a friend, all eyes turned on the transgressor in a scorching look of indignation.

The funeral procession reached its first goal, with the unremarkable and unmistakably provincial streets of East Cowes and the Trinity Pier opposite the town post office. Filling the little square was a phalanx of sailors from the royal yachts, ready to take the dead sovereign's body from the Royal Horse Artillery into the custody of the Senior Service. The band quit its funeral march, and only the dull roll of forty muffled drums continued as a party of eight bluejackets removed the coffin from its gun carriage and bore it to the waiting bier on board the *Alberta*. Princess May turned back, looking toward Osborne, as if to seek the support of her sick husband. With the rest of the family embarking in pinnaces to board the *Victoria and Albert*—because of its deeper draft it lay out in the roads with the *Osborne*—a tiny party of privileged royal aides went with their dead mistress to the *Alberta*: her ladies the Countess of Lytton and the Honorable Harriet Phipps, Sir John McNeill, V.C., two admirals—Sir Michael Culme-Seymour and Sir John Fullerton—and four naval aides-de-camp.

The Royal Standard suddenly fluttered out atop the *Alberta*'s masthead, and then immediately dropped to half-staff, the little black vessel creeping away from the dock all the while and passing into the roads. Alongside, the *Victoria and Albert*, the *Osborne*, the hulking mass of the *Hohenzollern*, and the Trinity House and Admiralty yachts—the *Siren* and the *Enchantress*—moved in behind in a single line. Eight low, black torpedo-destroyers led the royal flotilla, in pairs, out into the glassy-surfaced Solent. What followed was one of the most splendid and spectacular scenes in British history.

Waiting to salute this caravan was the lustiest fleet in the world, one that strung out in an eight-mile-long allée of floating steel. Battleships and cruisers of the line lay upon the waters as far as the eye could see. From the guardship *Australia* at the mouth of the Medina River, through the *Camperdown* and the *Majestic*, the *Hood* and the *Trafalgar*, the *Nile* and the *Benbow*, the *Resolution* and the *Edinburgh*, all the way to Portsmouth harbor rode these behemoths on the watery highway. At six knots speed, the *Alberta* steamed like little more than a toy between the ships that formed the emblem and instruments of Victoria's empire. As she passed, each vessel's guns fired a salute, every sailor, hand in hand with his mates, lined up alongside the decks.

Joining the British vessels was a throng of foreign warships, the four gray-masted ironclads flying the red, black and white German ensign overshadowing almost all the others; standing near them were the sharp-prowed *Dupuy de Lome* representing France, the Japanese battleship *Hatsuse*—the heaviest ship present—just beyond the tricolor of the *Dupuy*, and the *Dom Carlos I* of Britain's ancient Portuguese ally. Even Monaco was represented by its Prince's personal vessel. From Spain came word earlier that morning that the *Emperador Carlos V*, its engines crippled, had abandoned its trip to England. To the mortification of the Americans present, no vessel stood for the eldest and biggest of Britain's progeny; the American navy had no ship within ten days' sail of England when the Queen died. The one great commercial liner present, the *Campania*, carried the members of the two houses of Britain's Parliament. The ironclads, moored two and a half cables apart from each other, settled back a bit in the water as their powerful guns fired salutes, spitting billows of black smoke that rose straight heavenward in the almost eerily still air; only the tiniest breeze blew across the line of ships, taking long moments to disperse the dark clouds and keep them from obscuring the scene.

As the procession approached the embrace of Portsmouth harbor, the sun was beginning to sink behind it, turning the sea a molten gold and raising to high relief every detail of the *Alberta* for the thousands of spectators who lined the shore. It was, of course, the coffin lying athwartship that captured every eye, the Imperial State Crown and a huge wreath of white laurel from the Kaiser plainly visible, a single officer standing at attention in front. On the *Victoria and Albert*, behind the tiny *Alberta*, the King stood out from the rest of the party, his apartness an augury of every day of the remainder of his life. As the sun sank ever deeper into the west, it broke into a still brighter and more golden blaze of light, eventually backlighting the two towers of Osborne House some eight miles from Portsmouth harbor. A dim moon, almost full, stood in the not-yet-dark sky, and from far off the bands of one of the dreadnoughts set the air atremble with the deepening notes of a funeral march.

Aboard the *Victoria and Albert*, Bishop Davidson stared in astonishment at the Hampshire shoreline. Southsea Common, the park at the entrance of Portsmouth harbor, was packed with tens of thousands of spectators, as was indeed the whole line of beaches from Stokes Bay to Fort Cumberland. The excursion trains had brought thirty thousand people into the town, and as the shops were closed for the entire day, all spent much of their time on the esplanades skirting the city to see the royal flotilla arrive. While the little convoy entered the harbor, the Sea Lords, who had arrived the previous night on the Admiralty yacht *Enchantress*, issued a few last-minute orders to ensure that all was in readiness for the overnight stay of the royal visitors.

With the *Alberta* docking at the specially prepared Clarence Victualling Yard, the King remained aboard the *Victoria and Albert*, his vessel's lights now ablaze in the lowering mists. He was spending the evening greeting the senior officers of the great fleet that had just bade his mother a sublime farewell. When he had seen the last of the officers off, he hosted yet another gathering on board his yacht. The second group was considerably more humble, and included the workmen and carpenters who had built the *chapelle ardente* and had fitted up the catafalque on the *Alberta*, together with the petty officers from the royal yachts who had acted as the actual pallbearers moving Victoria's coffin from the island to Portsmouth. Paraded in front of the royal presence outside the yacht's main saloon, the three dozen or so men were told by their King that they had been employed in a "very grave and solemn duty," one which they had "admirably performed." The late Queen, he said, had some years earlier instituted the Victorian medal for just such service, and he then proceeded to confer the honor on each of them. He explained the accolade was not for his own sake, but was given in the name of Her late Majesty. Each man took the gift from King Edward's own hand.

The Household, on board the *Osborne*, were attending to less splendid duties than those occupying their King. Together with his fellow courtiers, Ponsonby was filled with concern for whatever challenges might come with the morning light. He had just returned from the *Victoria and Albert*, the King having briefly discussed with him the details of Monday's service at Frogmore. Fritz wrote of the evening: "There I was at Portsmouth on board the *Osborne* with nothing to refer to, no precedent to go by, and no idea who would attend this last ceremony. . . . I felt there was every possibility of the Windsor part being a fiasco." With the better part of European royalty present, he knew the most seemingly insignificant slipup, in precedence or priority, could mortally offend not only any of those who had come to England to honor the Queen, but the King himself. That was an outcome the courtier was most anxious to avoid.

The night remained fine and clear, the moon almost full. Victoria, lying peacefully on the now fully darkened *Alberta*, was left alone at the Clarence Yard dock, with only a detachment of Royal Marines guarding the approaches to the yacht. The temperature was dropping rapidly, giving rise to fears that the "Queen's weather" might not last through tomorrow's ceremonies.

# Saturday, February 2, and Sunday, February 3

## *SATURDAY*

### ❖ 1 ❖

The fears were borne out, as snow this morning had indeed begun to dust the hard frost that had blanketed Portsmouth overnight. Soon the watery flakes turned to a biting sleet, the sleet then degenerating into torrents of wind-driven rain whose violence increased by the hour. Rocked by pounding waves, the royal yachts pitched hard against their tethers. At Clarence Victualling Yard, a hundred bluejackets from the *Excellent* together with two hundred Marines from Forton Barracks began to form on the docks around the *Alberta*, preparing to remove Victoria's coffin to the royal train awaiting it in the nearby station.

Bertie had long since arisen on the *Victoria and Alberta*, facing a formidable day of rites he feared would be emotionally as well as physically draining. Protocol required that he wear the tightly unpliant uniform of a field marshal throughout the day, his bulk ill-suited to the demands this stiff costume imposed on him. Ready to take leave of his cabin, he placed atop his head the traditional cocked hat of the British military officer, his full-dress model accommodating a pride of white ostrich feathers erupting from the crown and spilling over the brim.

Accompanied by his brother Arthur, Bertie was taken on his pinnace alongside the *Alberta*. The small yacht, with its cluster of admirals on deck, was already lying low in the water. Doffing his hat, he saluted his mother's coffin, and waited while William came aboard from the *Hohenzollern*. Soon the Queen and the assorted princesses joined the men, and the Reverend Mr. Land, vicar of Portsea, presided over a brief prayer service. Throughout, the guns of the *Victory* and the *St. George* fired every minute, a salute that lasted until the coffin and the Royal Family had taken leave of the *Alberta* and boarded the royal train. During the transfer of the Queen's coffin from yacht to train, the wind had already risen to a half gale, with icy cold rain falling in slashing torrents. To the dismay of the women mourners, the umbrellas held over their heads quickly proved utterly insufficient to keep their voluminous black crepe skirts from becoming saturated.

With everyone finally having gotten aboard, the London and South Western train pulled out of the Portsmouth's Gosport Station a few minutes before nine o'clock. Steaming only a few miles to the northwest, it entered the small station at Fareham, where the entire party, coffin and all, was transferred onto a London, Brighton and South Coast train to complete the journey into London. It had been the King's idea to make the transfer, rather than completing the journey directly on the London and South Western line; Bertie thought the Brighton company's new royal train was "more in keeping with the times" than its rival. Had his mother been aware of his choice, she would most likely have been miffed. The late Queen thought the Brighton line vulgar, what with the mobs of overly enthusiastic excursionists it hauled to the coastal waters, not to mention her distaste for the seaside resort for which the line was named and where her uncle George IV had disgraced both himself and the monarchy.

Halfway up to London, there was a feeling of relief when the train passed out of the near-blizzard conditions of the south coast to enter clear skies, with the remainder of the trip passed once again in the vaunted "Queen's weather" by which Victoria's reign would be put to a close. As the train steamed past dozens of tiny stations between the south coast and London, the passengers peered out on platforms thronged with tens of thousands of people who had come to pay their last respects to the Queen. Many of those craning for a glimpse of the catafalque were able to see that the saloon in which the coffin was placed had been transformed, its interior fittings removed and the stark carriage lined with white cloth crossed by purple bands ringing the interior walls.

After the train had pulled out of Fareham a few minutes late, the punctilious King sent a message to the driver asking if he could make up the lost time. The engineer obligingly fired up his boilers, allowing the engine to get up to eighty miles per hour on some stretches. The result was that it arrived at Victoria two minutes early, a state of affairs that surprised and slightly discomfited Bertie, who liked royal arrivals to be carried out precisely on schedule. William thought the early arrival "capital," though, and through his equerry sent his imperial congratulations to driver Cooper and fireman Way. He magnanimously muttered to anyone listening about the superiority of the English engines over the ones he had at home.

For the dead Queen's last journey through her capital, the Earl Marshal's office had charted a route that would connect two of the metropolis's great railway terminals—Victoria, named for the sovereign and where her body would arrive from Portsmouth, and Paddington, where it would be transferred to another train for the journey on to Windsor. Victoria Station, the massive structure that acted as London's gateway to the south and the Channel coast, had been expensively glamorized for the day's ceremonies. From what was a vast shed that daily saw wriggling queues of travelers jostling amid the din of incoming and outgoing trains, the management had contrived to hide virtually every sign of its normal commercial life. The colorful hoardings that papered every available wall had all been taken down lest anything vulgar offend the occasion. The platform against which the funeral train would stop was hung from one end to the other with acres of swagged purple cloth. Directly opposite the point at which the coffin would be detrained, carpenters had erected a splendid little impromptu pavilion, covered with cream-colored drapery and hung with laurel leaves; its purpose was to shelter any members of the Royal Family who wished a few moments away from inquiring eyes, although the general public had been rigidly excluded from the entire station. Lined up in readiness on the arrival platform was a bearer party of sixteen non-commissioned officers from the Household regiments, each a specially chosen exemplar of British armed manhood.

At about ten o'clock, the mighty of the kingdom began to arrive along with the representatives of foreign governments. At the head of the official mourners, Field Marshal Lord Roberts entered astride a spirited brown mare, an equally lavishly mounted staff following the commander-in-chief. The King of the Belgians, the Grand Duke Michael of Russia, the King of the Hellenes and, representing the tenuous glories of the Austro-Hungarian conglomeration, the Archduke Francis Ferdinand, entered close behind in varying degrees of over-ornamented gorgeousness.

Just as the pilot engine—a machine running a few hundred yards ahead of the royal train that was meant to ensure a clear track—entered the station, the signal was given for the burnished gun-carriage to be brought up next to the platform, each of the eight great creams that pulled it being led by a royal groom. A murmur of general approbation passed through the ranks of the assembled reporters at the laudable behavior of the high-mettled beasts.

At the height of the gathering anticipation, the train itself appeared in the light at the south end of the vast train shed, the glint on the golden crown mounted on top the smokebox door visible to those waiting at the far end of the depot. Gliding virtually noiselessly into the station, it rolled to a smooth stop, the carriage bearing the King stopping precisely opposite the elegant little pavilion. As the Royal Family clambered out of their carriage, Alexandra and the rest of the ladies immediately ducked into the pavilion, leaving Bertie and the men waiting outside on the platform. The bearer party quickly assembled into a compact party and advanced toward the carriage with the Queen's coffin. Four aides-de-camp first entered the car to remove the white satin pall covering the coffin, taking the Imperial State Crown, the two scepters, and the orb with them. The bearers then entered and carefully lifted the now-denuded coffin, carrying it to the gun carriage waiting just outside the car's double doors. Throughout the entire procedure, Bertie stood stiff as a sword, his right arm raised in salute to his mother. The bearers quickly attached the straps and secured the coffin to the vehicle, so rehearsed at their task that none showed the least hurry or confusion. Barely a sound broke the cavernous hall's silence—even the engine having been brought to a complete hush—only a fretting and pawing of some of the horses occasionally breaking the stillness.

At a signal from one of the mounted hussars, the family was alerted that it was time to start their procession through the streets of London. Bertie, William and Arthur mounted bay chargers, the remainder of the princes of the royal families ascending their own mounts. Lord Roberts took again to his brown mare to lead the procession from a position forward of the coffin-bearing gun carriage. With the King and his kinsmen at its foot, followed by six closed coaches filled with the royal women—all of them indistinguishable under their flowing weeds—the procession took leave of the confines of Victoria Station.

Every foot of pavement along the route to Paddington was jammed with spectators, the mass of them quiet to an almost eerie degree. The only sounds came from thirty-two thousand slow-marching infantrymen who had fallen in behind the lead mourners, the hoof-clatter of their mounted leaders' horses resonating with a crystalline clarity along the route. The marching soldiers were filled with pride at just this morning having been told of a message from King Edward to Lord Roberts informing him that "one of the Queen's last inquiries was after yourself and the gallant army under your command." Passing by St. James's Palace and Piccadilly and Buckingham Palace, additional masses of stationary soldiery saluted their dead Queen, their new King, and their passing comrades-at-arms.

The branches of the trees in the royal parks along the procession route were heavy with spectators agile enough to have clambered onto them; many threatened to break, dropping their load onto the throngs underneath. So great were the crowds pressing in from every street along the route that the police began to fear that spectators might be crushed; in St. James's Square, the hordes spilling in from the tributary streets actually looked near to getting out of hand. At thirty-six stations over the three-mile route between Victoria and Paddington, the 701 doctors and nurses of the St. John Ambulance Brigade would this day treat more than

1,300 people, some injured but most having merely fainted in the crush. A few found a holiday atmosphere in the crowd. The novelist Arnold Bennett caustically wrote that "the people were not, on the whole, deeply moved, whatever the journalists may say, but rather serene and cheerful." Max Beerbohm was even more candid in his own assessment: "I have never seen such an air of universal jollity," and added trenchantly that "it is a city of ghouls." The afternoon newspapers noted that this was the first time in memory such a public procession had passed without the familiar voice of souvenir hawkers. They also noted something else: liberally sprinkled along the route stood conspicuous clusters of what one reporter called "foreign-looking" men. Word had spread through the crowds that these were representatives of the German secret police who had been sent to "protect" the Kaiser.

Among the myriad details that had confronted the metropolitan authorities was the feeding of the masses of soldiery that had descended on London for the day's ritual. Rather than setting up field kitchens, the War Office contracted with Messrs. R. Dickeson and Company to erect around the city some twenty-eight outdoor mess sites to serve the thirty-three thousand soldiers and sailors taking part in the funeral. Dickeson's served fifty tons of food, including a breakfast of sandwiches and tea and a dinner of meat pies, rolls, butter and cheese, along with a pint of beer or ginger beer. The *Times* duly reported that this represented the largest military contract supplied in so short a time in anyone's memory.

Around the caisson-borne coffin, four dismounted bands alternately played the funeral marches of Chopin and Beethoven, the latter slightly more upbeat. Forming a tight gauntlet around the coffin were many of the more resplendent and esoteric officers of the kingdom: the Earl Marshal accompanied by three Gold Sticks and two White Staves, the Vice-Chamberlain, the Comptroller of the Household and the Treasurer of the Household, the Lord Chamberlain and the Lord Steward, and a knot of aides-de-camp following close on their heels. Ranged along the sides of the carriage was a party of Victoria's aides-de-camp and equerries, any of whom might have retrieved the regalia atop the coffin in the event one of these fabulously valuable trinkets jostled loose from its moorings.

Thousands in the crowd wore colored outer garments to ward off the bitter chill of a day in which the sun appeared only fitfully in the perpetually smoky skies of the capital, but as the coffin itself passed, many as a mark of their mourning shed their coats to display perfectly black dresses and suits. Nearly everyone seemed to comment on the King's appearance. Bertie was covered by a black cape, so voluminous it concealed his horse's haunches; the front was thrown open to display a chestful of medals on his scarlet tunic. On his face was an expression many interpreted as grief, but which was certainly exacerbated by having to face an icy, biting wind as well as the difficulties of keeping his bulk securely astride his bay charger. As the cortege passed Hyde Park, the beast threatened to rear every time a shot came from the Royal Horse Artillery minute guns, whose cannon were fired for every year of the late monarch's life. In any case, the King seemed scarcely to drive the horse, letting the animal set its own pace and course, the steed occasionally even coming to a dead stop. William and Arthur were careful to observe protocol by keeping slightly behind Bertie, reining their own horses' heads level with the shoulder of that of the King.

The crowd viewing Queen Victoria's two-hour-long funeral march through London that day was among the largest in the history of the kingdom. Yet the occasion remained remarkably free of misbehavior on the part of the hundreds of thousands gathered. The *Times* commented: ". . . it might easily have been forgiven if, in the circumstances, there had been some manifestation of impatience or intractableness. A stationary position of nearly five hours, aherding together so that it was difficult, in some cases absolutely impossible, to move a single member of the body, with a keen, searching wind blowing all the time, are not, generally speaking, conditions conducive to amiability or good temper." It noted that when the approach of "the mourned, the loved, the lost" was heralded, "[the crowd's] demeanour was all that could be wished, all that could be expected of Englishmen and Englishwomen."

The lead elements of the march reached their objective, Paddington Station, two hours after leaving Victoria. Spacious and with a solid dignity elevating it over some of London's lesser terminals, Paddington seemed matched to the solemnity of the occasion. In 1901, it was neither gloomy nor yet dirty; advertisements had been kept off most of the building's gray stone surfaces—what few there were had been "decently" screened for the day with crimson hangings to shut out the vulgarity of trade.

Since railway stations aren't designed for ceremonial processions, many of the building's arrangements had to be altered to accommodate the day's events. The train that was to carry the Queen's body to Windsor was switched from the departures side to the arrivals platform, making street access less inconvenient. The change also allowed each detachment of the parade to be marched straight into the station, past the place where the gun carriage with the coffin was to be halted, and straight out again to a thoroughfare barred to crowds that might delay the marchers' drawing off. The station platform was spread with a thick crimson carpet, the sort common to royal occasions, and over which the caisson's wheels would pass soundlessly. For decoration, jungle-like masses of giant white flowers were strewn amongst typically Victorian palms and evergreens. Less decorous but unmistakable in their Prussian stiffness stood a cluster of German secret policemen, their presence officially tolerated by Scotland Yard.

The car that would bear the coffin on to Windsor was the same that had carried the Queen up from Portsmouth, and would on this leg be pulled by an engine that had recently been renamed *Royal Sovereign* specially for its role today; on its smokebox was hung a wreath of white immortelles, while the black-draped royal arms were affixed to both sides of the locomotive. (Two additional trains, carrying guests, politicians and diplomats, would depart the station for Windsor just ahead of the royal train.) At the time the cortege had been passing through London's street, the *Royal Sovereign* was taken from Victoria, driven around the West London connection to Paddington, and held waiting at the station's Platform 8 for the Queen's reappearance.

At half past one, the coffin was carried aboard the waiting coach. A bystander noted hearing the King stage-whispering to the Kaiser, "Come along, hurry up, we're twenty minutes late already." With the strains of Beethoven still emanating from the military band, the spectators now bareheaded and the masses of troops standing to the salute, colors lowered and everyone securely aboard, the train leisurely steamed out of Paddington as the stationmaster slowly dropped his green signal flag. London had looked its last upon Queen Victoria.

❖ 2 ❖

A nd, at last, home to Windsor. In this ordinary and extraordinary English town where royalty has dwelled since the haziest days of the kingdom's history, the sovereign who had made it her home for sixty-four years was on her way back, never to leave again. It was here, where so many of the seminal events of the Victorian era had come to pass, that the climax and culmination of this great national festival of mourning would be enacted.

Though almost everything had, so far, gone off with clockwork precision, that happy condition was about to end. The first signs of the trouble were the masses of mourners and day-trippers who had clogged the town's streets to near-impassability. Special trains had been disgorging people into Windsor's two stations for more than twenty-four hours, day-trippers who filled every corner of the town to the point of jelling. Fortunately, all but a handful of the thousands of onlookers comported themselves with respect in this their last chance to mourn the dead sovereign.

The first major hitch in the gears turned out to be the sort of mischance Fritz Ponsonby had dreaded. Shortly before two o'clock, the funeral train pulled into Windsor Station; its passengers had detrained and within minutes formed into neat ranks outside the main entrance, waiting patiently for the procession to start its advance to the castle and St. George's Chapel. The men would walk, while the women rode behind in closed carriages. Soldiers loaded the waiting gun carriage with the coffin and securely fixed the regalia in position atop the white pall. Ponsonby, in charge of this element of the day's whirlwind of undertakings, approached the King to ask for permission to order the cortege to start moving, the frazzled monarch only too happy to nod his acquiescence. Fritz stepped out to the side of the procession, as though he were a train conductor signaling an engine driver to start up. He lifted his arm, the drummers began their roll, and the lead marchers, including the band, started toward the castle.

The trouble began when it was time for the gun carriage to move out. To Ponsonby's horror, the lead horses that were to bear the caisson with the coffin stood absolutely still, utterly ignoring all efforts to get them to move. And worse, the rear horses of the team of eight had a different idea from those ahead of them.

The team of horses had been standing in the bitter cold for a long time, and when the lieutenant in charge gave them their command to move, the two trailing animals started up in spite of the leaders' defiantly standing their ground. One of the rear horses sensed the load was too heavy and reared up, kicking, which caused it to plunge to the slick pavement in a kind of near-dead heap. The traces tangled instantly, and all entreaties to the beasts to reform themselves went wholly in vain. The King, the Kaiser and the Duke of Connaught, standing immediately behind the jumble, viewed the fiasco in tight-jawed silence.

As the seconds ticked by, the reddening Ponsonby began to envision his court career heading straight toward oblivion. Taking measure of the situation, he knew that the first thing he had to do was stop the marchers who had already gone ahead from going any further. Evidently because of the band music, the first units hadn't noticed what was happening behind them and were, within less than a minute, already around the corner and on their way to the castle. Ponsonby sent a sergeant racing to stop them. Next he inspected the snarled traces, and saw that the weight of the collapsed horse had broken or hopelessly entangled almost all of them. Several officers were already doing what they could to get the mess cleared up, with no one having the slightest success. Fritz went to the King to explain what had happened. As he was leaving the sovereign, Prince Louis of Battenberg—the husband of Princess Victoria of Hesse and a highly respected naval officer—ran up to him with a suggestion that he thought would resolve the crisis.

Prince Louis explained to Fritz that since it appeared that the horses and their lines were hopelessly snarled, why not press his sailors—the naval guard-of-honor—into pulling the caisson, using manpower instead of horsepower? While Louis was presenting his case to the courtier, one of the officers who was trying to disentangle the horses interrupted to suggest cutting the lead horse and allow a single pair to pull the coffin-loaded carriage using a makeshift pair of traces. But Ponsonby immediately vetoed the idea, knowing the drive up the hill to the castle was far too steep for two horses alone to pull such a heavy load. Another officer suggested a shortcut to St. George's (in fact, the direct route by which the royal women were to proceed in their carriages while the men walked), but Ponsonby realized this would mean disappointing thousands of spectators who had been waiting for hours on the announced route.

Deciding to adopt Prince Louis's idea, Fritz went a second time to the King, this time to secure his permission for bluejackets to pull the Queen to St. George's. "Have I your Majesty's permission to take out the horses and let the men of the naval guard of honor drag the gun carriage?" "Certainly," Bertie exhaled, surprised but obviously relieved. Ponsonby hurried to the captain of the naval guard, ordering him to get the sailors up to the gun carriage on the double. He next told the officer in charge of the artillery team to cut away his horses, explaining that sailors on foot were going to take their place.

The honor of bearing the Queen to her final rest was an immense one, and the army officer was horrified at this change in plans. A "discussion" in sharp whispers immediately broke out among all concerned. The artillery officers hissed to Ponsonby that everything was going to be just fine if he'd leave them alone and let the army men get on with untangling the still very much tangled horses and traces. Ponsonby told the army faction—among them Arthur Bigge was particularly vocal, and angry, about the turn of events—that the King had already approved the new arrangements, and he had no intention of letting anyone alter them. Then Bigge himself went to see the King. But the dignified courtier met strong resistance from the monarch. Bertie sputtered, "Right or wrong, let him [Ponsonby] manage everything; we shall never get on if there are two people giving contradictory orders." It wasn't exactly a ringing endorsement of Ponsonby, but it demonstrated the sovereign's reluctance to brook any further delay.

Fritz, now concentrating on logistics, hurried off to the station master to see if any rope was available by which the sailors could pull the caisson. None could be found, but the station master came running out with some steel cable, having taken it from one of the trains' communication apparatus. Realizing that this would cut the bearers hands to pieces before they got anywhere near St. George's, the again-hopeful artillery officers thought the army just might be allowed to have another go with their horses. The hopes were quickly dashed when Ponsonby frantically asked the officer in charge of the naval guard what he might come up with. Responding if he could have the traces that were then being disentangled from horse-flesh, the young lieutenant gave them to the sailors, who quickly and expertly refashioned them into draw ropes that were then fastened to both the front and back of the gun carriage, those leading to pull, those behind to brake the caisson on the procession's few downhill patches. In little time, and with the several dozen sailors to the rescue, the procession was finally ready to again get under way.

All this had lasted only about fifteen minutes—to Ponsonby it seemed like hours—and the collected majesties, highnesses and assorted grand panjandrums were, at last, off. The bluejackets performed their work splendidly, the officer-in-charge even stationing a man at each wheel of the gun carriage to help check its descent on the downslope stretches. Almost everyone who saw this spectacle agreed that the effect was stunning.

Here in Windsor, the procession was deliberately less military in nature than the march through London. London's masses of troops had been replaced with a greater proportion of theatrically draped characters from Britain's past: heralds, pursuivants, kings-of-arms arrayed in medieval tabards, the gold-and-black-uniformed great officers of state, gentlemen-at-arms, yeomen of the guard, phalanxes of gorgeously caparisoned ambassadors and official representatives and, of course, the ethereal theatricality of a mass of royalty who formed the frosting on the ritual cake. To the boom of minute guns resounding in the Long Walk and the gaze of white-collared and high-hatted squadrons of Eton boys, this Babylonian procession snaked its slow and majestic way from the coziness of the town's streets to the arch-splendor of the castle's sequestered precincts, the latter strewn now with some 2,500 wreaths of every imaginable hue, their heavy scent weighing down the frigid air.

At the massive carved doors that led into the nave of St.

George's Chapel, the bluejackets handed over their burden to a party of Grenadier Guardsmen, men of the most prestigious regiment in the entire British military establishment. Here a true catastrophe nearly turned the day's rite into a historically memorable shambles. So heavy was the multiple-layered confabulation of coffins that made up the Queen's container—sources said it weighed more than half a ton—that the small detachment almost crumbled under their cargo, several of the Grenadiers visibly swaying as they struggled with their load up the triple flights of chapel steps. A sharp intake of breath came from Bertie, directly behind, as additional men quickly darted up to the bearer party to assist. Had the heavy coffin fallen to the stone chapel steps, the effect would most likely have been riveting.

This was not the last consternation of the day. As the chapel had begun to fill, it became apparent to the officials that the Earl Marshal had somehow neglected to assign any of the choir seats. Thus in a church packed elsewhere to overflowing, one entire and very conspicuous section stood embarrassingly vacant. Sir Spencer Ponsonby-Fane, in charge of seating under the Earl Marshal's authority, realized the blunder, and quickly snatched a number of likely looking congregants from the nave and spread them out in the forlorn choir section. The real misfortune, of course, was to the hundreds of "suitable" people who had applied for seats in St. George's and had been turned down by the Earl Marshal for lack of space.

The ceremony that followed the seating foul-up was, everyone agreed, impressive. The chapel itself was virtually aquiver with the golden glow emanating from a sea of candles, their rays reflecting magnificently off the diamonds in the state regalia that topped the coffin. The congregation was arrayed like the Pharaoh's court. The Prime Minister, Lord Salisbury, wore a velvet skullcap, perhaps to keep the chapel's chill drafts from worrying his cold. Most conspicuous for his finery was the Chinese minister, who looked as though he should have been under glass. Oddly, it was in almost every instance men who outshone the women. Loaded down with every chain and order, medal, collar and feather and cape, plume and button and golden frog to which their offices entitled them, they radiated a sort of aggregate unearthliness. In contrast, the ladies were to a woman hidden under the deepest mourning, their crepe hangings defying an onlooker to make out who was who. (Moreover, the new Queen and the other royal women were literally hidden—in the Royal Closet overlooking the altar.) Of the men, Mr. Joseph H. Choate, the American ambassador, dressed in the egalitarian black serge of young democracy.

One last blunder, although relatively innocuous, delayed the start of the service for several long minutes. The abundant collection of prelates couldn't work out which one was to start the service, forcing the congregation to bide its time while they mulled the situation over. Ultimately, it was Davidson who broke the logjam by leading off with a lesson entitled "Man That Is Born of Woman."

In a voice ringing with majestical consequence, the Norroy King-of-Arms, William Henry Weldon, at last delivered the central proclamation of the service:

> Forasmuch as it has pleased Almighty God to take out of this transitory life unto His Divine Mercy the late most high, most mighty, and most excellent Monarch Victoria, by the grace of God, of the United Kingdom of Great Britain and Ireland, Queen, Defender of the Faith, Empress of India, and Sovereign of the Most Noble Order of the Garter, let us humbly beseech Almighty God to bless with long life, health, and honour, and all worldly happiness the most high, most mighty, and most excellent Monarch our Sovereign Lord Edward, now, by the grace of God, of the United Kingdom of Great Britain and Ireland, King, Defender of the Faith, Emperor of India, and Sovereign of the Most Noble Order of the Garter. God save the King.

Bishop Davidson noted that the Bishop of Oxford was "rather unwell" afterward, probably from the strain, and that, furthermore, he himself was "thoroughly knocked up."

❖  3  ❖

At the same hour as the rites at Windsor were being conducted for the kingdom's highest, millions of ordinary Britons were themselves gathered in countless services reflecting on the just-ended reign. At St. Paul's and Westminster Abbey, great gatherings of remembrance were being played to packed congregations, both churches having filled every seat within moments of their doors being opened. At the exact moment the King-of-Arms was proclaiming Victoria's titles at St. George's, in every parish and street of Britain and Ireland a mandatory ten-minute pause from all commercial and social labors coincided with Weldon's ancient phrases. Wherever in the kingdom there was business, it ceased; wherever there was light, shades were drawn; wherever there was life, it seemed almost to stop. In Birmingham, a city stricken by a heavy snowstorm, dozens of mourners nonetheless piled up floral tributes at the foot of the statue of the late Queen in front of the Council House. Dublin's churches were full this Saturday, Catholic as well as Protestant. So were those in Edinburgh and Glasgow and the Channel Islands, in Leeds and Norwich, at Crathie on the Balmoral estate and Whippingham at Osborne—everywhere in these islands Victoria's people stopped to pay tribute, and to remember.

Nor was it only in the British Isles that the mourning was wide and deep. In New York, Saturday's stock market half-session was canceled. The overflowing Trinity Church celebrated a special service for the dead sovereign, the sextons being forced to turn away some six thousand people for lack of room. In the American capital city, the President and his entire cabinet rendered their tribute along with hundreds of Washington's notables in St. John's Episcopal Church; Admiral Dewey provided perhaps the brightest note in the blue and gold splendor of his formal naval uniform.

Everywhere in the world, from every British outpost to the metropolises of every continent, the world stopped for an hour this Saturday. From Dresden and Trieste and Tangier, Port Said and Copenhagen and Bombay, from the meanness of Calcutta to the splendors of St. Petersburg—where the Russian Imperial Family was being received at the English church—Victoria, and the serenity she represented, was mourned.

❖ 4 ❖

With the service at St. George's concluded, there were very many in the chapel who lingered for a while, knowing this day would be remembered and spoken of for years to come. The dead Queen still rested at the foot of the altar in her many-layered coffin. After a time, the family and the royalties having departed for a late luncheon in the palace range of the castle's vast precincts, a squad of soldiers reverently bore the coffin on their shoulders and took it next door to the Albert Chapel. There lay buried the dead Queen's son and grandson, and stood a massive marble memorial to her husband, and it was here that she would spend this night, the following day, and the early hours of Monday morning. Then the last little bit of this final journey would be done. It would be home to Frogmore, home to Albert, home to rest after the tasks of a lifetime.

Fritz Ponsonby was understandably relieved that the funeral ceremony had gone off without any overwhelming disasters, but he still felt a knot of anxiety about Monday's interment. Even now he wasn't sure how many would be at Frogmore, or exactly how the King wanted the rites to be handled. Leaving St. George's, he decided to ponder it over some lunch in the castle, where the royals would be eating in the palatial Dining Room in the East Wing, the remaining five hundred or so guests sitting down to their own banquet in St. George's Hall, in the North Wing's State Apartments.

Before Fritz managed to get to his meal, an equerry handed him a message that the King wanted to see him—immediately. Hurrying off to the Edward III Tower, the new sovereign's lodgings until his mother's apartments could be redecorated for him and his wife, Ponsonby found the monarch taking a much-needed pause from the day's rigors. What was on the King's mind was the incident with the horses and the sailors at Windsor Station. Bertie told Ponsonby that since the sailors had done "so well," he wanted them to repeat the performance at the burial.

Fritz saw at once the danger in the King's spontaneous proposal: if the sailors again dragged Victoria, this time on her last journey, the army's humiliation at today's fiasco would be far greater, doing that service an injustice he was sure the monarch would not want done. When Fritz expressed his concerns, Bertie told his aide that he fully realized the fault had not lain with the soldiers, that it was a mishap that might have happened under any circumstances—"an unlucky accident," as the King put it. Nonetheless, he believed the bluejackets had contributed a real degree of dignity to the day, and he wanted it repeated Monday. Risking the sovereign's wrath, Ponsonby pressed his objection. Eventually, the courtier talked the King out of the idea. Still miffed, though, the monarch conceded, "Very well, the gun carriage will be drawn by the artillery." But before Ponsonby could breathe too deep a sigh of relief, Bertie added, "But if anything goes wrong I will never speak to you again!"

One final duty kept Ponsonby from bed until very much later than he would have liked. Shortly before midnight, the ever-resourceful Reggie Esher suggested to Fritz a run-through of the interment part of Monday's ceremonies. Agreeing that it would likely be an effort well-spent, Ponsonby went with Esher to stage-manage an interment rehearsal at Frogmore. There, in the flickering light of lanterns, the bizarre scene unfolded. The two courtiers rounded up a five-foot-long box to stand in for the Queen's coffin, filling it with weights to represent the burden that would be carried by its military bearers. Two parties of soldiers—one from the Life Guards, the other from the Foot Guards—stood by. The box was hoisted onto a gun carriage, after which Fritz and the soldiers practiced getting it up the steps of the Frogmore Mausoleum until he and Esher were sure it could be done smoothly on Monday.

Only one problem became evident. The pair realized that, in the normal course of transporting the load, the coffin would be deposited on the tomb the wrong way, which is to say Victoria's head to Albert's toe. So the men worked out a way of transferring their load from the Life Guards to the Foot Guards halfway up the steps, turning it around, and thus getting it into the tomb so that Victoria's body would look face-to-face with that of her dead consort. Two more rehearsals of the intricate maneuver, and everything seemed as if it would go without a hitch at the real ceremony.

Late Saturday evening, William presented a little surprise to his aunt Alexandra. Much as she hated the "nasty, *Pickelhaube* Prussians," a category in which she unreservedly placed her noisome nephew, the fifty-six-year-old and still-beautiful consort graciously allowed the Kaiser to accord her an honorary colonelcy of the Prussian Dragoons, the regiment of which her late mother-in-law had been colonel. The new Queen appreciated the honor, especially so after William told her that he planned to leave for Germany on Tuesday.

# *SUNDAY*

## ❖ 1 ❖

Bishop Davidson reveled in the indulgence of lying in bed until ten. But he knew the treat would mean hurrying to get through breakfast and then rush off to St. George's chapel at noon for what was the umpteenth service for the late Queen. The entire Royal Family planned to hear the still-unwell Bishop of Oxford preach his sermon, though the near-voiceless prelate would turn out to be all but inaudible to almost everyone in the congregation.

Elsewhere in the castle this morning, Ponsonby continued to fret about Monday's interment. Still smarting from the King's threat "never to speak to [him] again," the courtier resolved to make absolutely certain the horses didn't become fractious again tomorrow. He ordered a number of ropes cut into suitable lengths, with hooks worked into them like traces. He then hid them in a handy place in the cloisters next door to St. George's. Finally, he told the chief of the bearers' party that if the horses refused to move, as had happened at Windsor Station yesterday, he was to instantly strip off their harness, hook up the jury-rigged traces waiting in the cloisters, and get the *artillerymen* to pull the Queen from the Albert Chapel to Frogmore. Furthermore, he warned, this was to be kept strictly confidential—Ponsonby didn't want the army to think he doubted their ability to handle the steeds. Fritz spent most of the rest of the morning walking the horses between the two venues, hopeful that they would become accustomed to what they were supposed to do on the morrow.

In the afternoon, Ponsonby, Davidson, and Esher went with the King to the mausoleum to see to the final arrangements. Each man shared a central worry: how to lower the heavy coffin into its tomb without it crashing. Davidson privately thought the coffin "needlessly huge," estimating it to be about a third larger than Albert's, even though the consort had been "a much larger person than she." Furthermore, he wasn't too crazy about the elmwood from which Victoria's outer coffin had been made ("unhappily at her own direction"), believing that it had "disfigured" the vault in the Albert Chapel for the short hours it rested there.

When workmen had—fortunately—earlier taken measurements to see if Victoria's container was going to fit into its stone receptacle next to Albert's, they discovered that it wouldn't. Masons quickly chipped out several inches from the inside of the great granite sarcophagus, a job Davidson felt had been "cleverly done." Meanwhile, Bertie was planning where everyone should stand on the following day, giving orders for the service while the others took notes.

The Royal Family's day ended in the Albert Chapel, where next to the Queen's coffin the penultimate service for Queen Victoria was celebrated. The Dean of Windsor and Davidson took turns with the prayers. It was now that Mme. Albani sang her songs— "Come unto Me" and "I Know That My Redeemer Liveth." Bertie was grateful that she seemed pleased. Sir Walter Parratt pumped out the accompaniment for the coloratura on a little harmonium that sat next to Prince Leopold's colossal sepulcher. Davidson felt the coloratura's voice "too strong" for the confined space, but admitted that the overall effect of the scene—it was held in the darkness, the chamber lit only by a few candles—was "very striking."

# *Monday,*
# *February 4*

Amazingly, the nasty winter weather that was enveloping much of the rest of Britain hadn't yet struck Windsor this morning. The biggest menace remained the chance that the high clouds would turn to snow. Since the entire Royal Family planned to walk en masse from their quarters in the castle to Frogmore Mausoleum, this possibility represented a matter of not inconsiderable concern. Still, the end of this exhausting series of rites was nearing, and most of the members of the Household were collectively emitting a quiet but nonetheless heartfelt sigh of relief.

Fritz Ponsonby had been up since dawn attending to the unending interment minutiae for which the King had made him responsible. Norfolk's role had ended with the funeral Saturday, and these final arrangements were considered a private family matter. As fate would have it, Fritz was in for one last misfortune this morning. An aide notified him of a serious social gaffe, news of which was making the rounds of the castle, a foul-up serious enough that he knew the King would be dangerously annoyed.

What happened was that the name of the Duke of Fife—the King's son-in-law—had been omitted from the list of those staying in the castle; furthermore, this erroneous list had been published in the morning papers; and, worst of all, the entire Royal Family was clucking about poor Fife's woeful omission from the aforesaid list. In the ranking of transgressions against princely sensibilities, this one, Ponsonby knew, stood embarrassingly high.

Directly after breakfast, Ponsonby recognized that the pot was about to boil when he got an ominous message that the King wanted to see him. The courtier found his sovereign in the Grand Corridor, the renowned passageway that extends the entire length of two of Windsor's wings and from which most of the castle's great family rooms are entered. He first saw, in a tight little knot, the Kaiser chatting with the Portuguese and Belgian kings. Fritz was shocked to see the trio smoking cigars, a long-held taboo of the ancien régime and one whose observance Victoria rigorously maintained. Obviously feeling his oats as the new master of the house, Fritz knew King Edward—who clearly approved of the free use of tobacco in his homes—was going to be doing certain things differently now.

Standing a bit away from his fellow sovereigns, Bertie was trapped in the middle of a harangue addressed at him from Fife. The son-in-law was all too plainly outraged at the omission of his name from the guest roster, and was in the midst of letting the King know that he expected scalp. The instant Bertie saw Ponsonby approaching, the King began to berate the courtier. Bertie bellowed that he was at a "loss to understand" how the Duke of Fife's name had been omitted from the list, and further, he couldn't understand how Ponsonby, of all people, could possibly have committed so grievous a mistake. For good measure, he added that he was sure he would no longer be able to trust such a servant, one who would treat "so important a person" as his son-in-law in this "shameful way."

It turned out that the rant was window-dressing, craftily designed by the King—a master at handling people—to placate Fife. As Bertie had hoped, the duke walked away from the encounter with a little grin of victory twisting his horsey features. While Fritz started to apologize to the sovereign, Bertie instead took him by the arm and in a conspiratorial stage whisper said, "I know how difficult it's been for you and I think you did wonders. I had to say something strong, as Fife was so hurt that he came to me and said that he presumed that he could go to London as he was apparently not wanted." That all this went on among grown men was the real wonder.

If Fritz thought this was the last of the day's snags, he miscalculated. What he would later describe as a "curious incident" began innocently, but could have ended with a far worse outcome than what actually happened. It began when Ponsonby was approached by a "dignified, gentlemanly-looking" man, dressed as an officer in informal field khaki and wearing an impressive brace of medals on his jacket. The man politely asked if he might obtain a ticket to the mausoleum service. Ponsonby responded that the service was closed to the public, being held only for the Royal Family and a few Household members. The officer left without further comment, and Fritz quickly forgot the encounter.

Although the interment itself would be private, the King had given permission for the public to line the walkway from the castle, through the Long Walk, and up to the mausoleum's gates. The distance was only a few hundred yards, and the entire route would be bordered with scarlet-coated Grenadier Guards standing shoulder to shoulder. At about half past two, the ranks of mourners began to form up outside the Albert Chapel, an area which serjeants-at-arms had just cleared of all outsiders. With the King at their head, and the Royal Artillery in charge of the horse-drawn gun carriage bearing the dead Queen, the massed royalty—only slightly leavened with a sprinkling of specially invited courtiers and members of the Kaiser's suite—started the ten-minute walk to Frogmore. The women were on foot, directly alongside the men. Queen Alexandra held the gloved hand of the six-year-old Prince Edward of Cornwall and York, the small, blond second heir to the throne patriotically garbed in a blue sailor suit then the rage for boys his age. Ringing out above the mourners' heads was the massive bell in the Round Tower, captured at Crimea a half century earlier and, as it was reserved for the funeral of a sovereign, never before rung.

Just before the procession reached the gates leading through the George IV Archway and on to the Long Walk, Ponsonby's "dignified, gentlemanly-looking" officer again appeared, this time stepping out from a cluster of spectators. Comporting himself as if his presence were expected, he joined the German suite, which had clotted into its own little clique. Since the Germans naturally believed him to be some sort of Household official, they paid little attention to the British officer, regardless of the quirkiness of his dress, which the fastidious Prussians probably didn't think too odd for an Englishman. As it happened, the interloper marched right through the gates into Frogmore grounds, the furthest point the public had been allowed to penetrate, and, together with the entire Royal Family, up to the steps of the mausoleum. From his position at the rear of the line of march, Ponsonby hadn't been able to see the intruder.

Frogmore Mausoleum was especially beloved to Victoria, a place where she had often ordered church services celebrated on the summer Sundays she passed at Windsor. Towering over the Florentine-style temple were majestic yews and junipers and firs, all lending a filigreed beauty to the setting unmatched almost anywhere else in the kingdom. This morning, snowdrops—the earliest blossoms of the new year and the unmistakable sign of the coming spring—were the sole flower to grace the wintry setting. Contrasting with the delicate blooms were the bright scarlets of the massed kings and princes and soldiers, their lustrous gold and silver breastplates flashing like mirrors under the struggling sun.

The mausoleum's interior had been lavishly transformed for the interment. High above the tall candles around the altar hung great gasoliers, their flickering light bouncing off the heavy silver Communion vessels adorning the altar. Acres of purple hangings swathed the interior walls, with the whiteness of great masses of corpulent lilies of the valley relieving the sober shrouds. To minimize congestion for this afternoon's service, workmen had removed the four great bronze angels guarding the corners of Albert's sarcophagus. The enormous recumbent statue of the Prince Consort, the details of his field marshal's uniform chiseled out in wondrously lifelike relief, had been taken off the top of Albert's tomb. A viewing platform that entirely enclosed the sarcophagi awaited the mourners; the platform was, like the rest of the building's interior, swagged with purple cloth, with a huge golden representation of the Queen's monogram on its front, facing the entrance. At the center of the platform, an opening was provided for lowering Victoria's coffin into the marble vault.

Shortly after three, the service began, with the strains of Beethoven's "Funeral March" hanging on the frigid February air. When the coffin reached the entrance, the music changed to a more poignant funeral march, that of the Black Watch, granting particular honor to the regiment which was suffering so disproportionately on the battlefields of South Africa.

Just as the bearers shouldered the Queen's coffin into the mausoleum, Ponsonby—who was now standing directly behind the caisson—saw from the corner of his eye a khaki-clad officer approach him from the group of Germans. Getting next to Fritz's ear, the intruder startled the courtier by whispering, "Who's the old bird with the beard?" obviously referring to the grizzled Belgian King. Fritz was stunned that the man had somehow managed to crash the service in the company of the now-suspicious Germans. Realizing the man must be out of his mind, Fritz hissed at him, "Hush," and took him firmly by the arm, leading him to the doors, where he quickly evicted him, hoping it would put an end to any more importuning. (When after the service had concluded Ponsonby saw the man mingling with the Royal Family in the castle quadrangle, he finally had a castle policeman arrest him; he later discovered the officer had been sent home from South Africa with sunstroke, a condition that he had evidently suffered to a greater than usual degree.)

The intruder's presence unknown to the King, the service proceeded to its dignified close, a conclusion that was in Davidson's phrase "touching beyond words." Soldiers reverently lowered Victoria's coffin into the crypt that awaited her. After all the various bishops and canons and ecclesiastics had spoken their brief last eulogies to the late Queen's memory, the Royal Family passed in single file across the temporary platform over the tombs, giving each the chance to look upon the coffins of Victoria and Albert for the last time.

Bertie went first. He stopped at the center of the little bridge for a few moments, and with a sad gaze looked down at the containers enclosing his parents' bodies. God knows the thoughts that crossed his mind. Perhaps they were of a father who had so long ago made it clear to the boy that he would never achieve the greatness that was his mother's. Perhaps of a mother who had all his life, without surcease, made it clear how little she appreciated his character and capabilities. Perhaps of parents whose larger-than-life reputations he could not hope to emulate in what he knew couldn't be more than a few years left of life.

Alexandra followed her husband. Still holding her hand was her grandson, little Prince Edward, a boy who would grow into a troubled manhood, and in an act of stunning disregard for his heritage, give up a throne for a woman unfit to be his queen. Like Bertie, Alexandra too stopped to look in the crypts, bending to one knee in homage. But the child was frightened so high up on the structure, and started to pull away. The King turned back and joined his wife in her genuflection, gently bidding the boy to join them. The three knelt together for a few unforgettable moments, the sight capturing for all in this gilded temple the final reality of an era's end.

Immediately after Bertie and Alexandra, William walked by his grandparents' coffins, and like his uncle and aunt, he too knelt for a moment. He was quickly followed by all the rest of the family, and then the few members of the Court and Household who had been invited by the King to this most private part of his mother's funeral rites.

As the mourners departed Frogmore Mausoleum, the lengthy ceremonies finally concluded, long lines of carriages awaited to carry them back to the castle. Lord Esher, who had stage-managed today's ceremonies, remained alone for a few minutes to watch workmen place the stone over the Queen's vault. He was the last of her servants to take leave of his royal mistress. He left the mausoleum holding the wreath of bay leaves which had hung over the graves, and which the new King allowed him to keep.

The threatening skies finally opened up in the failing light, the rain lasting for only a few minutes before it turned into snowflakes. Quickly the scene was covered with a white blanket of soft snow. In the now deserted mausoleum, the only sign of life was the yellow rays from the oil lamps, trying with little success to cut through the gathering gloom. Victoria and Albert had it to themselves, and were alone, together, at long last.

# BIBLIOGRAPHY

Alice, HRH Princess, Countess of Athlone. *For My Grandchildren.* Cleveland: World, 1966.

Allison, Ronald & Sarah Riddell, eds. *The Royal Encyclopedia.* London: Macmillan, 1991.

Anonymous [A Member of the Royal Household]. *The Private Life of the Queen.* New York: D. Appleton, 1897.

Aronson, Theo. *The Kaisers.* Indianapolis: Bobbs-Merrill, 1971.

Baedeker's *Great Britain,* various editions.

Baedeker's *London,* various editions.

Bagehot, Walter. *The English Constitution and Other Political Essays.* New York: D. Appleton, 1905.

Battiscombe, Georgina. *Queen Alexandra.* Boston: Houghton Mifflin, 1969.

Bell, G. K. A. *Randall Davidson—Archbishop of Canterbury.* New York: Oxford, 1935.

Benson, E. F. *Queen Victoria's Daughters.* New York: D. Appleton-Century, 1938.

Besant, Walter. *Fifty Years Ago.* New York: Harper & Bros., 1888.

Blackburne, Harry W. & Maurice F. Bond. *The Romance of St. George's Chapel Windsor Castle.* Windsor: 1933.

Bland, Olivia. *The Royal Way of Death.* London: Constable, 1986.

Blunt, Wilfrid Scawen. *My Diaries.* London: Martin Secker, 1921.

Bolitho, Hector. *The Widow and Her Son.* New York: D. Appleton-Century, 1934.

Byrde, Penelope. *Nineteenth Century Fashion.* London: B.T. Batsford, 1992.

Caesar, Egon [Conte Corti]. *The English Empress—A Study in Relations between Queen Victoria and her Eldest Daughter, Empress Frederick of Germany.* London: Cassell, 1957.

Cannadine, David. *The Pleasures of the Past.* New York: W.W. Norton, 1989.

Cannon, John & Ralph Griffiths. *The Oxford Illustrated History of the British Monarchy.* Oxford: Oxford, 1988.

*Catalogue of the Principal Items on View at Osborne House.* London: HMSO, 1980.

Cecil, Lamar. *Wilhelm II—Prince and Emperor, 1859–1900.* Chapel Hill: University of North Carolina Press, 1989.

Chapman, Caroline & Paul Raben, compilers. *Debrett's Queen Victoria's Jubilees 1887 & 1897.* New York: Viking, 1977.

Charlton, John. *Osborne House.* London: HMSO, 1977.

Chesney, Kellow. *The Victorian Underworld.* London: Penguin, 1970.

Curl, James Stevens. *A Celebration of Death.* New York: Charles Scribner's Sons, 1980.

Cust, Sir Lionel. *King Edward VII and His Court—Some Reminiscences.* New York: E.P. Dutton, 1930.

Dangerfield, George. *Victoria's Heir—The Education of a Prince.* New York: Harcourt Brace, 1941.

Davidson Papers. Volume XIX, Item 101. Lambeth Palace Library, London.

Duff, David. *The Shy Princess—the Life of HRH Princess Beatrice.* London: Evans Brothers, 1958.

Eckardstein, Baron von. *Ten Years at the Court of St. James' 1895–1905.* London: Thornton Butterworth, 1921.

*Edwardian London,* vol. 1. London: Village Press, 1990.

Edwards, Anne. *Matriarch.* New York: William Morrow, 1984.

Farago, Ladislas & Andrew Sinclair. *Royal Web—The Story of Princess Victoria & Frederick of Prussia.* New York: McGraw-Hill, 1982.

Farwell, Byron. *Eminent Victorian Soldiers—Seekers of Glory.* New York: W.W. Norton, 1985.

Fletcher, Ifan Kyrle. *The British Court—Its Traditions and Ceremonial.* London: Cassell, 1953.

Florance, Arnold. *Queen Victoria at Osborne.* London: Yelf Bros., 1977.

Fulford, Roger, ed. *Dearest Mama—Letters Between Queen Victoria and the Crown Princess of Prussia.* New York: Holt, Rinehart and Winston, 1968.

Girouard, Mark. *The Victorian Country House.* Oxford: Oxford, 1979.

Grey, Lt. Col. the Hon C. *The Early Years of His Royal Highness the Prince Consort.* New York: Harper & Bros., 1867.

Hardie, Frank. *The Political Influence of the British Monarchy 1868–1952.* London: B.T. Batsford, 1970.

————. *The Political Influence of Queen Victoria 1861–1901.* London: Frank Cass, 1963.

Harrison, J.F.C. *Late Victorian Britain 1875–1901.* London: Fontana, 1990.

Hayden, Ilse. *Symbol and Privilege—The Ritual Context of British Royalty.* Tucson: University of Arizona Press, 1987.

Hibbert, Christopher. *The Court at Windsor—A Domestic History.* New York: Harper & Row, 1964.

————. *Edward VII—A Portrait.* London: Allen Lane/Penguin, 1976.

Holmes, Sir Richard, ed. *Edward VII—His Life and Times.* London: Amalgamated, 1910 (vol. 1), 1911 (vol. 2).

Jullian, Philippe. *Edward and the Edwardians.* New York: Viking, 1967.

*Kelly's Handbook to the Titled, Landed & Official Classes for 1898.* London: Kelly's Directories, 1898.

Kingston, Patrick. *Royal Trains.* London: Spring, 1985.

Lee, (Sir) Sidney. *King Edward VII—A Biography.* New York: Macmillan, 1927.

———. *Queen Victoria—A Biography.* London: John Murray, 1904.

Leech, Margaret. *In the Days of McKinley.* New York: Harper & Bros., 1959.

Lees-Milne, James. *The Enigmatic Edwardian—The Life of Reginald, 2nd Viscount Esher.* London: Sidgwick & Jackson, 1986.

Longford, Elizabeth, ed. *Louisa Lady in Waiting.* New York: Mayflower, 1979.

———. *The Oxford Book of Royal Anecdotes.* Oxford: Oxford, 1989.

Longford, Elizabeth. *Queen Victoria—Born to Succeed.* New York: Harper & Row, 1964.

Lutyens, Mary, ed. *Lady Lytton's Court Diary.* London: Rupert Hart-Davis, 1961.

MacDonagh, Michael. *The English King.* Port Washington, N.Y.: Kennikat, 1929 (reissued 1971).

Magnus, Philip. *King Edward the Seventh.* London: John Murray, 1964.

Mallet, Victor, ed. *Life with Queen Victoria—Marie Mallet's Letters from Court 1887–1901.* Boston: Houghton Mifflin, 1968.

Marie Louise, Princess. *My Memories of Six Reigns.* London: Evans Brothers, 1956.

Martin, Kingsley. *The Magic of the British Monarchy.* Boston: Little, Brown, 1962.

Massie, Robert K. *Dreadnought.* New York: Random House, 1991.

Matson, John. *Dear Osborne.* London: Hamish Hamilton, 1981.

Maurois, André. *King Edward VII and His Times.* London: Cassell, 1933.

Merrill, Arthur Lawrence. *Life and Times of Queen Victoria.* New York: D.Z. Howell, 1901.

Montgomery, John. *1900—The End of an Era.* London: George Allen & Unwin, 1968.

Morley, John. *Death, Heaven and the Victorians.* Pittsburgh: University of Pittsburgh Press, 1971.

Morris, Charles & Murat Halstead. *Life and Reign of Queen Victoria.* Chicago: International Publishing Society, 1901.

Morton, Andrew. *Theirs Is the Kingdom—The Wealth of the British Royal Family.* New York: Summit, 1989.

Mullen, Richard & James Munson. *Victoria—Portrait of a Queen.* London: BBC Books, 1987.

Nevill, Barry St. John, ed. *Life at the Court of Queen Victoria 1861-1901.* Exeter: Webb & Bower, 1984.

Nicolson, Harold. *King George V—His Life & Reign.* London: Constable, 1952.

*Ordnance Survey Leisure Guide, Isle of Wight.* Basingstoke, Hampshire: Automobile Association, 1988.

Palmer, Alan. *Crowned Cousins—The Anglo-German Royal Connection.* London: Weidenfeld and Nicolson, 1985.

Patchett-Martin, A. *The Queen in the Isle of Wight.* Shanklin, Isle of Wight: Vectis, 1898.

Pearsall, Ronald. *Edwardian Life & Leisure.* New York: St. Martin's, 1973.

Petrie, Sir Charles. *Monarchy in the Twentieth Century.* London: Andrew Daker, 1952.

Ponsonby, Arthur. *Henry Ponsonby, Queen Victoria's Private Secretary—His Life from His Letters.* New York: Macmillan, 1943.

Ponsonby, Sir Frederick. *Recollections of Three Reigns.* New York: E.P. Dutton, 1952.

Pope-Hennessy, James. *Queen Mary 1867–1953.* New York: Alfred A. Knopf, 1960.

Reid, Michaela. *Ask Sir James.* London: Hodder & Stoughton, 1987.

Rhodes James, Robert. *Prince Albert—A Biography.* New York: Alfred A. Knopf, 1984.

Röhl, John G. C. & Nicholas Sombart, eds. *Kaiser Wilhelm II—New Interpretations: The Corfu Papers.* Cambridge: Cambridge, 1982.

Rose, Kenneth. *Kings, Queens & Courtiers.* London: Weidenfeld and Nicolson, 1985.

Rusk, John. *The Beautiful Life and Illustrious Reign of Queen Victoria.* Chicago: Monarch, 1901.

St. Aubyn, Giles. *Edward VII—Prince & King.* New York: Atheneum, 1979.

———. *Queen Victoria—A Portrait.* New York: Atheneum, 1992.

Salway, Lance. *Queen Victoria's Grandchildren.* London: Collins & Brown, 1991.

Sibbick, Edward A. "Abbreviated History of Osborne 1066–1904." Unpublished.

Sitwell, Edith. *Victoria of England.* London: Faber and Faber, 1937.

Strachey, Lytton. *Queen Victoria.* New York: Harcourt, Brace and Company, 1921.

Thompson, Dorothy. *Queen Victoria—The Woman, the Monarchy, and the People.* New York: Pantheon, 1990.

Tisdall, E. E. P. *Queen Victoria's Private Life.* New York: John Day, 1961.

Topham, Anne. *A Distant Thunder—Intimate Recollections of the Kaiser's Court.* New York: New Chapter, 1992.

Tschumi, Gabriel. *Royal Chef—Recollection of Life in Royal Households from Queen Victoria to Queen Mary.* London: William Kimber, 1954.

Turner, Michael. *Osborne House.* London: English Heritage, 1991.

Van der Kiste, John. *Edward VII's Children.* Wolfeboro Falls, N.H.: Alan Sutton, 1991.

———. *Queen Victoria's Children.* Wolfeboro Falls, N.H.: Alan Sutton, 1986.

Wake, Jehanne. *Princess Louise—Queen Victoria's Unconventional Daughter.* London: Collins, 1988.

Weintraub, Stanley. *Victoria—An Intimate Biography.* New York: E. P. Dutton, 1987.

*Whittaker's Almanac,* various issues.

Whittle, Tyler. *The Last Kaiser—A Biography of William II.* New York: Times Books, 1977.

William II. *My Ancestors.* London: Wm. Heinemann, 1929.

———. *My Early Life.* New York: George H. Doran, 1926.

————. *My Memoirs 1878–1918*. London: Cassell, 1922.

Woodham-Smith, Cecil. *Queen Victoria—From her birth to the death of the Prince Consort*. New York: Alfred A. Knopf, 1972.

Yearsley, Macleod. *Le Roy Est Mort!—An Account of the Deaths of the Rulers of England*. London: Unicorn, 1935.

York, HRH the Duchess of, with Benita Stoney. *Victoria and Albert— A Family Life at Osborne House*. New York: Prentice Hall, 1991.

## Newspapers & Periodicals

*The Times* (London)
*The Manchester Guardian*
*The Sportsman*
*Windsor and Eton Express*
*The Daily Graphic*
*The Daily Telegraph*
*Eastern Daily Press*
*The Morning Post*

*The Queen*
*The Outlook*
*The Lancet*
*The Illustrated London News*
*The Graphic*
*The Sphere*
*The New York Times*
*The Oregonian*

# NOTES

*Chapter I*
5 **elegant than words**: Hibbert, *Court at Windsor*, 221–222
14 **great stinks there**: Florance, 5
15 **Chinese-looking thing**: York, 22
19 **won't be interrupted**: Mullen & Munson, 145
20 **value to me**: Pakenham, 256

*Chapter II*
23 **think of it**: Hardie, *QV*, 226
28 **her pretty presents**: Reid, 199
28 **should have thought**: ibid., 259
28 **abrupt and unsympathetic**: ibid., 259
28 **was a little worse**: ibid., 200
32 **did some work**: Rose, 265

*Chapter III*
43 **cerebral degeneration**: St. Aubyn, *QV*, 593
45 **will be a prince**: Farago, 1
49 **this Kaiser madness**: Farago, 193
50 **wishes to avoid**: Röhl, 170
52 **against his parents**: Röhl, 173

54 *question of time*: Reid, 91
55 frank with me: Count Corti, 250
55 to his wife: ibid., 254
56 for no good: ibid., 254
56 carefully been preparing: Farago, 253
58 has gone through: in Van der Kiste, *QV*, 116
66 officers' social equals: Reid, 35
66 prepared to do: ibid., 46
67 his new job: Reid, 39
68 confused and aphasic: ibid., 201

*Chapter IV*
71 as a "charlatan": Reid, 222
72 as a "stimulant": Weintraub, 630
72 [at home] twice: Reid, 200
72 to 'help' me: ibid., 202
73 in the rain: ibid., 202
74 the Bishop's passing: Reid, 202
74 that understands me: Reid, 202
75 heart of Berlin: Eckardstein, 188
75 one knows whither: Kohut, 164
76 one so young: Longford, *QV*, 373
76 a military clique: Jullian 157
77 actually an Englishman: Kohut, 178

*Chapter V*
84 quiet, graceful manners: Rose, 137
85 of her habit: Reid, 136
88 to old age: Rose, 30
92 at all hazards: Reid, 205
94 it at present: Reid, 203

*Chapter VI*
98 business is impossible: H. Ponsonby, 101
99 Victoria knew better: H. Ponsonby, 109
106 ever existed before: Massie, 197
106 cheer him up: Van der Kiste, *QV*, 139
107 are better now: Reid, 205
108 a little longer: ibid., 205
110 they were before: St. Aubyn, *QV*, 525

## Chapter VII
115 **of the world**: Eckardstein, 189
117 **coming of yours**: Kaiser's Memoirs, 102
120 **dissolute old harridan**: Morris, 86
121 *way departed from*: Reid, 208
124 **we were born**: Leech, 567

## Chapter VIII
127 **come to you**: Reid, 210
137 **Kiss my face**: ibid., 210

## Chapter IX
142 **is here too**: Reid, 210–211
145 **on without her**: F. Ponsonby, 128
145 **Wales wishes it**: Reid, 211
147 **is very kind**: Reid, 211
148 **slums of Windsor**: St. Aubyn, *QV*, 349
168 **much to do**: Reid, 213
173 **in the sky**: St. Aubyn, *QV*, 597

## Chapter X
182 **never forget it**: Reid, 214

## Chapter XI
188 **what a woman**: St. Aubyn, *QV*, 507
190 **in the Courtyard**: Reid, 214
191 **any other sensations**: Pearsall, 13

## Chapter XII
198 **travelling with me**: Reid, 215
207 **Pce of Wales**: Pope-Hennessy, 348

## Chapter XIII
210 **insignificant of mechanics**: Rose, 227
216 **to that figure**: Davidson Memorandum
230 **found "absolute chaos"**: F. Ponsonby, 132

## Chapter XIV
243 **being a fiasco**: F. Ponsonby, 134–135

*Chapter XV*
246 **had at home**: Kingston, 40ff.
260 **to you again**: F. Ponsonby, 139

*Chapter XVI*
265 **dignified, gentlemanly-looking**: F. Ponsonby, 143

# INDEX